Excel 2000
Short Course

Carole Tobias
Patrick Henry Community College
Martinsville, VA

Glencoe McGraw-Hill

New York, New York   Columbus, Ohio   Woodland Hills, California   Peoria, Illinois

This program has been prepared with the assistance of Gleason Group, Inc., Norwalk, CT.

Editorial Director: Pamela Ross

Developmental Editor: Michele Ruschhaupt

Copy Editor: Beth Conover

Composition: PDS Associates, Creative Ink, Inc.

Screens were captured using FullShot 97 For Windows from Inbit Incorporated, Mountain View, CA.

Glencoe/McGraw-Hill

A Division of The **McGraw·Hill** Companies

Excel 2000: A Professional Approach, Short Course
Student Edition
ISBN 0-02-805586-1

Copyright © 2000 by The McGraw-Hill Companies, Inc. All rights reserved. Printed in the United States of America. Except as permitted under the United States copyright Act of 1976, no part of this publication may be reproduced or distributed in any form or by any means, or stored in a data base or retrieval system, without the prior written permission of the publisher.

1 2 3 4 5 6 7 8 9 10   058/058   04 03 02 01 00 99

Microsoft, Microsoft Excel, and Windows are either registered trademarks or trademarks of Microsoft Corporation in the United States and/or other countries.

PostScript is a registered trademark of Adobe Systems, Inc.

Contents

Preface — xi

- Case Study — xi
- Organization of the Text — xi
- Features of the Text — xi
- MOUS Certification Program — xii
- Conventions Used in the Text — xii
- If You Are Unfamiliar with Windows — xii
- Screen Differences — xiii
- Acknowledgments — xiii

Installation Requirements — xv

- Hardware — xv
- Software — xv
- Installing New Features — xv

Case Study   1

Kearney-Sansome Accounting, Inc.   2
Working As an Intern   4
Your Clients During the Intern Period   5
ALPHA Pharmaceuticals   6
Beautiful Belle Company   7
Preview   8

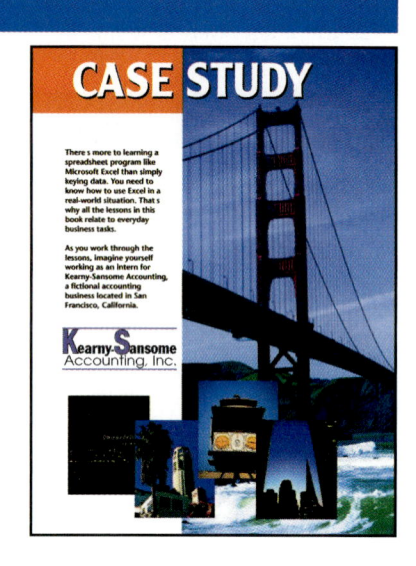

CONTENTS

UNIT 1

Basic Skills — 9

Lesson 1 What Is Excel? — 11

- Starting Excel — 11
- Changing the Active Cell — 17
- Navigating Between Worksheets — 18
- Closing and Opening Worksheets — 20
- Navigating within a Worksheet — 21
- Keying Data in a Worksheet — 26
- Saving a Workbook — 27
- Printing a Worksheet and Exiting Excel — 30
- USING HELP — 32
- CONCEPTS REVIEW — 33
- SKILLS REVIEW — 34
- LESSON APPLICATIONS — 38

Lesson 2 Creating a Simple Worksheet — 42

- Entering and Editing Data — 42
- Using Pick from List and AutoComplete — 47
- Entering Data in Selected Cells — 49
- Constructing Basic Formulas — 54
- Using the SUM Function — 58
- Using AutoCalculate — 61
- USING HELP — 63
- CONCEPTS REVIEW — 64
- SKILLS REVIEW — 65
- LESSON APPLICATIONS — 71

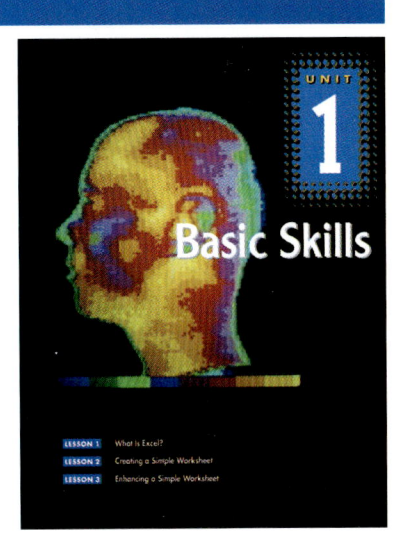

Lesson 3 Enhancing a Simple Worksheet — 77

Selecting Multiple Columns and Rows	77
Inserting Cells, Columns, and Rows	79
Deleting Cells, Columns, and Rows	82
Using the Undo and Redo Commands	83
Using Shortcut Menus	84
Moving Data to a New Location	85
Formatting Numbers: The Basics	88
Applying Text Attributes and Cell Borders	89
USING HELP	92
CONCEPTS REVIEW	94
SKILLS REVIEW	95
LESSON APPLICATIONS	100

UNIT 1 APPLICATIONS — **106**

UNIT 2

Developing a Worksheet 113

Lesson 4 Designing and Printing a Worksheet 115

Planning a Worksheet on Paper 116
Putting the Worksheet Plan on Screen 118
Keeping Row and Column Labels in View 125
Selecting Display Options 128
Creating User Documentation 130
Protecting Files 132
Printing Workbooks and Print Areas 133
Printing Formulas 140
USING HELP 142
CONCEPTS REVIEW 143
SKILLS REVIEW 144
LESSON APPLICATIONS 151

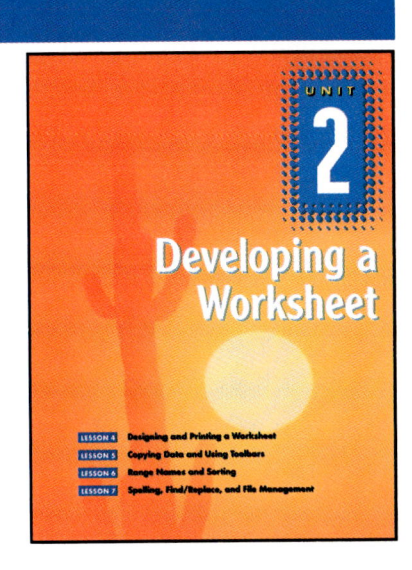

Lesson 5 Copying Data and Using Toolbars 158

Building a Worksheet with Copy and Paste 158
Copying Using Drag and Drop 162
Copying Using Fill and AutoFill 163
Using Toolbars in Excel 165
USING HELP 171
CONCEPTS REVIEW 173
SKILLS REVIEW 174
LESSON APPLICATIONS 179

Lesson 6 Ranges Names and Sorting 185

Naming Ranges and Constants	186
Using Names in Formulas	188
Changing and Deleting Range Names	189
Navigating Using Range Names	190
Pasting Names into Worksheets	191
Sorting Information in a Worksheet	193
USING HELP	195
CONCEPTS REVIEW	196
SKILLS REVIEW	197
LESSON APPLICATIONS	202

Lesson 7 Spelling, Find/Replace, and File Management 208

Checking Spelling	208
Using AutoCorrect	211
Finding and Replacing Data	213
Finding Files	216
Renaming, Copying, and Deleting Files	218
USING HELP	220
CONCEPTS REVIEW	222
SKILLS REVIEW	223
LESSON APPLICATIONS	228

UNIT 2 APPLICATIONS 233

CONTENTS

Portfolio Builder — P-1

Building a Résumé	P-5
Identifying Prospective Employees	P-16
Building Your Portfolio	P-19
Targeting Your Résumé and Portfolio	P-22
Writing a Cover Letter	P-24
Filling Out an Employment Application	P-27
Employment Interviews	P-28
Following Up the Interview	P-30

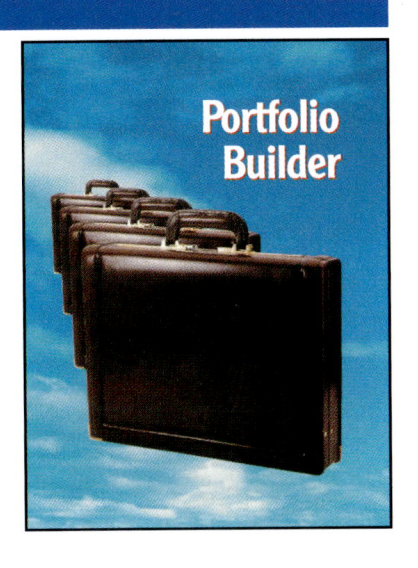

Appendices A-1

Appendix A: Windows Tutorial — A-2
Appendix B: Using the Mouse — A-11
Appendix C: Using Menus and Dialog Boxes — A-12
Appendix D: File Management — A-14
Appendix E: Proofreaders' Marks — A-16
Appendix F: MOUS Certification — A-18

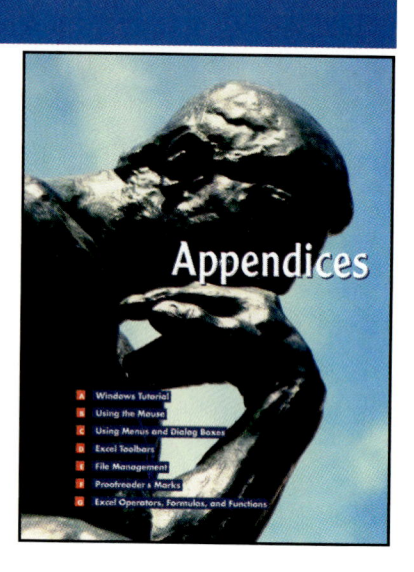

Glossary G-1

Index I-1

Preface

Excel 2000 is written to help you master Microsoft Excel for Windows. The text takes you step-by-step through the Excel features that you're likely to use in both your personal and business life.

Case Study

Learning about the features of Excel is one thing, but applying what you've learned is another. That's why a *Case Study* runs throughout the text. It offers you the opportunity to learn Excel within a realistic business context. Take the time to read the Case Study about Kearny-Sansome Accounting, Inc., a fictional business set in San Francisco. All the worksheets for this course deal with the clients of Kearny-Sansome.

Organization of the Text

The text includes two *units*. Each unit is divided into smaller *lessons*. There are seven lessons, each building on previously learned procedures. This building block approach, together with the Case Study and the features listed below, enable you to maximize the learning process.

Features of the Text

- ☑ *Objectives* are listed for each lesson
- ☑ Required skills for the *Microsoft Office User Specialist (MOUS) Certification Program* are listed for each lesson
- ☑ The *estimated time* required to complete each lesson (up to the "Concepts Review") is stated
- ☑ Within a lesson, each *heading* corresponds to an objective
- ☑ Easy-to-follow *Exercises* emphasize "learning by doing"
- ☑ *Key terms* are italicized and defined as they are encountered
- ☑ Extensive *graphics* display screen contents
- ☑ *Toolbar buttons* and *keyboard keys* are shown in the text when they are used
- ☑ *Large toolbar buttons in the margins* provide easy-to-see references
- ☑ Lessons contain important *Notes* and useful *Tips*
- ☑ A *Command Summary* lists the commands learned in the lesson
- ☑ *Using Help* introduces you to a Help topic related to lesson content
- ☑ *Concepts Review* includes true/false, short answer, and critical thinking questions that focus on lesson content

- ✔ *Skills Review* provides skill reinforcement for each lesson
- ✔ *Lesson Applications* ask you to apply your skills in a more challenging way
- ✔ *Unit Applications* give you the opportunity to use the skills you learn in a unit
- ✔ Appendices
- ✔ Glossary
- ✔ Index

MOUS Certification Program

The Microsoft Office User Specialist (MOUS) certification program offers certification at two skill levels—"Core" and "Expert." This certification can be a valuable asset in any job search. For more information about this Microsoft program, go to www.mous.net. For a complete listing of the MOUS skills for the Excel 2000 "Core" certification exam (and a correlation to the lessons in the text), see Appendix F: "MOUS Certification."

Conventions Used in the Text

This text uses a number of conventions to help you learn the program and save your work.

- Text that you're asked to key appears either in **boldface** or as a separate figure.
- Filenames appear in **boldface**.
- You're asked to save each document with your initials, followed by the Exercise name. For example, an Exercise may end with the instruction: "Save the workbook as *[your initials]***5-12.xls**." Workbooks are saved in folders for each lesson after the first lesson.
- Menu letters you can key to activate a command are shown as they appear on screen, with the letter underlined (for example, "Choose Print from the File menu"). Dialog box options are also shown this way, and they appear in title case to increase readability (for example, in the Find dialog box, "Find What" rather than "Find what").

If You Are Unfamiliar with Windows

If you're unfamiliar with Windows 98, you'll want to work through *Appendix A: "Windows Tutorial"* before beginning Lesson 1. You may also need to review *Appendix B: "Using the Mouse," Appendix C: "Using Menus and Dialog Boxes,"* and *Appendix D: "File Management"* if you've never used a mouse or any version of Windows before.

Screen Differences

As you read about and practice each concept, illustrations of the screens help you follow the instructions. Don't worry if your screen is different from the illustration. These differences are due to variations in system and computer configurations.

Acknowledgments

We want to thank the reviewers of this text for their valuable assistance. We would particularly like to thank: Kathleen Anderson, Empire College, Santa Rosa, CA; Susan Olson, Northwest Technical College, East Grand Forks, MN; and John F. Walker, Dona Ana Community College (New Mexico State University), NM.

Installation Requirements

You'll need Microsoft Excel 2000 to work through this textbook. Excel needs to be installed on the computer's hard drive (or on a network). Use the following checklist to evaluate installation requirements.

Hardware

- ☑ Pentium computer with 32 MB or more of RAM
- ☑ 3.5-inch high-density disk drive and CD-ROM drive
- ☑ 200 MB or more of hard disk space for a "Typical" Office installation
- ☑ VGA or higher-resolution video monitor
- ☑ Printer (laser or ink-jet recommended)
- ☑ Mouse
- ☑ *Optional:* Modem

Software

- ☑ Excel 2000 (from Microsoft Office 2000)
- ☑ Windows 95 (or later) or Microsoft Windows NT Workstation 4.0 with Service Pack 3.0 installed
- ☑ *Optional:* Browser (and Internet Service Provider)

Installing New Features

While working in Excel, you may come across a file or a feature that requires installation. For example, some templates, wizards, add-in features, and Office Assistant characters must be installed from the Microsoft Office CD-ROM.

To install a feature:

1. Close all programs.
2. Click the Windows Start button, point to Settings, and click Control Panel.
3. Double-click the Add/Remove Programs icon.
4. Display the Install/Uninstall tab, if necessary.
5. If you installed Excel using the Office Setup program, choose Microsoft Office from the list of programs and click Add/Remove. If you installed Excel individually, choose Microsoft Excel from the list and click Add/Remove.

6. Click the plus sign to the left of an Office feature to expand the options. Click the down arrow to the right of a feature you want to add and choose Run All From My Computer. When you're done choosing features, click Update Now. Follow the onscreen instructions (which include loading the Office CD-ROM).

CASE STUDY

There's more to learning a spreadsheet program like Microsoft Excel than simply keying data. You need to know how to use Excel in a real-world situation. That's why all the lessons in this book relate to everyday business tasks.

As you work through the lessons, imagine yourself working as an intern for Kearny-Sansome Accounting, a fictional accounting business located in San Francisco, California.

Kearny-Sansome
Accounting, Inc.

EXCEL CASE STUDY

EXCEL 2

Kearny-Sansome Accounting, Inc.

Kearny-Sansome Accounting, Inc. was formed in 1908 by a group of San Francisco businesspeople to provide accounting services to small San Francisco businesses trying to recover from the earthquake of 1906. The company has grown over the years, but still focuses on smaller businesses.

Located in San Francisco's busy Financial District, Kearny-Sansome has clients from all across the nation, although the majority of clients are still from California. The company provides accounting, data processing, and consulting assistance to its clients.

**Kearny-Sansome Accounting, Inc.
240 Montgomery St.,
San Francisco, CA 94101**

4 EXCEL

EXCEL CASE STUDY

Working As an Intern

You'll be working as an intern at Kearny-Sansome. This involves working with one client for a few weeks, then working with another client for a few weeks, and so on. Kearny-Sansome feels that it's important for new employees to gain experience working with a variety of clients before they begin working on their own.

Kearny-Sansome expects that any incoming employee will have a solid foundation of skills.*

• Basic Skills
Reading, writing, arithmetic/mathematics, listening, and speaking

• Thinking Skills
Creative thinking, decision making, problem solving, being able to visualize problems and solutions, knowing how to learn, and reasoning

• Personal Qualities
Responsibility, self-esteem, sociability, self-management, and integrity/honesty

In addition, Kearney-Sansome believes that the five competencies identified below are the keys to job-performance.

Keys to Successful Job-Performance*

1. **Resources: Identifies, organizes, plans, and allocates resources**
   A. *Time*—Selects goal-relevant activities, ranks them, allocates time, and prepares and follows schedules.
   B. *Money*—Uses or prepares budgets, makes forecasts, keeps records, and makes adjustments to meet objectives.
   C. *Material and Facilities*—Acquires, stores, allocates, and uses materials or space efficiently.
   D. *Human Resources*—Assesses skills and distributes work accordingly, evaluates performance and provides feedback.

2. **Interpersonal: Works with others**
   A. *Participates as a Member of a Team*—Contributes to the group effort.
   B. *Teaches Others New Skills*
   C. *Serves Clients/Customers*—Works to satisfy customers' expectations.
   D. *Exercises Leadership*—Communicates ideas to justify a position, persuades and convinces others, responsibly challenges existing procedures and policies.
   E. *Negotiates*—Works toward agreements involving exchanges of resources, resolves differing interests.
   F. *Works with Diversity*—Works well with men and women from diverse backgrounds.

3. **Information: Acquires and uses information**
   A. *Acquires and Evaluates Information*
   B. *Organizes and Maintains Information*
   C. *Interprets and Communicates Information*
   D. *Uses Computers to Process Information*

4. **Systems: Understands complex relationships**
   A. *Understands Systems*—knows how social, organizational, and technological systems work and operates effectively with them.
   B. *Monitors and Corrects Performance*—Distinguishes trends, predicts impacts on system operations, diagnoses systems' performance and corrects malfunctions.
   C. *Improves or Designs Systems*—Suggests modifications to existing systems and develops new or alternative systems to improve performance.

5. **Technology: Works with a variety of technologies**
   A. *Selects Technology*—Chooses procedures, tools or equipment including computers and related technologies
   B. *Applies Technology to Task*—Understands overall intent and proper procedures for setup and operation of equipment.
   C. *Maintains and Troubleshoots Equipment*—Prevents, identifies, or solves problems with equipment, including computers and other technologies.

* These skills and competencies were identified by the Secretary of Labor and the Secretary's Commission on Achieving Necessary Skills (SCANS). They are included in the report *What Work Requires of Schools: A SCANS Report for America 2000*, published in June, 1991, by the U.S. Department of Labor.

EXCEL CASE STUDY   EXCEL 5

Your Clients During the Intern Period

During your intern period at Kearny-Sansome, you will be working with two clients.

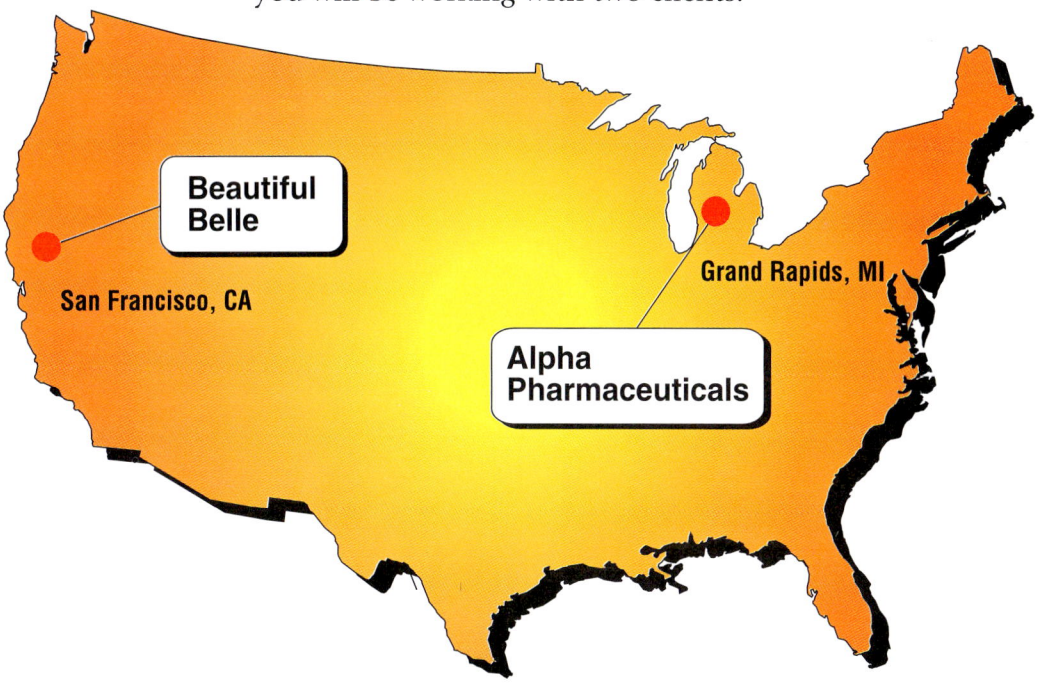

Beautiful Belle
San Francisco, CA

Alpha Pharmaceuticals
Grand Rapids, MI

6 EXCEL

EXCEL CASE STUDY

ALPHA Pharmaceuticals

Alpha Pharmaceuticals
145 Bostwick Ave., NE
Grand Rapids, MI 49503
(616) 555-4698

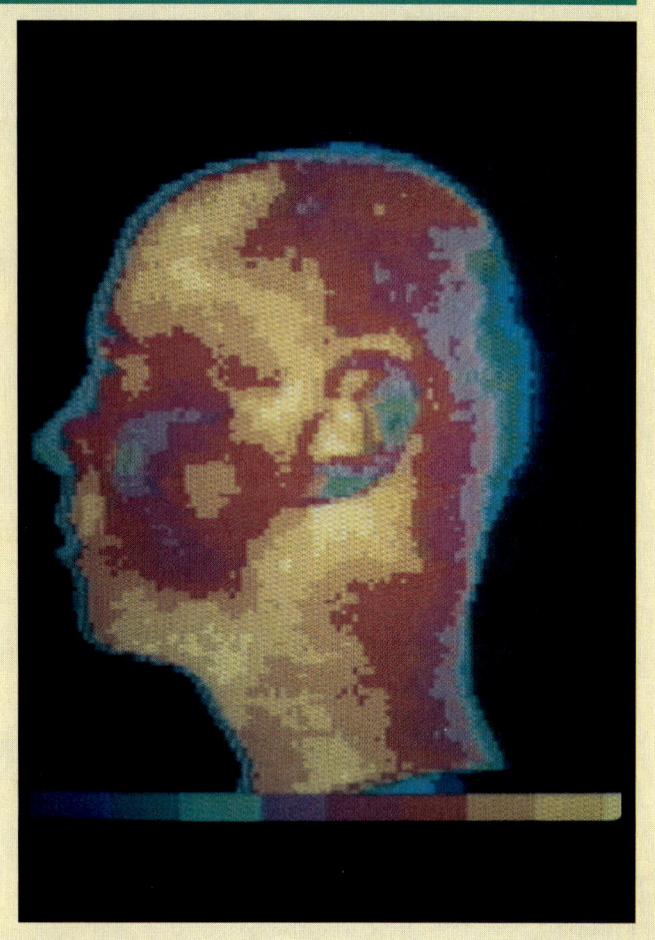

Alpha Pharmaceuticals manufactures generic over-the-counter drugs, such as ibuprofen, acetaminophen, and aspirin, for large grocery and drug-store chains. You'll be helping Alpha Pharmaceuticals study historical data about pain relievers. Alpha's president, Mark Latzko, thinks that people are switching from aspirin to ibuprofen. Your worksheets will indicate if he's right.

EXCEL CASE STUDY   EXCEL **7**

Beautiful Belle Company

Beautiful Belle Company
103 Professional Center Drive
Santa Rosa, CA 95403
(707) 555-2398

The Beautiful Belle Company manufactures a moderately priced line of cosmetics. The company is currently promoting a product called "Sun Soft," a natural, hypo-allergenic lotion that has refined almond and sesame oils as main ingredients. Renata Santo, the Southwest regional sales manager, is test marketing Sun Soft in the Phoenix area. You'll be developing worksheets that track Sun Soft's sales performance against a competing product.

8 EXCEL

EXCEL CASE STUDY

Preview

As you learn Microsoft Excel, you'll produce professional worksheets similar to the ones shown below for the clients of Kearny-Sansome Accounting. By "working" as an intern at Kearny-Sansome Accounting, you'll gain experience that you can apply to a real-world situation.

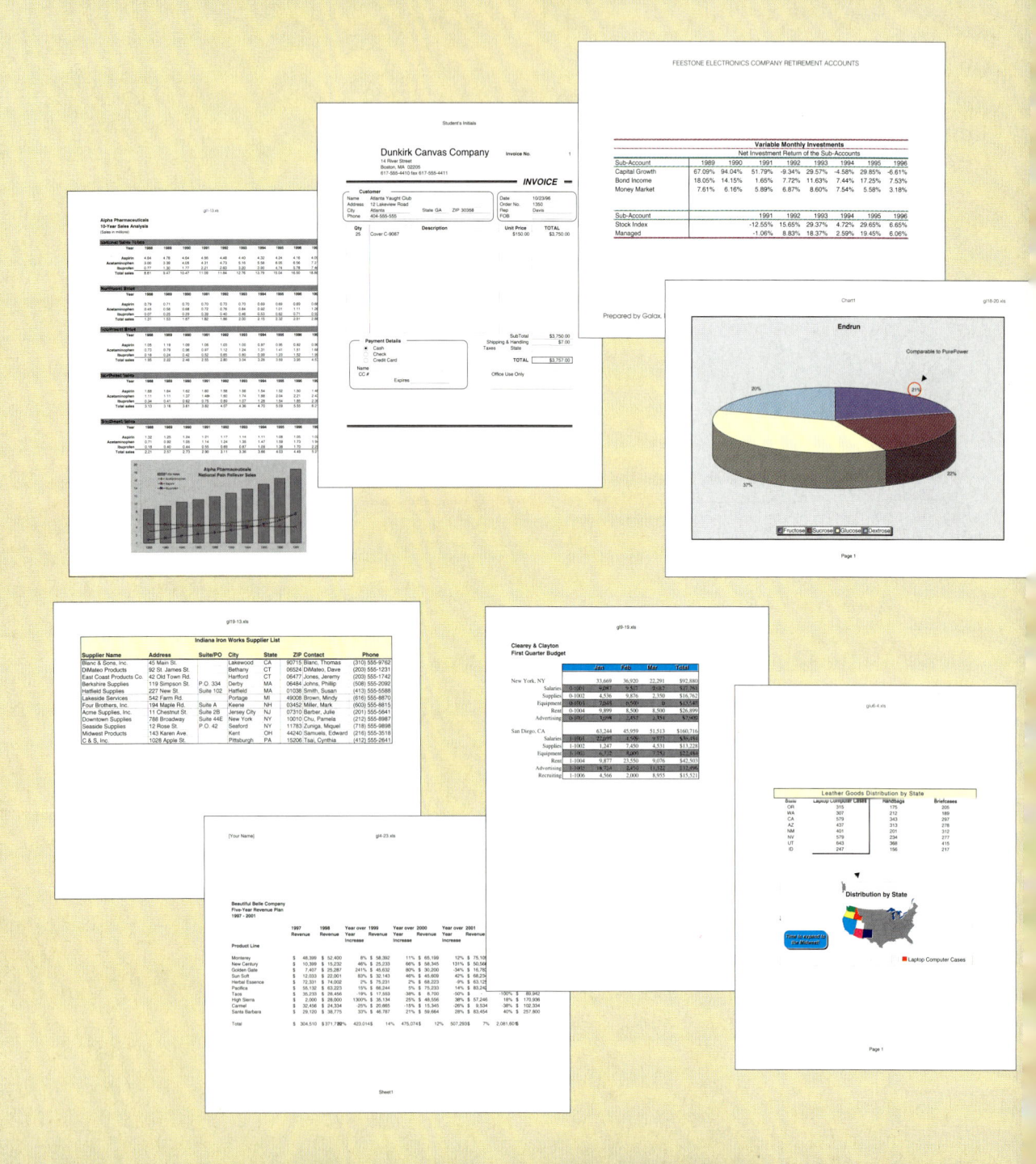

UNIT 1

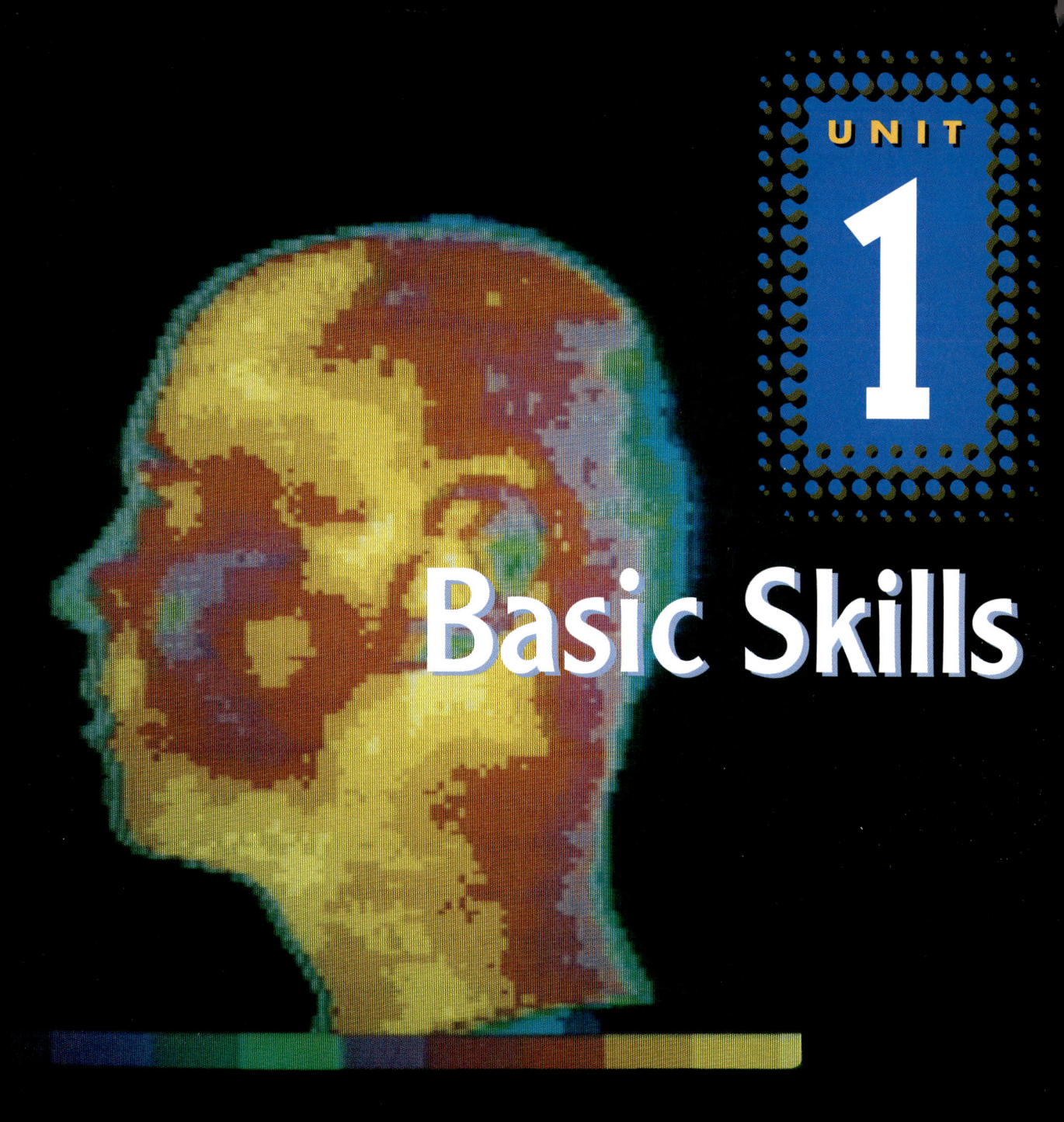

Basic Skills

LESSON 1 What Is Excel?

LESSON 2 Creating a Simple Worksheet

LESSON 3 Enhancing a Simple Worksheet

Alpha Pharmaceuticals

ALPHA Pharmaceuticals

Drug Company Banks on Growing Pains

Alpha Pharmaceuticals manufactures generic over-the-counter drugs, such as ibuprofen and aspirin, for large grocery and drug-store chains. Because demographic studies are showing that the average age of the general population is trending upward, and since older people tend to have more minor aches and pains than younger people, Alpha anticipates that the pain-reliever business will grow steadily into the 21st century.

Alpha's president, Mark Latzko, has asked his market-research team to study the company's historical data to confirm his belief that people are switching from aspirin to ibuprofen as the pain reliever of choice.

Jean Brody, who heads up the market-research team, has requested the following information to fulfill Mark's request:

✔ A detailed worksheet showing sales of aspirin, acetaminophen, and ibuprofen for the past ten years in each of the four national sales regions, with a chart illustrating trends. **(Lesson 1)**

✔ A summary sheet showing Alpha's sales of each product for the last four years and projected sales for the current year. **(Lesson 2)**

✔ An attractively styled worksheet showing the five-year sales analyses developed in Lesson 2. **(Lesson 3)**

LESSON 1

What Is Excel?

OBJECTIVES

After completing this lesson, you will be able to:
1. Start Excel.
2. Change the active cell.
3. Navigate between worksheets.
4. Close and open workbooks.
5. Navigate within a worksheet.
6. Key data in a worksheet.
7. Save a workbook.
8. Print a worksheet and exit Excel.

MOUS ACTIVITIES

In this lesson:
XL2000 **1.5**
XL2000 **2.1**
XL2000 **2.2**
XL2000 **2.3**
XL2000 **2.6**
XL2000 **2.8**
XL2000 **4.1**
XL2000 **4.2**
XL2000 **5.5**

See Appendix F.

Estimated Time: 1½ hours

Microsoft Excel is an electronic workbook that gives you the ability to perform business and scientific calculations effortlessly. It provides powerful charting, database management, and macro programming capabilities allowing you to produce professional worksheets and reports. Although Excel is powerful, it's very intuitive and easy to use. Once you learn a few basics, you'll become a productive Excel user very quickly.

Starting Excel

There are several ways to start Excel, depending on your system setup and personal preferences. For example, you can use the Start button on the Windows

FIGURE 1-1
Shortcut icon to start Excel

taskbar or double-click an Excel shortcut icon that may appear on your desktop.

NOTE: Windows provides many ways to start applications. If you have problems, ask your instructor for help.

EXERCISE 1-1 Start Excel

1. Turn on your computer. Windows loads.
2. Click the Start button on the Windows taskbar and point to Programs.

FIGURE 1-2
Starting Excel from the Windows taskbar

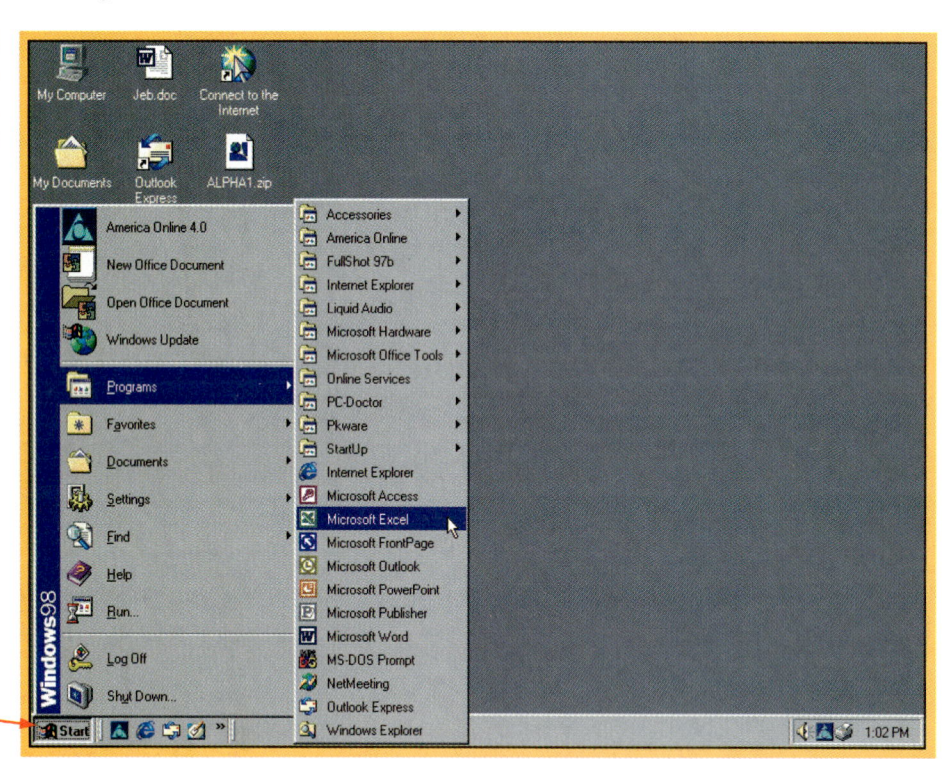

Start button

NOTE: Your screen may differ from the screen shown in Figure 1-2 depending on the programs installed on your computer.

3. On the Programs menu, click Microsoft Excel. The program is loaded in a few seconds and the Excel window appears.

LESSON 1 ■ WHAT IS EXCEL? EXCEL **13**

FIGURE 1-3
Excel window

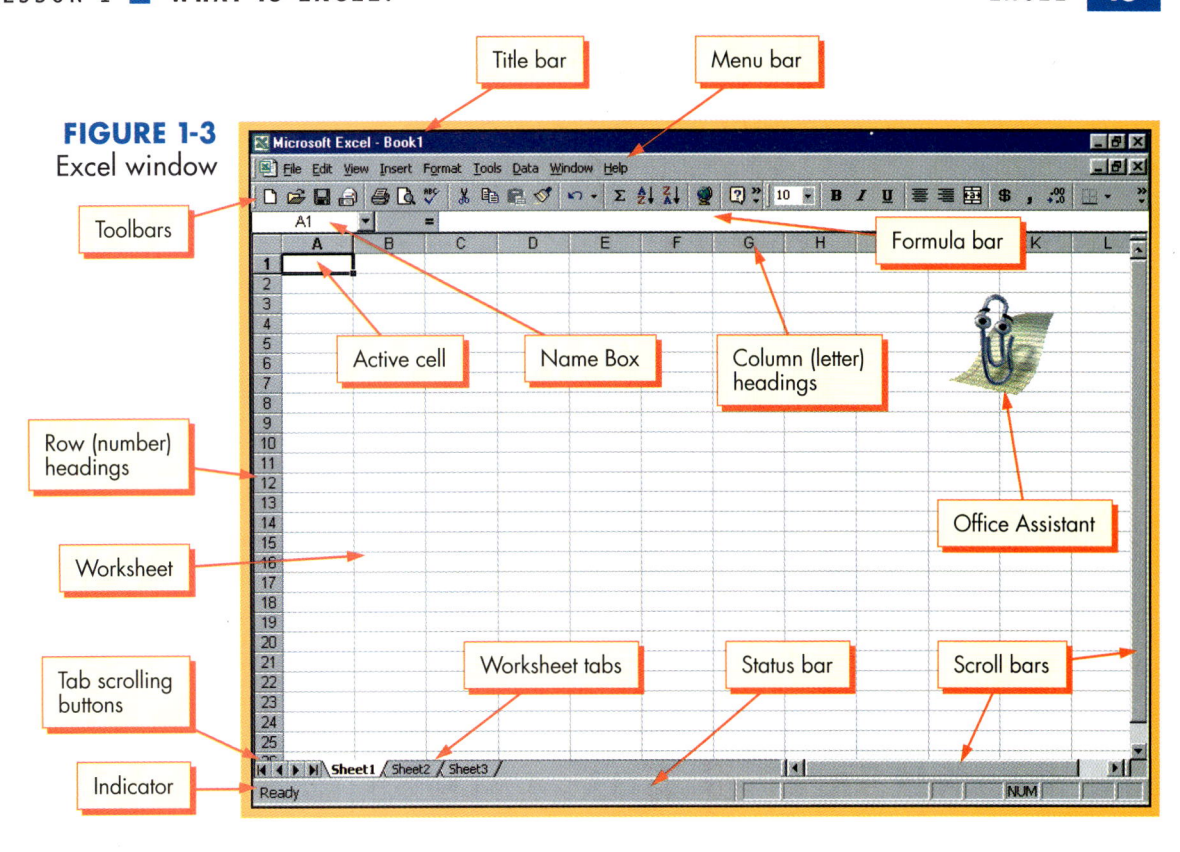

Callouts identifying parts of the Excel window: Title bar, Menu bar, Toolbars, Active cell, Name Box, Formula bar, Column (letter) headings, Office Assistant, Row (number) headings, Worksheet, Tab scrolling buttons, Worksheet tabs, Status bar, Scroll bars, Indicator.

TABLE 1-1 Parts of the Excel Screen

PART OF SCREEN	PURPOSE
Title bar	Displays the name of the workbook. The opening Excel window is always named "Book1."
Menu bar	Contains the menus you use to perform various tasks. You can open menus using the mouse or the keyboard.
Toolbars	Contain buttons you click to initiate commands. Each button is represented by an icon. Excel typically opens with the Standard and Formatting toolbars displayed in abbreviated form on one line.
Name Box	Indicates where data being keyed or edited appears on the worksheet.
Formula bar	Displays the formula in the current cell.
Worksheet	Area where you enter and work with data.

continues

TABLE 1-1   **Parts of the Excel Screen** *continued*

PART OF SCREEN	PURPOSE
Column headings	Indicates columns on the worksheet. Columns are labeled with letters.
Row headings	Indicates rows on the worksheet. Rows are labeled with numbers.
Scroll bars	Used with the mouse to move right or left and up or down within the worksheet.
Tab scrolling buttons	Used to scroll between worksheet tabs.
Worksheet tabs	Used to move from one worksheet to another.
Status bar	Displays information about a selected command or an operation in progress.
Indicators	Displays modes of operation, such as NUM when the number keypad is on.
Active cell	Cell that is current—that is, ready to receive information.
Office Assistant	Provides tips as you work and suggests Help topics related to the work you're doing.

EXERCISE 1-2   Identify Toolbar Buttons

When you start Excel, the Standard and Formatting toolbars typically appear side by side below the menu bar. The Standard toolbar has a variety of buttons for controlling the file and manipulating data. The Formatting toolbar contains buttons for controlling your worksheet's appearance.

Only the basic buttons and those that were used most recently are displayed in the toolbars. To see more buttons for either toolbar, click the More Buttons button at the end of each toolbar. To identify a toolbar button or any other onscreen button by name, point to it with the mouse.

FIGURE 1-4 Identifying a toolbar button

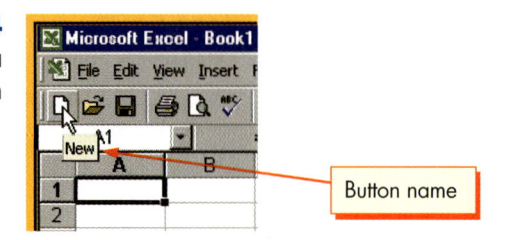

LESSON 1 ■ WHAT IS EXCEL? EXCEL **15**

1. Position the pointer over the New icon on the Standard toolbar. This button opens a new workbook. The icon appears as a button when you point to it and a *ScreenTip* (a box with the button name) appears below the button. (See Figure 1-4.)

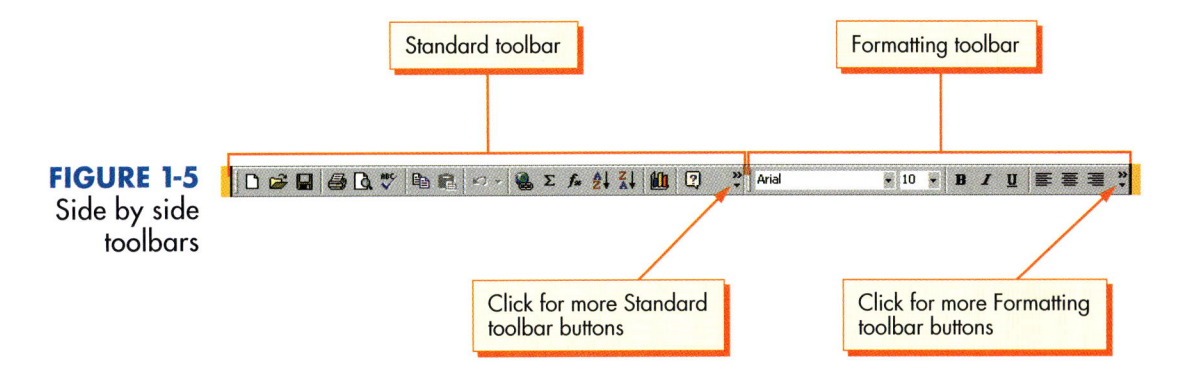

FIGURE 1-5
Side by side toolbars

Standard toolbar — *Formatting toolbar*

Click for more Standard toolbar buttons — *Click for more Formatting toolbar buttons*

NOTE: The buttons shown in Figure 1-5 and any other figure containing toolbar buttons may differ from the ones you see on your screen. Your computer may be set to display expanded Standard and Formatting toolbars on top of one another, rather than side by side.

2. Click the More Buttons button at the end of the Standard toolbar to see the rest of the toolbar's buttons. Move the mouse pointer over any button to identify it.

NOTE: Light gray icons are currently not available. Even if an icon is gray, you can identify it by positioning the mouse pointer over it.

3. Position the pointer over the Microsoft Excel Help button on the Standard toolbar. You may need to click the More Buttons button first to locate the button. Click the button to display the Office Assistant balloon. Notice that when you click (or "press") a button, its appearance changes.

TIP: Use the Office Assistant to discover quicker, easier ways to work. It provides Help topics and tips that can simplify and speed up your tasks. The Using Help section at the end of the lesson provides helpful information on using the Office Assistant.

4. Click the Microsoft Excel Help button 🔲 again to close the Office Assistant balloon. The Office Assistant remains on the screen.

5. Click the More Buttons button 🔲 on the Formatting toolbar. Identify the additional buttons, and then click in the worksheet area to hide them. Be careful not to click a menu option or toolbar button. If you do, click in the worksheet or ask your instructor for help.

EXERCISE 1-3 Identify Menus and Menu Commands

Each item on the menu bar is an individual menu that contains a list of commands.

1. Move the pointer to Edit on the menu bar and click to open the menu. Excel displays a short version of the Edit menu with the most commonly used Edit menu commands.

TIP: A menu shows commands with corresponding toolbar buttons and keyboard shortcuts. For example, you can save a workbook by choosing Save from the File menu, by clicking the Save button 🔲 on the Standard toolbar, or by pressing Ctrl+S.

2. Point to or click the arrows at the bottom of the menu to expand the Edit menu. Notice the additional commands on the expanded menu.

NOTE: The menu may already be expanded. Excel expands menus on its own if you wait a few seconds. Also, Excel's short menus are adaptive—they change as you work, listing the commands you use most frequently.

3. Without clicking the mouse button, move the pointer to View on the menu bar. Continue moving the pointer slowly across the menu bar until you display the Help menu.

4. Click Help on the menu bar to close the menu. You can also close a menu by clicking within the worksheet area of the screen or by pressing Esc.

5. Click View to open the View menu. Without clicking the mouse button, move the pointer to the Toolbars command. The right-pointing arrow indicates a submenu that shows which toolbars are currently displayed. (See Figure 1-6 on the next page.)

6. Press Esc twice to close the submenu and then the menu.

LESSON 1 ■ WHAT IS EXCEL? EXCEL **17**

FIGURE 1-6
Displaying menu options

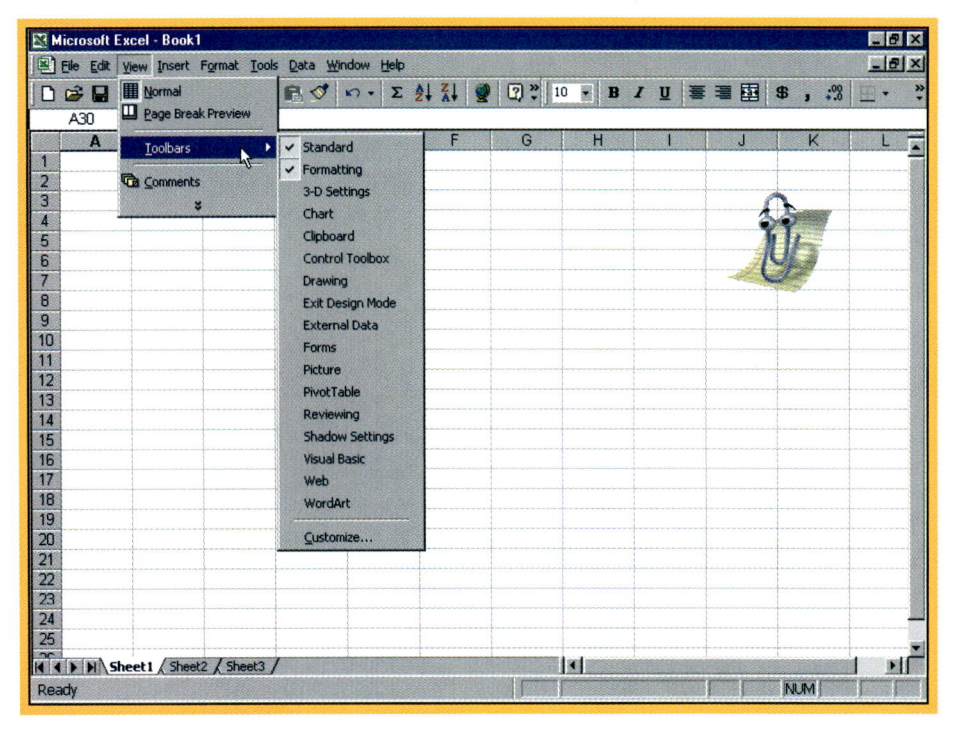

Changing the Active Cell

When you start Excel, a blank *workbook* named "Book1" appears, ready for you to create a new worksheet. The workbook contains three *worksheets* that you can visualize as pages bound in a notebook. You can add or remove worksheets from the workbook. A workbook can contain from 1 to 255 worksheets.

Each worksheet contains a grid that defines a series of rows and columns. A worksheet can use as many as 65,536 rows and 256 columns to store data. Rows are numbered. Columns are labeled A through Z, then AA through AZ, and so forth, up to column IV.

The intersection of a row and a column forms a rectangle called a *cell*. Each cell in a worksheet has a unique *cell address* that is determined by the column and row in which it is located. A cell address always indicates the column letter followed by the row number (for example, A1, C25, or AF14).

The cell that is current—that is, ready to receive information—is called the *active cell*. The active cell has a heavy border and its address is displayed in the Name Box.

EXERCISE 1-4 Change the Active Cell

1. Click in cell B3. It becomes the active cell. You can tell it's active because a heavy border surrounds it. The Name Box displays the address of the active cell, B3.
2. Press [↓] twice. Notice that the active cell changes.
3. Hold down [Ctrl] and press [Home]. Cell A1 becomes active.

NOTE: Whenever keyboard combinations (such as [Ctrl]+[Home]) are indicated, hold down the first key while you press the second key. Release the second key and then release the first key. An example of the entire sequence is: Hold down [Ctrl], press [Home], release [Home], and release [Ctrl]. With practice, you'll find it natural to execute this sequence.

FIGURE 1-7
The Name Box shows the address of the active cell.

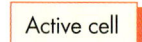

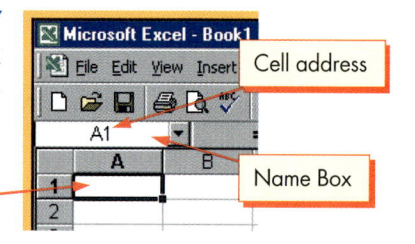

4. Notice that the pointer is a white cross. Point to cell A4 and click it. It becomes active.
5. Press [→] five times. F4 is now the active cell.
6. Press [Tab] twice to make cell H4 active.
7. Press [Ctrl]+[Home] to return to cell A1.

Navigating Between Worksheets

To move between worksheets in a workbook, you can use:
- Keyboard commands
- Worksheet tabs, which also allow you to move to a specific worksheet in a workbook

EXERCISE 1-5 Navigate Between Worksheets

1. Press [Ctrl]+[PgDn]. The next worksheet appears in the window. The worksheet tab for Sheet2 is highlighted. The active cell is A1. (See Figure 1-8 on the next page.)
2. Using the white cross pointer, click cell B3.

LESSON 1 ■ WHAT IS EXCEL? EXCEL 19

FIGURE 1-8
Worksheet tab Sheet2 is highlighted.

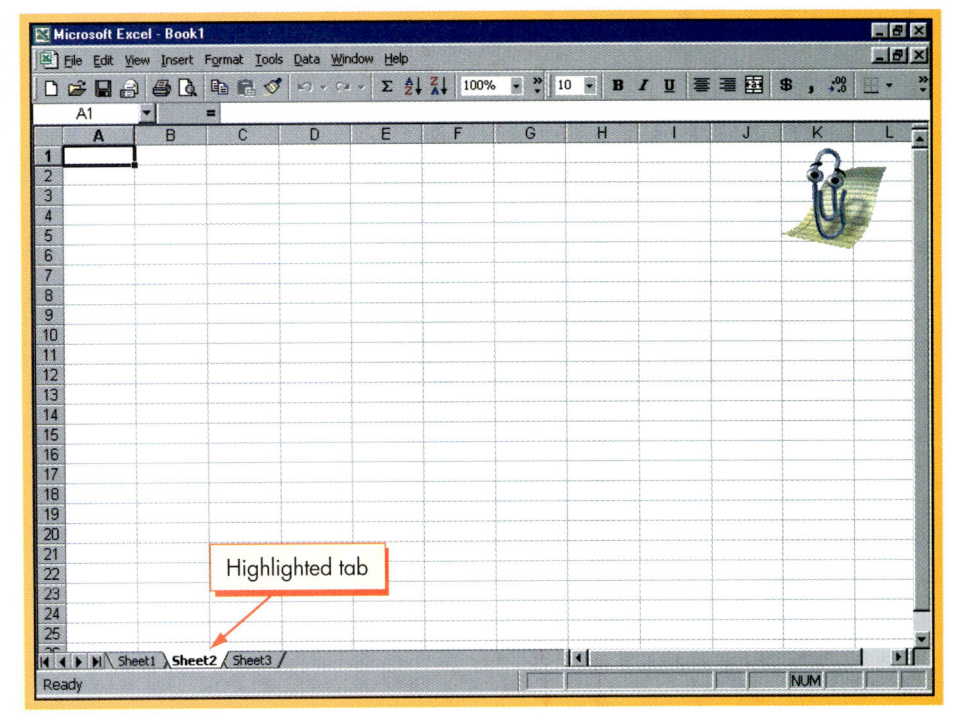

[Screenshot of Microsoft Excel - Book1 window with Sheet2 tab highlighted at the bottom, labeled "Highlighted tab"]

3. Press Ctrl + PgUp to return to Sheet1.
4. Click the worksheet tab for Sheet2. Worksheet 2 appears in the window again.
5. Click the worksheet tab for Sheet1 to return to worksheet 1.

FIGURE 1-9
Tab scrolling buttons

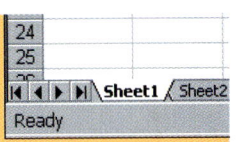

TIP: You can use the tab scrolling buttons to scroll between sheet tabs if there are so many worksheets that all of the tabs are not visible on the screen. For example, the First Tab Scrolling button and the Last Tab Scrolling button display the first and last tabs in the workbook. Note that the tab scrolling buttons only scroll the tabs. To open a worksheet, you can click the worksheet tab.

TABLE 1-2   Keyboard Commands for Navigating Between Worksheets

KEYSTROKE	ACTION
Ctrl + PgDn	Move to the next worksheet in the workbook.
Ctrl + PgUp	Move to the previous worksheet in the workbook.

Closing and Opening Workbooks

In the following exercises, you look at a workbook containing a 10-year sales analysis for Alpha Pharmaceuticals as you learn basic Excel skills. The worksheet is fairly large, showing historical data for Alpha's four sales regions and each of its products: aspirin, acetaminophen, and ibuprofen. Though it may seem confusing to you now, please keep in mind that this worksheet is an example of what you will be able to accomplish when you complete this course.

To open an existing workbook that's stored on a hard disk or floppy disk, you can:

- Choose Open from the File menu.
- Click the Open button on the Standard toolbar.

In the next exercise, you use the Open button.

EXERCISE 1-6 Close and Open Workbooks

Before you open Alpha's workbook, you close "Book1," the workbook you were just examining. Normally, you would save the file before you close it, but since you didn't key any data in "Book1," it isn't worth saving. You learn how to save a file later in this lesson.

1. Click File to open the File menu. Click Close to close the file.

   NOTE: If no workbook is open, the workbook window is gray. You can open an existing workbook or start a new one.

2. Click the Open button on the Standard toolbar. You are going to open a file called **Alpha1.xls**, but first you must locate it.

3. Click the down arrow to the right of the Look In box and choose the appropriate drive according to your instructor's directions. (See Figure 1-10 on the next page.)

   TIP: The *Places bar* on the left side of the Open dialog box contains folders that provide easy access to files or folders that you placed in them or recently accessed. "My Documents" and "Web Folders" are folders created by Windows to help you organize your files. "History" lists the most recently opened files or folders. "Desktop" lists files or folders you want to open that are on your desktop. "Favorites" contains shortcuts to files or folders that you added.

LESSON 1 ■ WHAT IS EXCEL? EXCEL 21

FIGURE 1-10
Open dialog box

Places bar

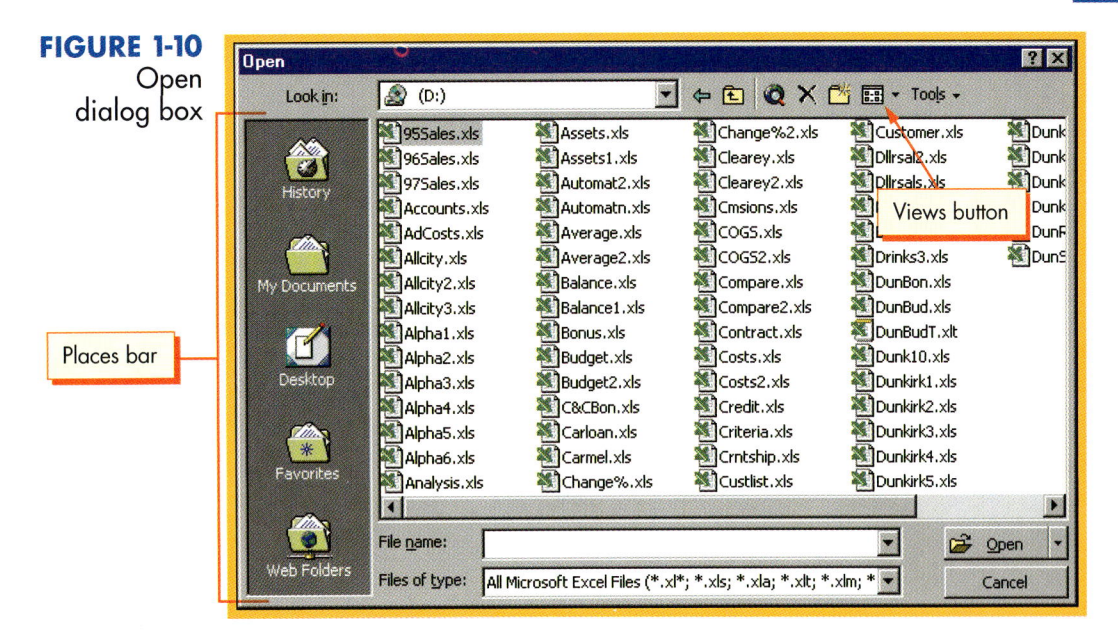

> **NOTE:** If file extensions are not visible in the Open dialog box, ask your instructor how to use Windows Explorer to change the View settings on your computer.

4. Once you locate the student files, click the arrow next to the Views button in the Open dialog box to display a menu of view options.

5. Choose <u>L</u>ist to list all files by filename.

> **NOTE:** Your files may already be shown in a list. You can click other views to see what they look like, but return to the List view before you proceed.

6. Locate the file **Alpha1.xls** and double-click it (you could also click it and then click <u>O</u>pen). Excel opens the Alpha Pharmaceuticals worksheet.

The Alpha Pharmaceuticals worksheet is formatted using shading, varying column widths, and several type sizes and number formats that will be discussed in later lessons. This worksheet provides an example of what you will be able to accomplish when you complete this course. This lesson provides an overview of Excel.

Navigating within a Worksheet

As you learned when you changed the active cell, you can move to any location in the worksheet by pressing the Arrow keys. You can move to distant cells quickly using the scroll bar and keyboard commands.

Notice that "Alpha Pharmaceuticals" appears in both the formula bar and the active cell. The cell address A1 appears in the Name Box.

EXERCISE 1-7 Navigate within a Worksheet Using Keyboard Commands

1. Press ↓ four times. "National Sales Totals" appears in the formula bar and the cell address A5 appears in the Name Box.
2. Using ↓ and →, move to cell C8. A formula that adds data in cells C17, C25, C34, and C43 appears in the formula bar. The formula result, 4.78, appears in the active cell.
3. Press Home. The active cell moves to column A in the current row.
4. Press PgDn to move down one screen.

> **NOTE:** The actual rows or columns that are visible vary from screen to screen, depending on the screen's size and settings.

5. Press PgUp to move up to the previous screen.
6. Press Alt + PgDn to move one screen to the right.
7. Press Alt + PgUp to move back to the original column.
8. Press Ctrl + ↓ four times. Cell A17 is now the active cell. Each time you press Ctrl + ↓, the active cell jumps to the edge of a group of cells containing data.
9. Press Ctrl + ↑ three times. Cell A11 is now active.
10. Press Ctrl + → once. The active cell jumps to cell K11, the last column in the table that starts at cell A5.
11. Press Ctrl + → again. Column IV, the very last column in the worksheet, is displayed.
12. Press Ctrl + ↓. Row 65536, the last row in the worksheet, appears. Move up or across the worksheet to get an idea of its huge size.
13. Press Ctrl + Home. Pressing this key combination always brings you back to cell A1.
14. Press Ctrl + End. The active cell moves to the cell in the last row in the last column that contains data or formatting instructions. (See Figure 1-11 on the next page.)

> **NOTE:** A chart showing Alpha Pharmaceuticals' sales figures appears at the bottom of the worksheet. Excel uses the numbers contained in the worksheet to create the chart.

LESSON 1 ■ WHAT IS EXCEL? EXCEL **23**

FIGURE 1-11
Cell K67 is now active.

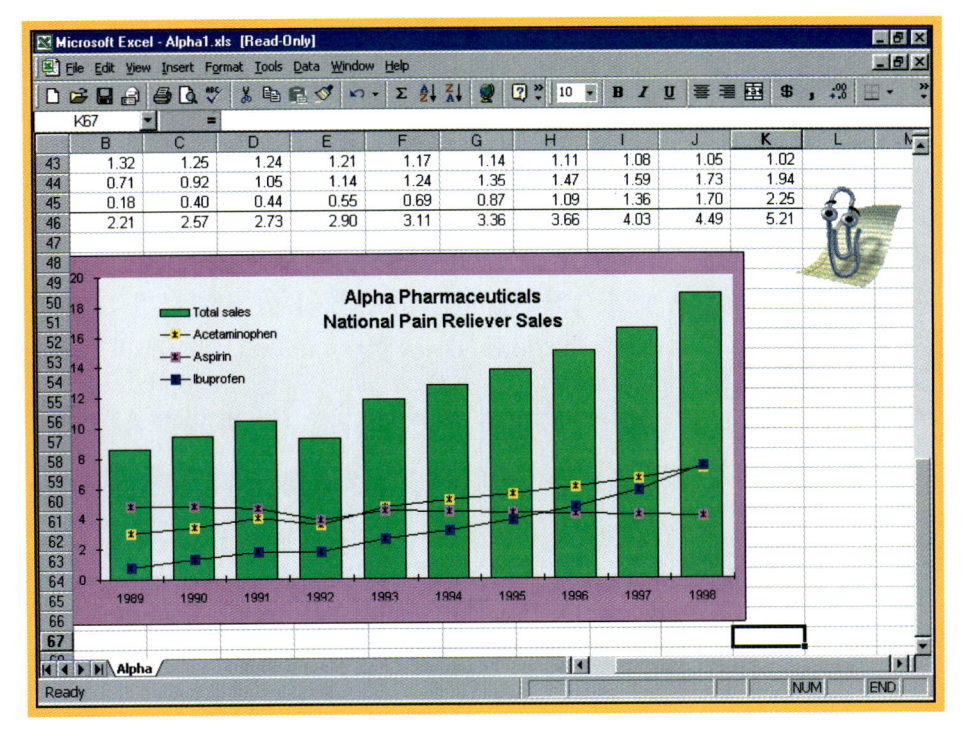

TABLE 1-3 Keyboard Commands for Navigating within a Worksheet

KEYSTROKE	ACTION
Arrow keys	Move one cell in the direction of the arrow.
Ctrl+Arrow keys	Move to the edge of a group of cells containing data.
Home	Move to the beginning of the row.
Ctrl+Home	Move to the beginning of the worksheet (cell A1).
Ctrl+End	Move to the lower right corner of the data in the worksheet.
PgDn	Move down one screen.
PgUp	Move up one screen.
Alt+PgDn	Move right one screen.
Alt+PgUp	Move left one screen.
Ctrl+Backspace	Move to the active cell if it is not visible on your screen.

24 EXCEL   UNIT 1 ■ BASIC SKILLS

EXERCISE 1-8 Navigate within a Worksheet Using Scroll Bars

You use the scroll bars to move through a worksheet using the mouse. When you use the scroll bars, the active cell does not move. You must click a cell to make it active.

1. Press Ctrl+Home to move back to cell A1.
2. Click the down arrow ▼ on the vertical scroll bar five times. The active cell scrolls out of view. The cell in the top left corner of the worksheet is A6. Notice that the Name Box still displays A1.

FIGURE 1-12
Scroll bars

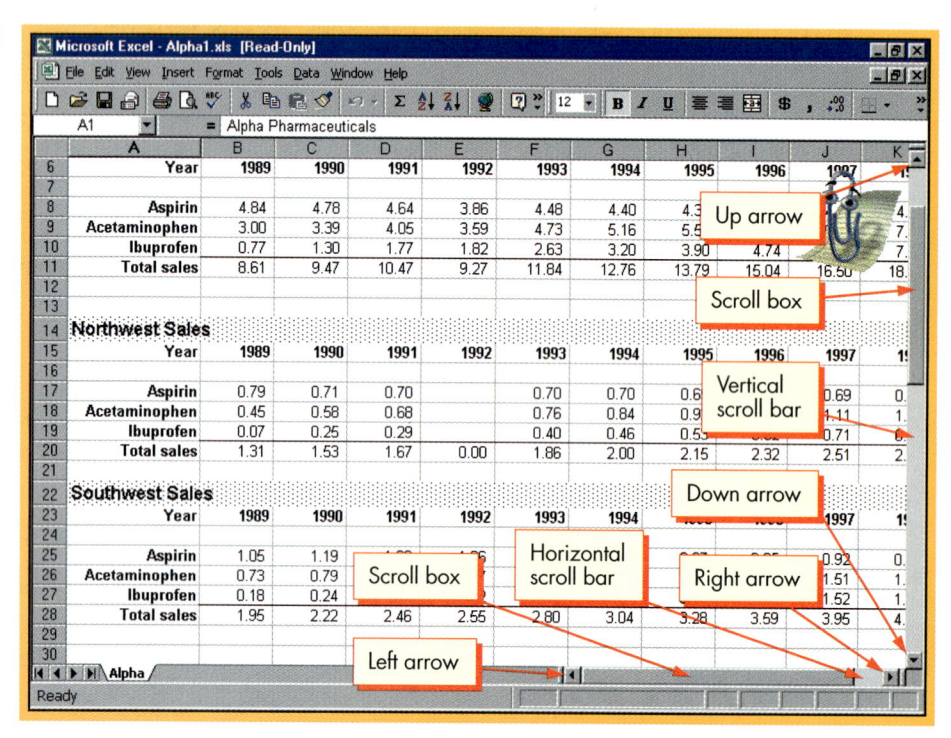

3. Click cell A6 to make it active. Remember that scrolling in a worksheet doesn't change the active cell. You must click a cell to make it active.
4. Click the up arrow on the scroll bar ▲ until you can see cell A1 again. Cell A6 is still the active cell. This is indicated by the Name Box.
5. Click the right arrow on the horizontal scroll bar ▶ six times to move to the right in the worksheet.
6. Drag the scroll box back to the left arrow ◀. Excel displays the column names that you pass over as you move to the left. Column A becomes visible.

LESSON 1 ■ WHAT IS EXCEL?   EXCEL 25

> **TIP:** To "drag" the scroll box, move the pointer to the box, hold down the left mouse button, and move the mouse.

7. On the vertical scroll bar, click between the scroll box and the down arrow ▼. Excel moves down the worksheet one screen (13 or more rows, depending on the size of your screen).

8. Click between the scroll box and the up arrow ▲ to move back up one screen in the worksheet.

9. In steps 4 through 8, cell A6 remained the active cell. Change the active cell back to cell A1 by clicking it.

TABLE 1-4   Navigating with Scroll Bars

ACTION	RESULT
Click up or down scroll arrow once	Scroll up or down one row.
Click left or right scroll arrow once	Scroll left or right one column.
Click between scroll arrow and scroll box	Scroll up, down, left, or right one screen (at least 9 columns or 13 rows).
Drag scroll box	Scroll a variable amount, depending on the distance you drag the scroll box.

EXERCISE 1-9 Use the Go To Command

You use the Go To command on the Edit menu to move to a specific cell address quickly.

1. Click Edit to open the Edit menu and choose Go To. (You may have to expand the menu.) The Go To dialog box appears.

FIGURE 1-13
Go To dialog box

2. Key **J17** in the Reference text box and click OK (or press Enter). The dialog box closes and cell J17 becomes the active cell.

> **NOTE:** Cell J17 displays the number 0.69, but notice that the formula bar displays the number 0.6869. The two differ because the number format for this cell is set for two decimal places. You learn about basic number formatting in Lesson 3.

3. Press F5, the shortcut key for the Go To command. (Ctrl+G also opens the Go To dialog box.)
4. Key **BX94** and press Enter. The active cell moves to column BX, row 94.
5. Press Ctrl+Home to return to cell A1.

> **TIP:** Go To maintains a list of the cells you moved to. You can select a cell from this list to return to it.

Keying Data in a Worksheet

In the following exercises you key data into the Alpha Pharmaceuticals worksheet.

EXERCISE 1-10 Key Data in a Worksheet

1. Click cell E17 to make it active.
2. Key **0.7023**. Notice that the Cancel button ✗ and the Enter button ✓ appear in the formula bar, indicating the formula bar is active. (See Figure 1-14 on the next page.)

> **TIP:** If you make a mistake while keying data, press Backspace to delete the error.

3. Press Enter. The numeric value 0.70 appears in cell E17 and cell E18 becomes active. Notice that the formula bar is no longer active because you have not keyed data in this cell.
4. Key **0.7193** in cell E18 and press ↓. The value 0.72 appears in cell E18 and cell E19 becomes active. Notice the change in cell E20.

> **TIP:** You can complete a cell entry by pressing Enter or an Arrow key.

LESSON 1 ■ WHAT IS EXCEL? EXCEL **27**

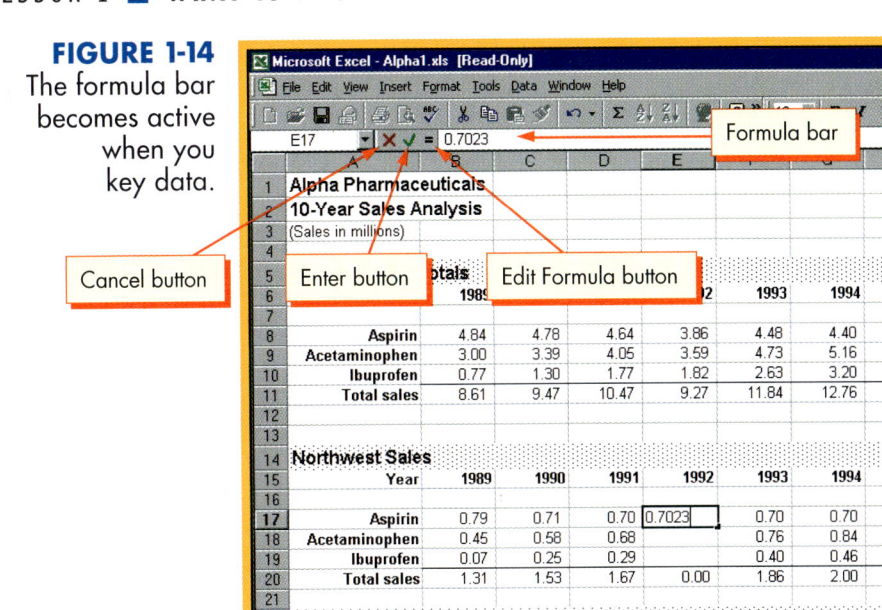

FIGURE 1-14
The formula bar becomes active when you key data.

Cancel button — *Enter button* — *Edit Formula button* — *Formula bar*

5. Key **3.941** in cell E19 and press Enter. Cell E20 reflects the new total, 5.36, which is the sum or total of the column of numbers entered.

EXERCISE 1-11 Change Data in a Worksheet

To change data in a worksheet, you move to the cell that contains the incorrect data, key the correct data, and press Enter or an Arrow key. The new data replaces the old data.

1. Press ↑ to move to cell E19.
2. Key **0.3941** and press Enter. The new corrected total is 1.82.
3. Press Ctrl + Home to move to cell A1.

Saving a Workbook

In Excel, workbooks are saved as files. When you create a new workbook or make changes to an existing one, you must save the workbook to make your changes permanent. Until you save your changes, they can be lost if you have a power failure or hardware problem. It is always a good idea to save your work frequently.

The first step in saving a workbook for future use is to give it a *filename*. In Windows, filenames can be up to 255 characters and are generally followed by a period and a three-character extension. Filename extensions are used to distinguish different types of files. For example, Excel workbooks have the extension .xls, and Word documents have the extension .doc.

Throughout the exercises in this book, filenames consist of three parts:

- *[your initials]*, which may be your initials or the identifier your instructor asks you to use, such as **rst**
- The number of the exercise, such as **4-1**
- The **.xls** extension that Excel uses automatically for workbooks

An example of a filename is: **rst4-1.xls**

> **NOTE:** Filenames can include uppercase letters, lowercase letters, or a combination of both. They can also include spaces. For example, a file can be named "Business Plan.xls."

You can use either the Save command or the Save As command to save a workbook. Use Save As when you name and save a workbook the first time or when you save an existing workbook under a new name. Use Save to resave an existing workbook as you key and edit.

Before you save a new workbook, decide where you want to save it. Excel saves workbooks in the current drive and folder unless you specify otherwise. For example, to save a workbook to a floppy disk, you need to change the drive to A: or B:, whichever is appropriate for your computer.

> **NOTE:** Your instructor will advise you on the proper drive and folder to use in this course.

EXERCISE 1-12　Name and Save a Workbook

1. Click <u>F</u>ile to open the <u>F</u>ile menu and choose Save <u>A</u>s. The Save As dialog box appears.
2. In the File <u>N</u>ame text box, the suggested filename, **Alpha1.xls**, should be highlighted. Replace the filename by keying *[your initials]***1-12**. You don't have to key the filename extension, .xls. Excel applies the extension automatically.

> **NOTE:** If file extensions are not visible in the Save As dialog box, ask your instructor how to use Windows Explorer to change the View settings on your computer.

LESSON 1 ■ WHAT IS EXCEL? EXCEL **29**

3. At the top of the dialog box, click the down arrow in the Save In box and choose the appropriate drive for your data disk (3½ Floppy (A:), for example). Make sure a formatted disk is inserted in the drive.

4. Click Save. Your workbook is named and saved for future use.

FIGURE 1-15
Save As dialog box

EXERCISE 1-13 Choose Another File Type

When you save a file with an .xls extension, you need to open and read the file using Excel. However, when you save a file using the HTML (*Hypertext Markup Language*) file format, anyone can open and read the workbook using a browser. This means that an Excel workbook saved using the HTML file format can be read by anyone with a browser, without opening Excel.

> **NOTE:** Workbooks saved in the HTML file format are often used to create Web pages.

1. Click File to open the File menu and choose Save as Web Page. At the bottom of the Save As dialog box, notice that Web Page is indicated as the file format in the Save As Type box. The file will have the extension .htm (which is short for HTML).

2. Key the filename *[your initials]*1-13 in the File Name text box.

> **TIP:** You can save only the active worksheet or the entire workbook as an HTML file by selecting either option beside Save in the Save As dialog box.

30 EXCEL

UNIT 1 ■ BASIC SKILLS

3. Choose the appropriate location in the Save In box and click Save. The file is saved in HTML format and it can now be read in a browser.

4. Open the File menu and choose Web Page Preview. Excel opens your browser and displays the file.

NOTE: When you convert a file to HTML format and view it in a Web browser, be aware that some formatting may be lost.

5. Close the browser window by clicking the window's Close button ⊠.

Printing a Worksheet and Exiting Excel

Once you create a worksheet, it's easy to print it. You can use any of these methods:

- Click the Print button 🖨 on the Standard toolbar.
- Choose Print from the File menu.
- Press [Ctrl]+[P].

The menu and keyboard methods open the Print dialog box, where you set printing options. Pressing the Print button 🖨 sends the active worksheet, not the entire workbook, directly to the printer using Excel's current print settings.

EXERCISE 1-14 Print a Worksheet

1. Choose Print from the File menu to open the Print dialog box. The dialog box displays Excel's default settings and shows your designated printer.

FIGURE 1-16
Print dialog box

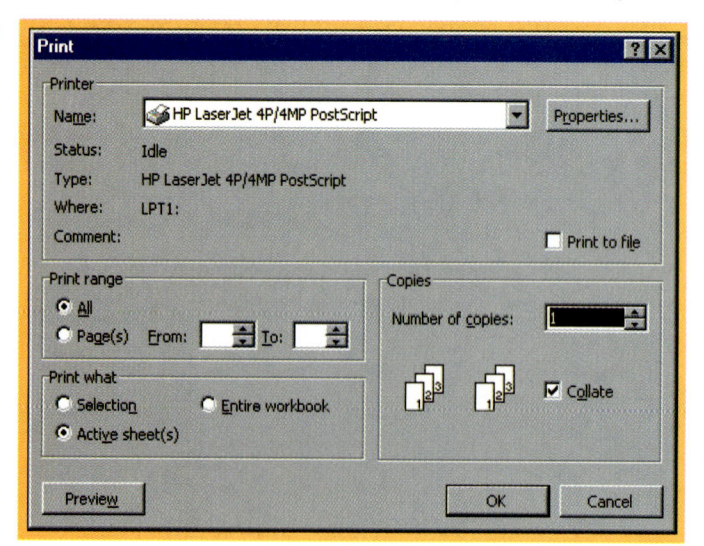

LESSON 1 ■ WHAT IS EXCEL? EXCEL **31**

  2. Click OK or press Enter to accept the settings. A printer icon appears on the taskbar as the worksheet is sent to the printer.

> **TIP:** To print all worksheets in the workbook, you would click the Entire Workbook option in the Print dialog box under Print What.

EXERCISE 1-15 Close a Workbook and Exit Excel

When you finish working with a workbook and save it, you can close it and open another workbook or you can exit Excel.

The easiest ways to close a workbook and to exit Excel include using:

FIGURE 1-17 Close buttons

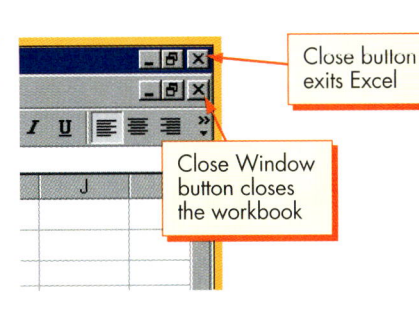

- Close button exits Excel
- Close Window button closes the workbook

- The Close Window button ☒ in the upper right corner of the workbook window and the Close button ☒ in the upper right corner of the Excel window.
- The File menu. You already learned how to close a workbook using Close. To exit Excel, choose Exit. Closing Excel is the same thing as exiting Excel.
- Keyboard shortcuts. Ctrl+W closes a workbook and Alt+F4 exits Excel.

  1. Click the Close Window button ☒ to close the workbook.
  2. Click the Close button ☒ to exit Excel and display the Windows desktop.

COMMAND SUMMARY

FEATURE	BUTTON	MENU	KEYBOARD
Save	💾	File, Save	Ctrl+S
Print	🖨	File, Print	Ctrl+P
Go to a specified address		Edit, Go To	F5 or Ctrl+G
Close current workbook	☒	File, Close	Ctrl+W
Exit Excel	☒	File, Exit	Alt+F4

USING HELP

The Office Assistant is your guide to Excel online Help. The Office Assistant provides tips based on the kind of work you're doing and directs you to relevant Help topics. It may also amuse you with its animated movements. If you find it annoying, you can hide it or choose another character.

Get acquainted with the Office Assistant:

1. Start Excel, if necessary.
2. Click the Office Assistant figure. If the Office Assistant is hidden, press F1. A balloon appears with the question "What would you like to do?"
3. Key **use office assistant** in the text box and click Search. The Office Assistant locates Help topics related to the text you keyed.

FIGURE 1-18
Using Office Assistant

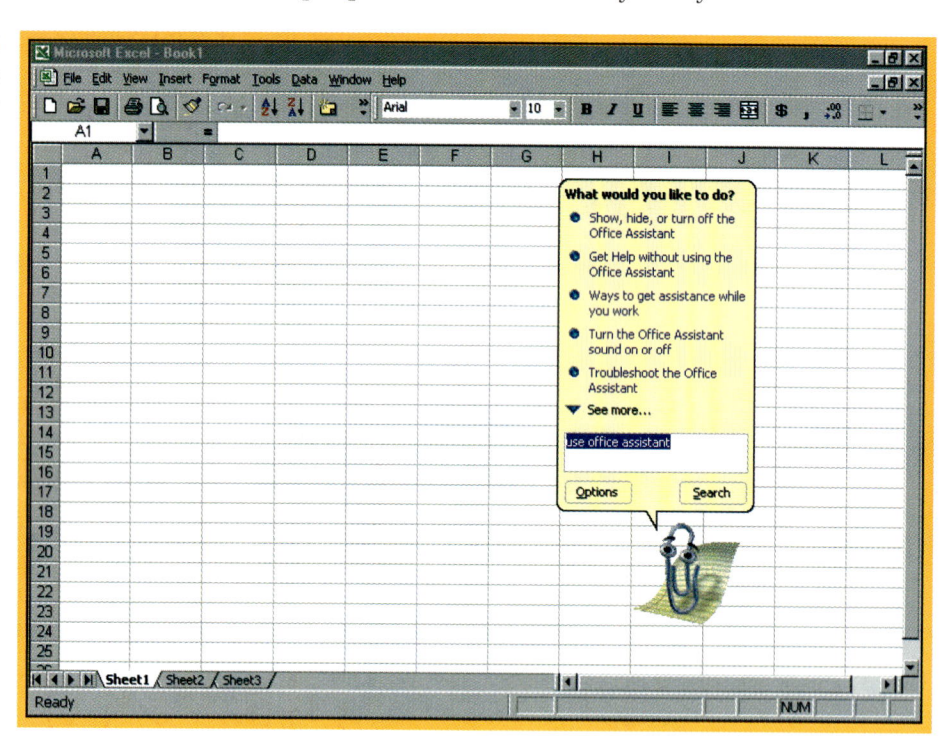

4. Review the displayed topics and click "See more" to display additional related topics.
5. Click "See previous" and then click the topic "Ways to get assistance while you work." A Microsoft Excel Help window with the same topic name is displayed beside the Excel window.
6. Scroll the Help window to review its contents.
7. Click the window's Close button to close Help.

LESSON 1 ■ WHAT IS EXCEL?   EXCEL 33

Concepts Review

TRUE/FALSE QUESTIONS

Each of the following questions is either true or false. Indicate your choice by circling **T** or **F**.

T F   **1.** There is only one way to start Excel.

T F   **2.** The Standard toolbar indicates the location of data being keyed in the active cell.

T F   **3.** The default number of worksheets in a workbook is 3.

T F   **4.** `PgDn` moves one screen down.

T F   **5.** Columns are numbered and rows are labeled with letters.

T F   **6.** The address of the active cell is displayed in the Name Box.

T F   **7.** Scrolling with the scroll bar doesn't change the active cell.

T F   **8.** Moving to a cell using the Go To dialog box doesn't change the active cell.

SHORT ANSWER QUESTIONS

Write the correct answer in the space provided.

1. What is the name of the area on the screen that displays information about a selected command or an operation in progress?

2. What is the name of the rectangle formed by the intersection of a row and a column?

3. What is the name of the area within a worksheet that is current, or ready to receive information?

4. Which keyboard command moves you to the beginning of a row?

5. Which keyboard command moves to the beginning of a worksheet (cell A1)?

6. What command allows you to move to a specific cell address quickly?

_____

7. Which filename extension is used for Excel workbooks?

_____

8. Which filename extension is used for HTML files?

_____

CRITICAL THINKING

Answer these questions on a separate piece of paper. There are no right or wrong answers. Support your answer with examples from your own experience, if possible.

1. What advantages would a worksheet program like Excel offer for a business compared with a noncomputerized pencil and paper worksheet? What advantages for an individual?
2. Excel allows great flexibility when naming files. Many businesses and individuals establish their own rules for naming files. What kinds of rules would you recommend for naming files in a business? For personal use?

Skills Review

EXERCISE 1-16

Start Excel, change the active cell, navigate between worksheets, and close the workbook without saving it.

1. Start Excel, if necessary, by following these steps:
   a. Click the Start button [Start] on the Windows taskbar.
   b. Point to Programs and click Microsoft Excel.
2. Use the Arrow keys to change the active cell to AB15 by following these steps:
   a. Press [↓] until the active cell is A15.
   b. Press [→] until the active cell is AB15.
3. Change to Sheet3 by pressing [Ctrl]+[PgDn] twice.
4. Make D5 the active cell.

LESSON 1 ■ WHAT IS EXCEL?   EXCEL 35

5. Use the mouse to make Sheet1 the current worksheet by following these steps:
   a. Move the pointer over the Sheet1 tab.
   b. Click the worksheet tab for Sheet1.
6. Change the active cell to A1 by pressing Ctrl+Home.
7. Close the workbook by clicking the Close Window button ✕. (You don't save this workbook.)

EXERCISE 1-17

Open a file, change the active cell, and use keyboard commands to navigate within the worksheet.

1. Open the file **Alpha1.xls** by following these steps:
   a. Click the Open button 📂 on the Standard toolbar.
   b. Locate the file in the Look In box.
   c. Double-click the file **Alpha1.xls**.
2. Use ↓ and → to move to cell K19.
3. Return to cell A1 by pressing Ctrl+Home.
4. Press PgDn three times to move down three screens.
5. Press PgUp twice to move up two screens.
6. Press Alt+PgDn two times to move two screens to the right.
7. Press Alt+PgUp once to move one screen to the left.
8. Use ↑ and ← to make cell I17 active.
9. Press Ctrl+→ to move to the last column in this group of cells.
10. Press Ctrl+↓ to move to the last row in this group of cells.
11. Press Ctrl+End to move to the last cell in the last row that contains data or formatting instructions.
12. Press Ctrl+↑. The active cell jumps to the edge of the previous group of cells containing data.
13. Press Ctrl+↑ two more times. K41 becomes the active cell.
14. Return to cell A1.
15. Close the workbook without saving it.

EXERCISE 1-18

Open a file, change the active cell, use the scroll bars and the Go To Command to navigate within the worksheet, key data, print a worksheet, and save and close the workbook.

1. Open the file **Alpha1.xls**.

2. Make cell A1 active (if it isn't already).
3. Click the down arrow on the vertical scroll bar seven times to scroll down seven rows.
4. Click the right arrow on the horizontal scroll bar eight times to scroll eight columns to the right.
5. Drag the scroll box on the horizontal scroll bar to the left so the first column becomes visible again.
6. On the vertical scroll bar, click between the scroll box and the down arrow to move down one screen.
7. Use the Go To command by performing the following steps:
    a. Press F5.
    b. Key **E17** in the Reference box and click OK.
8. Key **0.59** and press Enter.
9. Key **0.55** in cell E18, press ↓, key **0.78** in cell E19, and press Enter.
10. Return to cell A1.
11. Save the file by following these steps:
    a. Choose Save As from the File menu.
    b. In the File Name box, key *[your initials]*1-18
    c. If necessary, change the drive to your data disk by clicking the down arrow in the Save In drop-down list and choosing the appropriate drive.
    d. Click Save.
12. Print your worksheet by following these steps:
    a. Choose Print from the File menu.
    b. Click OK.
13. Close the workbook.

EXERCISE 1-19

Change the active cell, open an existing file, navigate within a worksheet, change data, print a worksheet, save the workbook in different file formats, and close Excel.

1. Open the file **Alpha3.xls**.
2. Change the data as shown in Figure 1-19 by following these steps:
    a. Make the cell containing data you want to change active.
    b. Key the new data.
    c. Move to another cell or press Enter.

LESSON 1 ■ WHAT IS EXCEL?　　　　　　　　　　　　　　　　　　　　　EXCEL　**37**

FIGURE 1-19

Salesperson	Qtr 1	Qtr 2	Qtr 3	Qtr 4	Total	% of Total
Robert Johnson	*65.3*	*62.7*	*58.6*	*52.9*		
Ewald Rhiner	61.0	65.5	70.1	75.3	271.9	10.0%
~~Ruth Seuratadot~~	~~81.7~~	~~60.7~~	~~54.0~~	~~47.3~~	243.7	9.0%
Buster Manatee	50.8	56.1	57.5	58.5	222.9	8.2%
Jose Garcia	75.2	77.9	72.4	73.8	299.3	11.0%
Colleen Masterhouse	65.3	70.9	54.6	74.5	265.3	9.8%
Anthony Chen	88.5	74.6	66.4	68.9	298.4	11.0%
Elouise Swift	66.7	73.9	64.7	69.9	275.2	10.1%
~~Lloyd Polaski~~	~~87.5~~	~~42.3~~	~~57.6~~	~~50.3~~	237.7	8.7%
Murray Diamond	61.0	65.8	74.6	74.2	275.6	10.1%
Barbara Bloomberg	70.0	87.7	82.3	90.2	330.2	12.1%
Richard Daniels	*53.1*	*51.1*	*56.7*	*72.8*		

These will change automatically

 3. Press Ctrl + Home to return to cell A1.
 4. Save the workbook as *[your initials]*1-19.xls.
 5. Click the Print button 🖨 on the Standard toolbar to print the worksheet.

> **NOTE:** This worksheet should print with gridlines to give a different worksheet appearance.

 6. Save the workbook as an HTML file by following these steps:
    a. Choose File, Save As Web Page. (You may have to extend the menu.)
    b. Verify that the filename is *[your initials]***1-19.htm** in the File Name box.
    c. Choose the appropriate location in the Save In box, if necessary.
    d. Click Save.
 7. Close the workbook and close Excel by following these steps:
    a. Choose Close from the File menu.
    b. Click the Close button ❌ in the upper right corner of the Excel Window.

Lesson Applications

EXERCISE 1-20

Start Excel, open an existing file, change the active cell, enter data, use the Save As command, print the worksheet, and close the workbook.

When proofing Alpha Pharmaceuticals' 10-year sales analysis worksheet, the marketing manager's administrative assistant found errors in some of the Northwest region's 1989 figures. You must correct them and add 1992 data to make the worksheet accurate.

1. Start Excel.
2. Open the file **Alpha1.xls**.
3. Make cell B17 active.
4. Change the data in cell B17 to **0.6314**
5. Change the data in cell B18 to **0.5563**
6. Add the following data for "Northwest Sales" in 1992:

Aspirin	**0.7233**
Acetaminophen	**0.7036**
Ibuprofen	**0.3179**

7. Return to cell A1.
8. Save the workbook as *[your initials]***1-20.xls**.
9. Print the worksheet and close the workbook.

EXERCISE 1-21

Open a file, change the active cell, navigate within a worksheet, key data, save and print the worksheet, and close the workbook.

After reviewing the 10-year sales analysis numbers, the marketing manager found several mistakes in the data. You must correct these before the worksheet goes to the president.

1. Open the file **Alpha4.xls**.
2. Make K10 the active cell and change the data to **6.8431**
3. Use the Go To command to move to the following cells and change the data as shown:

LESSON 1 ■ WHAT IS EXCEL?

Cell	Change Data to:
D18	**0.6219**
J19	**0.6891**
B25	**1.0618**
K27	**2.0662**
G34	**1.4817**
C36	**0.3993**
K43	**1.4216**
D45	**0.5225**

4. Go to cell A1.
5. Save the workbook as *[your initials]***1-21.xls**.
6. Print the worksheet.
7. Close the workbook.

EXERCISE 1-22

Open a file, change the active cell, navigate in the worksheet, enter data, print a worksheet, save the workbook in different file formats, and close the workbook.

Because the sales volume in Alpha Pharmaceuticals' Northwest region is significantly lower than the other regions, the company president requested detailed figures for each salesperson. Complete the worksheet containing the sales data by entering the second- and fourth-quarter.

1. Open the file **Alpha5.xls**.
2. Move to cell C8 and key **66.4** (Ewald Rhiner's second-quarter sales).
3. Press Enter to enter the data and move down one cell.

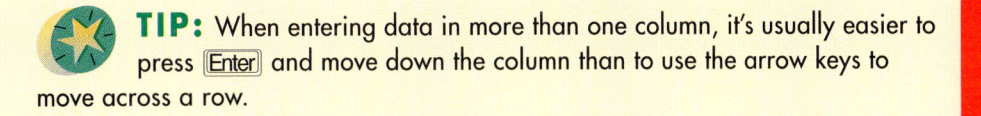

> **TIP:** When entering data in more than one column, it's usually easier to press Enter and move down the column than to use the arrow keys to move across a row.

4. Continue keying the second-quarter data from Figure 1-20 (on the next page). When you finish entering it, enter the fourth-quarter data.
5. When you finish entering the data, verify that the total figure in cell F19 is 2,726.87. If it isn't, check the figures you keyed and correct them where necessary.
6. Go to cell A1 and save the workbook as *[your initials]***1-22.xls**.
7. Print the worksheet.
8. Save the workbook as *[your initials]***1-22.htm**.
9. Close the workbook.

FIGURE 1-20

Salesperson	Qtr 2	Qtr 4
Ewald Rhiner	66.4	54.6
Ruth Seuratadot	82.2	86.0
Buster Manatee	73.8	74.1
Jose Garcia	50.3	81.6
Colleen Masterhouse	57.7	74.6
Anthony Chen	81.2	69.7
Elouise Swift	45.9	60.7
Lloyd Polaski	71.0	67.0
Murray Diamond	65.3	70.6
Barbara Bloomberg	79.8	52.4

EXERCISE 1-23

Open a file, navigate between worksheets, enter data, navigate in the worksheet, and save, print, and close the workbook.

The final sales figures for the Northwest and Southeast regions are now available. Complete the worksheets and print each region's worksheet for the marketing manager.

1. Open the file **Alpha2.xls**.
2. Go to cell B10 on the Northwest worksheet.
3. Key the following data in cells B10, C10, and D10:
   0.074
   0.071
   0.036
4. Go to cell B7 on the Southeast worksheet.
5. Key the following data in cells B7, C7, and D7:
   0.135
   0.097
   0.037
6. Go to cell A1 and save the workbook as *[your initials]***1-23.xls**.

LESSON 1 ■ WHAT IS EXCEL? EXCEL **41**

7. Print all the worksheets and close the workbook.

> **TIP:** To print all the worksheets in a workbook, click Entire Workbook in the Print dialog box under Print What.

EXERCISE 1-24 Challenge Yourself

Open a file, change the active cell, key data in four worksheets within one workbook, and save, print, and close the workbook.

Alpha Pharmaceuticals' sales force is divided into four regions. Annual company sales are shown in a workbook that consists of four worksheets—one worksheet for each region. Some adjustments are needed in the Annual Sales figures for each region.

1. Open the file **Alpha6.xls**.
2. Add the following data for "May" to Sheet2:

Aspirin	**0.074**
Acetaminophen	**0.070**
Ibuprofen	**0.042**

3. Add the following data for "February" to Sheet3:

Aspirin	**0.126**
Acetaminophen	**0.080**
Ibuprofen	**0.030**

4. Change the amounts for "Ibuprofen" on Sheet4 as shown below:

October	**0.201**
November	**0.210**
December	**0.212**

5. Change the amounts for "September" on Sheet1 as shown below:

Aspirin	**0.132**
Acetaminophen	**0.202**
Ibuprofen	**0.207**

6. Save the workbook as *[your initials]***1-24.xls**.
7. Print the entire workbook, close the workbook, and close Excel.

LESSON 2

Creating a Simple Worksheet

OBJECTIVES

After completing this lesson, you will be able to:
1. Enter and edit data.
2. Use Pick From List and AutoComplete to enter labels.
3. Enter data in selected cells.
4. Construct basic formulas.
5. Use the SUM function.
6. Use AutoCalculate.

MOUS ACTIVITIES

In this lesson:
XL2000 **1.2**
XL2000 **1.3**
XL2000 **1.4**
XL2000 **2.4**
XL2000 **6.1**
XL2000 **6.2**
XL2000 **6.3**
XL2000 **6.5**
XL2000 **6.7**
XL2000 **6.8**

See Appendix F.

Estimated Time: 1½ hours

In Lesson 1, you opened an existing worksheet, examined its contents, and keyed data. In this lesson, you create a simple worksheet from scratch—one that contains text, numeric values, and formulas.

Entering and Editing Data

Excel recognizes text and numbers automatically and formats them differently. For example:

- An entry that begins with a number or mathematical sign is recognized as a *value*. Values are aligned at the right margin of the cell by default and are included in calculations.

LESSON 2 ■ CREATING A SIMPLE WORKSHEET   EXCEL **43**

- An entry that begins with a letter is recognized automatically as a *label*. Labels are aligned at the left margin of the cell and are excluded from calculations.

> **TIP:** You can format a number as a label if you begin the entry with an apostrophe (') or if the cell is formatted for text. The number is then excluded from calculations.

When you key data, the information appears in both the formula bar and the active cell. Before you complete the entry, you can use [Backspace] to edit the text or [Esc] to start over. To complete the entry, you can use one of several mouse or keyboard methods.

TABLE 2-1 **Methods for Completing an Entry**

ACTION	RESULT
Click another cell	Completes the entry and makes the selected cell active.
Click ✓	Completes the entry. The current cell remains active.
Press [Enter]	Completes the entry and the cell below becomes active.
Press [Tab]	Completes the entry and the cell to the right becomes active.
Press an Arrow key	Completes the entry and the cell above, below, to the right, or to the left becomes active.

EXERCISE 2-1 Enter Labels and Values in a Worksheet

1. Start Excel. The workbook Book1 appears and cell A1 on Sheet1 is the active cell.
2. Hide the Office Assistant, if necessary. (Choose Hide the <u>O</u>ffice Assistant from the <u>H</u>elp menu.)
3. Key **Sales Analysis** in cell A1. (Do not press [Enter] yet.) Notice that the status bar indicates you are in Enter mode. The text appears in both the formula bar and the active cell. Notice also that the Enter button ✓ and the Cancel button ✗ appear on the formula bar in Enter mode. (See Figure 2-1 on the next page.)
4. Delete three of the characters you just keyed by pressing [Backspace] three times.

44 EXCEL

UNIT 1 ■ BASIC SKILLS

FIGURE 2-1
Text appears in the formula bar in Enter mode.

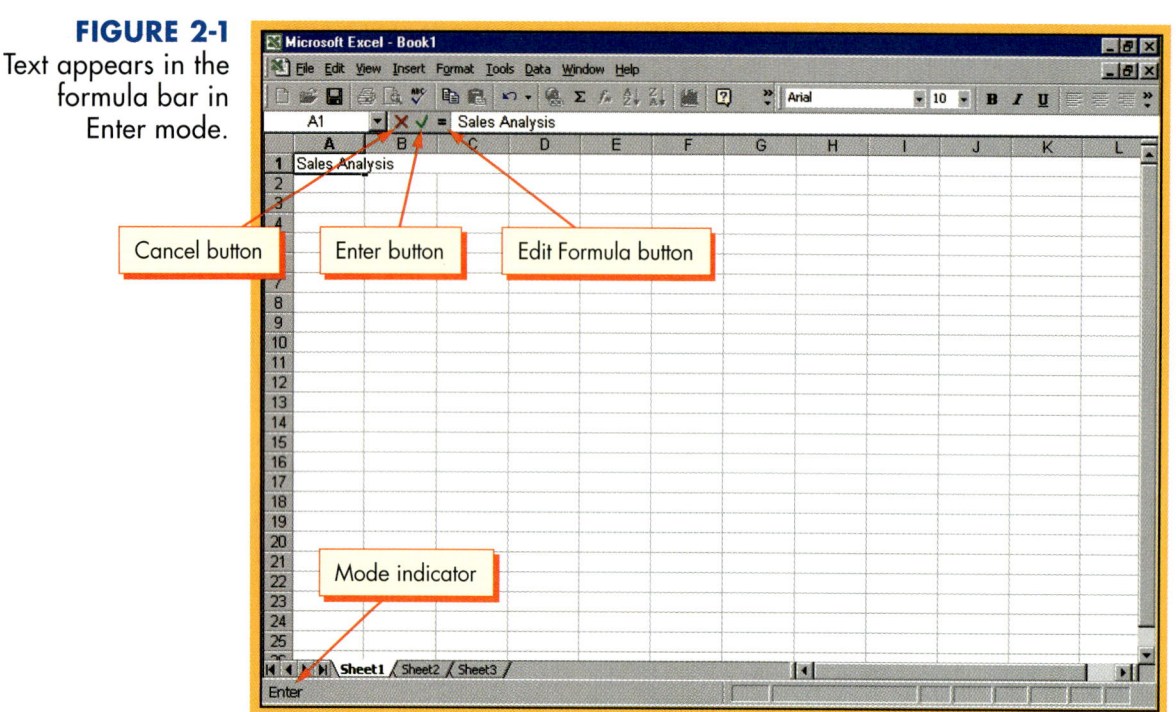

- Cancel button
- Enter button
- Edit Formula button
- Mode indicator

5. Key **sis** to complete the word "Analysis" and click the Enter button ✓ in the formula bar. A1 remains the active cell. Notice that the mode returns to Ready upon completion of the entry. The text appears in cell A1 and overlaps cell B1.

6. Key **Alpha Pharmaceuticals** and press [Enter]. The new text replaces "Sales Analysis" in cell A1 and cell A2 becomes the active cell.

7. In cell A2, key **Regional Sales** and press [Enter] to complete the cell entry. Cell A3 becomes the active cell. Whenever you press [Enter], the active cell moves down one row.

8. In cell A3, key **Sales in $ millions** and press [Enter].

9. Press [↑] and key **1995** as a correction to cell A3, but do not press [Enter]. Cell A3 now contains "1995." However, you actually want it to contain "Sales in $ millions."

10. Press [Esc]. The correction is not made and the original cell content is restored.

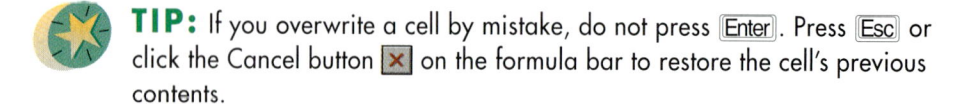

> **TIP:** If you overwrite a cell by mistake, do not press [Enter]. Press [Esc] or click the Cancel button ✕ on the formula bar to restore the cell's previous contents.

11. Move to cell B7. Key an apostrophe ('), then key **1995**. The apostrophe tells Excel this entry is a label, not a value. Press [Tab], C7 is now the active cell, the apostrophe disappears from the 1995 label, and the year is left-aligned.

LESSON 2 ■ CREATING A SIMPLE WORKSHEET															EXCEL **45**

    12. Key **'1996** in cell C7 (note the apostrophe) and press Tab. The year is entered as a label and cell D7 becomes the active cell.

    13. Key the remaining text as shown in Figure 2-2, entering all years as labels. The years all appear left-aligned.

FIGURE 2-2
The Alpha Pharmaceuticals worksheet layout

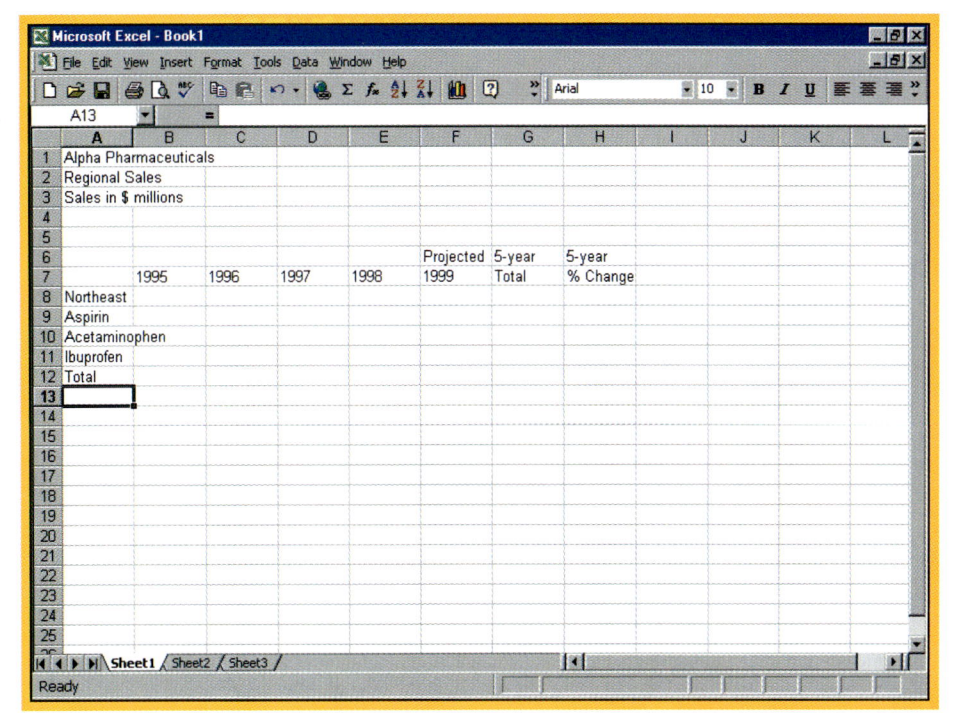

	A	B	C	D	E	F	G	H
1	Alpha Pharmaceuticals							
2	Regional Sales							
3	Sales in $ millions							
4								
5								
6						Projected	5-year	5-year
7		1995	1996	1997	1998	1999	Total	% Change
8	Northeast							
9	Aspirin							
10	Acetaminophen							
11	Ibuprofen							
12	Total							

    14. Widen column A to accommodate the column entry "Acetaminophen." To do this, click anywhere in column A, choose Column from the Format menu, and choose Width. Key **13** in the text box and click OK. (If the column is still not wide enough to accommodate the label, repeat the command, keying a larger value in the text box.)

EXERCISE 2-2 Create a New Folder

    1. Choose Save As from the File menu. You're going to save the document in a new folder that will contain all the files you create in this lesson.

    2. Choose the folder location from the Save In drop-down list. (For example, to save your files to a floppy disk, put a disk in the drive and make sure Save In indicates drive A:.)

> **NOTE:** Check with your instructor about where to save the new folder.

46 EXCEL   UNIT 1 ■ BASIC SKILLS

3. Click the Create New Folder button and key the folder name *[your initials]***Lesson 2**.

4. Enter the filename *[your initials]***2-2** and click **S**ave.

EXERCISE 2-3 Clear the Contents of a Cell

If you key incorrect data into a cell, you can clear the cell's contents by making the cell active and pressing Delete. Another way to clear a cell is to use the Cle**a**r option on the **E**dit menu.

1. In the current workbook, move to cell A8, which contains "Northeast."

FIGURE 2-3
Edit menu, Cle**a**r submenu

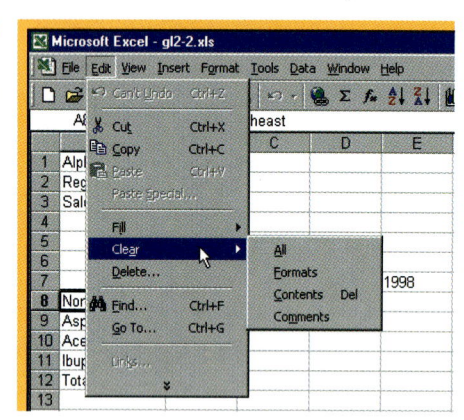

2. Choose Cle**a**r from the **E**dit menu. A submenu appears.

3. Choose **C**ontents to clear cell A8.

4. Key **Southeast** in cell A8 and press Enter.

5. Press ↑ to reactivate cell A8 and press Delete to clear the cell.

6. Key **Northeast** in cell A8 and press Enter.

EXERCISE 2-4 Edit the Contents of a Cell

If a cell contains a long or complicated entry, you might want to edit the contents rather than rekey the entire entry.

To change to Edit mode you can:

• Double-click the cell.

• Click the cell to make it active and click the formula bar.

• Press F2.

1. Double-click cell A3. You are now in Edit mode, as indicated on the status bar. Notice that the pointer changes from a white cross to an I-beam and you can position the insertion point (the flashing vertical bar) to edit text.

2. Click the I-beam between "in" and "$" to position the insertion point.

LESSON 2 ■ CREATING A SIMPLE WORKSHEET   EXCEL   **47**

3. Press `←` and `→` several times. The insertion point moves to the left or right, one character at a time.

4. Press `Home`. The insertion point moves to the left of "Sales." In Edit mode, keys such as `Home` and `End` operate within the cell, rather than within the entire worksheet as they do in Ready mode.

5. Press `Delete` nine times to delete "Sales in" and the space after "in."

6. Key **(** (open parenthesis) and press `End` to move to the end of the text in the cell.

7. Key **)** (close parenthesis) and press `Enter` to complete the entry and exit Edit mode. Cell A3 now contains "($ millions)."

TABLE 2-2   **Keystrokes in Edit Mode**

KEYSTROKE	RESULT
`Enter`	Completes the entry and returns to Ready mode.
`Esc`	Restores the previous cell contents and returns to Ready mode.
`←` or `→`	Moves the insertion point left or right by one character.
`Home`	Moves to the beginning of the cell contents.
`End`	Moves to the end of the cell contents.
`Delete`	Deletes one character to the right of the insertion point.
`Ctrl`+`Delete`	Deletes text to the end of the line.
`Backspace`	Deletes one character to the left of the insertion point.
`Ctrl`+`←` or `Ctrl`+`→`	Moves left or right by one word.

Using Pick From List and AutoComplete

Labels for rows are usually keyed in a single column and often are repeated. For instance, if your worksheet shows sales for three products in four regions, the product names appear four times, once in each region.

Excel provides two features that make it easier to enter labels:
- Pick From List
- AutoComplete

Both features use information that you already entered in the worksheet.

EXERCISE 2-5 Use the Pick From List and AutoComplete Features

1. In cell A13, key **Southeast** and press Enter.
2. Right-click cell A14 (position the mouse pointer in cell A14 and click the right button). The shortcut menu appears.

FIGURE 2-4
Shortcut menu

3. Choose Pick From List from the shortcut menu. The list contains the labels that you keyed in consecutive cells A8 through A13.

> **NOTE:** The labels appearing in the Pick From List are from consecutive cells that appear above the current cell.

4. Click "Aspirin" in the list. (See Figure 2-5.) Excel automatically inserts this row label in cell A14.
5. Right-click cell A15, choose Pick From List, and click "Acetaminophen" in the list. Excel inserts this label in the active cell.
6. Move to cell A16 and key **I**. The AutoComplete feature highlights "buprofen" as a choice to complete the entry. AutoComplete chooses an item from the Pick From List when you key the first letters of that item. Because "Ibuprofen" is the only item that begins with an "I," you needed to key only one letter in this case. (See Figure 2-6.)

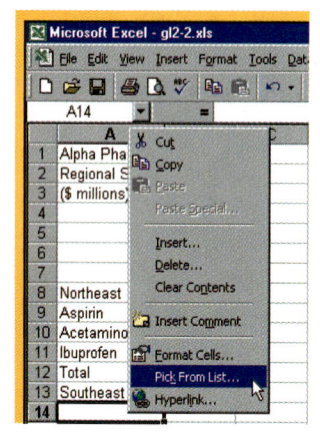

FIGURE 2-5
Using the Pick From List feature

7. Press Enter to accept "Ibuprofen."
8. Key **As** in cell A17, but do not press Enter. AutoComplete suggests "Aspirin."
9. Press Esc to start over and key **T**. AutoComplete suggests "Total." Press Enter to complete the entry.
10. Complete the labels in column A as shown in Figure 2-7 (on the next page). Key text for the new entries. Use AutoComplete or the Pick From List feature to insert items that you already keyed.

FIGURE 2-6
AutoComplete suggests an item from the Pick From List.

LESSON 2 ■ CREATING A SIMPLE WORKSHEET   EXCEL   **49**

FIGURE 2-7

	A
18	Northwest
19	Aspirin
20	Acetaminophen
21	Ibuprofen
22	Total
23	Southwest
24	Aspirin
25	Acetaminophen
26	Ibuprofen
27	Total
28	Grand Total

Entering Data in Selected Cells

In many cases, you may find it convenient to work with a group of selected cells. One way to group selected cells is as a block. A *block* is a group of cells that are next to one another.

Excel provides three methods of selecting cells to form a block:
- Using the Keyboard
- Using the Mouse
- Using the Name Box

EXERCISE 2-6 Select a Block of Cells Using the Keyboard

When you make a cell active, you have actually selected it. To extend the selection using the keyboard, press [Shift] in combination with the navigation keys.

1. Make cell B9 active.

2. Hold down [Shift] and press [→] three times. A dark border surrounds the selected cells, B9 through E9. The first cell in the selection, B9, which is also the active cell, appears white. Cells C9 through E9 appear highlighted by transparent blue through which you can easily see data.

3. With [Shift] held down, press [↓] twice. The selected block now extends from B9 through E11.

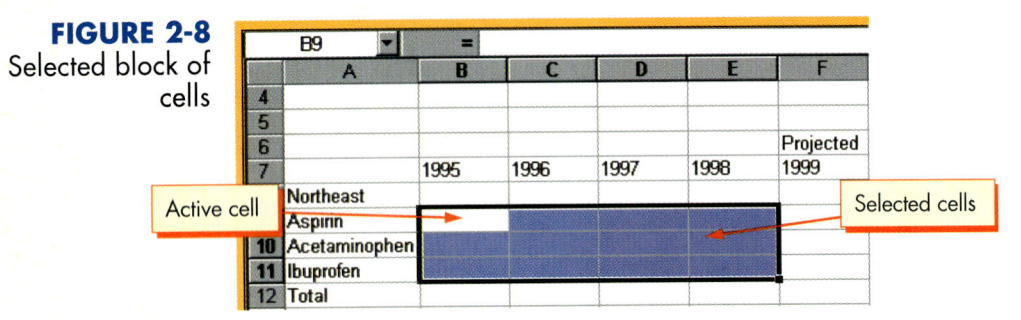

FIGURE 2-8
Selected block of cells

4. Key **1.112** and press [Enter]. The value appears in cell B9 and B10 becomes active.

5. Key **1.465** and press [Enter]. The value appears in cell B10 and B11 becomes active.

6. Key **1.085** and press [Enter]. The value appears in cell B11. The next cell in the block, C9, becomes active.

TIP: Entering data in selected cells can be a very efficient technique, because [Enter] or [Tab] then moves only *within* the selected cells.

7. Key the remaining data for the selected block as shown in Figure 2-9.

FIGURE 2-9

	A	B	C	D	E
9	Aspirin	1.112	1.082	1.053	1.024
10	Acetaminophen	1.465	1.592	1.73	1.94
11	Ibuprofen	1.085	1.36	1.704	2.225

NOTE: Using the arrow keys or the mouse to position the active cell deselects the block.

LESSON 2 ■ CREATING A SIMPLE WORKSHEET   EXCEL   **51**

   8. Press ↓. The block is deselected.
   9. Click cell F11 to make it active, hold down Shift, and press Home. The selection extends from F11 through A11.
   10. Press Shift+Ctrl+Home. The selection extends from F11 through A1.
   11. Press Shift+↓. The selection shrinks by one row.
   12. Press any arrow key to deselect the block.

TABLE 2-3 **Navigation Key Combinations**

KEY COMBINATION	ACTION
Shift+Arrow key	Extend the selection one cell in the direction indicated by the Arrow key.
Shift+PgUp or Shift+PgDn	Extend the selection one screen up or down.
Shift+Ctrl+Home	Extend the selection to the beginning of the worksheet.
Shift+Home	Extend the selection to the beginning of the row.
Shift+Ctrl+End	Extend the selection to the end of the data in the worksheet.
Shift+Ctrl+Arrow key	Extend the selection to the edge of a block of data in the direction indicated by the Arrow key.
Ctrl+Spacebar	Select an entire column.
Shift+Spacebar	Select an entire row.
Ctrl+A or Ctrl+Shift+Spacebar	Select an entire worksheet.

EXERCISE 2-7   Select Cells Using the Mouse

Excel provides several ways to select cells in a block using the mouse:
- Click a column-heading letter to select an entire column or click a row-heading number to select an entire row.
- Click the Select All button to select the entire worksheet.
- Drag across adjacent cells to select a block.
- Hold down Shift and click a cell to select a block beginning with the active cell and ending at the new location.

You can also use the mouse to add a non-adjacent block of cells to an existing block of cells. Once the first block is selected, you can select additional blocks by holding down Ctrl and dragging across the cells in the additional block.

1. Click cell B14, hold down the mouse button, and then drag the pointer down and over to cell E16.
2. Release the mouse button. Cells B14 through E16 are selected and B14 is the active cell.
3. Click any cell to deselect the block.
4. Click column-heading A to select the entire column.

FIGURE 2-10
Selecting a column

Select All button
Column heading
Row heading

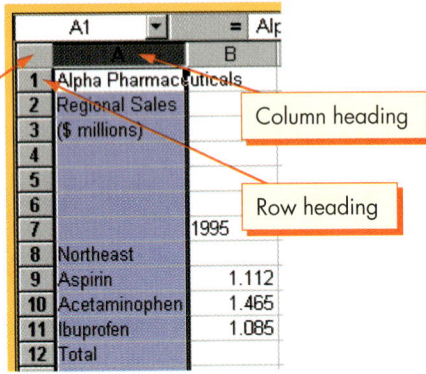

5. Click anywhere in the worksheet to deselect the column. Click row-heading 1 to select the entire row.
6. Click the Select All button (the gray square to the left of column heading A) to select the entire worksheet. (See Figure 2-10 for the location of the Select All button.)
7. Click cell B7 (containing "1995"), hold down Shift, and click cell E7. Cells B7 through E7 are selected.
8. Press Delete to clear the cells. The block is still selected and B7 is the active cell.
9. Rekey **1995**, **1996**, **1997**, and **1998** in cells B7, C7, D7, and E7, respectively, pressing Enter or Tab between each entry. Remember to enter the years as labels by beginning each entry with an apostrophe.

TIP: Tab moves the active cell to the right. Shift+Tab moves the active cell to the left.

10. Press ↓ once to deselect the block of cells.
11. Drag from cell B14 to E16 to select this block.
12. Click the down arrow in the vertical scroll bar to display row 28 of the worksheet. To add a second block of cells to the range, hold down Ctrl and drag the mouse from cell B19 to E21.
13. Hold down Ctrl and drag the mouse from cell B24 to E26. A third block is added to the range.
14. Hold down Ctrl and click B14 to make it the active cell. (See Figure 2-11 on the next page.)
15. Key **1** and press Enter twice. B15 becomes the active cell.
16. Press Enter repeatedly to move through the range. Notice that the active cell moves from the end of one block to the beginning of the next block and from the end of the range to the beginning of the range.

LESSON 2 ■ CREATING A SIMPLE WORKSHEET   EXCEL   **53**

FIGURE 2-11
Selected range of non-adjacent blocks

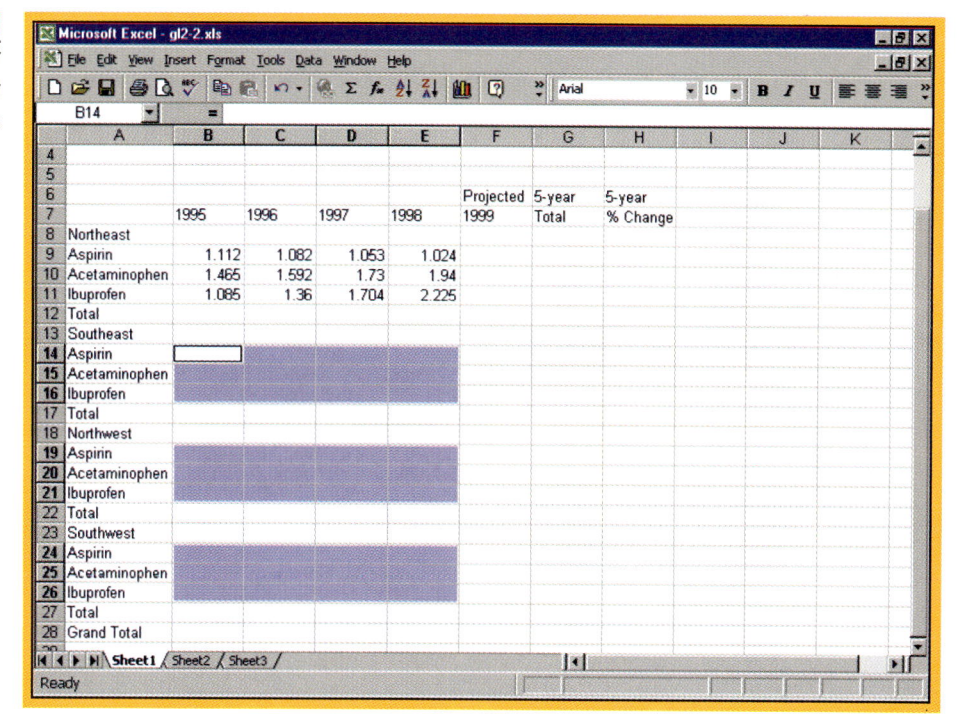

TIP: Enter moves the active cell down. Shift+Enter moves the active cell up.

17. Press Delete to clear the range contents.
18. Click anywhere in the worksheet to deselect the range.

NOTE: If you're using the Microsoft IntelliPoint Mouse, additional navigating options are available. For example, you can roll the wheel forward and backward instead of using the vertical scroll bars; hold down the wheel and drag in any direction to pan the document; or hold Ctrl and roll the wheel to change magnification.

EXERCISE 2-8 Select Cells Using the Name Box

You can select a range of cells by keying the first and last cells separated by a colon in the Name Box. For example, you can enter C9:E10 to select the block that includes cells C9, C10, D9, D10, E9, and E10.

FIGURE 2-12
Using the Name Box to select cells

1. Click in the Name Box and key **b14:e16**. (Cell references are not case-sensitive, so you can key lowercase letters.)

2. Press [Enter]. The cells in the specified range are selected.

3. Click any cell to deselect the block. Return to cell A1.

4. Save the worksheet as *[your initials]*2-8.xls in your Lesson 2 folder.

Constructing Basic Formulas

Formulas are instructions that tell Excel how to perform calculations. Formulas can contain mathematical operators, values, cell references, cell ranges, and functions. Excel performs the operations indicated in the formula in a specific order.

TABLE 2-4   **Commonly Used Mathematical Operators**

OPERATOR	PRECEDENCE	DESCRIPTION
^	1st	Exponentiate
*	2nd	Multiply
/	2nd	Divide
+	3rd	Add
-	3rd	Subtract
( )		Used to control the order of mathematical operations

NOTE: The exponentiation operator (^) raises a value to a power. The expression 2^3 means "two to the third power," or 2^3, or 2x2x2.

Excel's *order of precedence* defines the order in which it performs formula operations. In a formula, Excel performs exponentiation operations first, multiplication and division next, and addition and subtraction last. Operations with equal precedence are performed from left to right. You can use parentheses ( ) to override the order of precedence. Excel performs operations inside parentheses first. You can also "nest" expressions—that is, put parenthetical expressions within parentheses. The innermost operations are handled first. The following figure shows how parentheses change the order of precedence for operations.

LESSON 2 ■ CREATING A SIMPLE WORKSHEET   EXCEL 55

FIGURE 2-13
These two formulas include the same numbers and operators, but parentheses change the order of operations.

     2nd 1st 3rd   1st 2nd 3rd

1 + 2 * 3 - 1 =   ((1 + 2) * 3) - 1 =
1 + 6 - 1   = 6   ((3) * 3) - 1   =
                                                     9 - 1   = 8

You can create formulas using the keyboard or by entering a combination of keystrokes and mouse clicks. As you key a formula, it appears in both the active cell and the formula bar. When you complete the entry, the result of the calculation appears in the active cell, but the formula bar displays the formula. Excel formulas begin with = (an equal sign). Because cell references in a formula are not case-sensitive, you can enter them in either uppercase or lowercase.

TABLE 2-5 Typical Excel Formulas

FORMULA	ACTION
=245+374	Adds the values 245 and 374.
=F4+F5	Adds the values in cells F4 and F5.
=c3+b3-d5	Adds the values in cells C3 and B3 and subtracts the value in cell D5 from the result.
=(A3+B3)/C9	Adds the values in cells A3 and B3 and divides the result by the value in cell C9.
=F5*1.02	Multiplies the contents of cell F5 by 1.02 (or 102%).
=F5*C10	Multiplies the contents of cell F5 by the contents of cell C10.

EXERCISE 2-9 Key an Addition Formula

1. In the current workbook, select and clear the contents of cells A13 through A28.
2. Move to cell B12, which will display the total of 1995 sales.
3. Key **=B9+B10+B11** and press Enter. The result, "3.662," appears in cell B12.

> **TIP:** Remember, cell references are not case-sensitive—you can enter them in either uppercase or lowercase.

4. Press ↑ to make B12 the active cell. The formula is displayed in the formula bar.

56 EXCEL UNIT 1 ■ BASIC SKILLS

EXERCISE 2-10 Build an Addition Formula with the Mouse

You can enter a cell reference in a formula by clicking the cell with the mouse. While building a formula, clicking another cell switches the worksheet into Point mode, which appears in the status bar. If you click the wrong cell or make another error, just press [Backspace] to delete the incorrect characters. You can then continue building the formula.

1. Move to cell C12 and click the Edit Formula button [=]. Excel changes to Edit mode, expands the formula bar, and enters an equal sign to start the formula. Notice the addition of the Function box.

FIGURE 2-14
The formula bar expands when the Edit Formula button is clicked.

TIP: You can drag the expanded formula bar out of the way to see cells it covers.

2. Click cell C9. Excel changes to Point mode and a moving dashed border surrounds cell C9. Notice that "=C9" appears in both the active cell and the formula bar.
3. Key **+** (the plus sign). The plus sign is added to the formula and the moving border disappears. Excel changes to Edit mode.
4. Click cell C10 and key **+** (the plus sign). The formula "=C9+C10+" appears.
5. Click cell C11 and then press [Enter]. The result, "4.034," appears in cell C12. C13 is now the active cell.

TIP: You can also click the Enter button [✓] or OK on the formula bar to get the formula result. C12 would then remain the active cell.

EXERCISE 2-11 Build Multiplication Formulas

Alpha Pharmaceuticals' sales figures are available for the years 1995 through 1998, but a projection must be calculated for 1999. The company is predicting that aspirin sales will decrease by 5% in 1999 and acetaminophen and ibuprofen sales will increase by 2% and 3%, respectively.

1. In cell F9, key **=** (the equal sign) and click cell E9.

LESSON 2 ■ CREATING A SIMPLE WORKSHEET   EXCEL **57**

2. Key ***** (the multiplication operator), key **.95**, and click the Enter button ☑ on the formula bar.

3. The formula "=E9*0.95" appears in the formula bar and "0.9728" appears in cell F9. This formula is equivalent to 5 percent less than E9, which is the projected decrease in aspirin sales for 1999.

4. Move to cell F10, key **=E10*1.02**, and press Enter. The result, "1.9788," appears in cell F10. The formula "=E10*1.02" is equivalent to the formula "=E10+E10*0.02," which is the projected 2 percent increase in acetaminophen sales for 1999.

5. In cell F11, key the formula **=E11*1.03,** and click the Enter button ☑. The result "2.29175" appears.

EXERCISE 2-12   Calculate a Percentage Change

The Alpha Pharmaceuticals worksheet needs calculations to determine the percentage change in each product over the five-year sales period. The general formula for a percentage change is (new-old)/old*100. The subtraction must be performed before division. The resulting decimal must be multiplied by 100 to convert it to a percentage.

1. Move to cell H9 and key **=(**

2. Click cell F9 and key **-** (the minus sign).

3. Click cell B9 and key **)**

4. Key **/** (the forward slash, which is the division operator).

5. Click cell B9, key *****, key **100**, and press Enter.

6. Move back to cell H9. The formula "=(F9-B9)/B9*100" appears in the formula bar and the result "-12.518" appears in cell H9.

7. In cell H10, enter the formula **=(F10-B10)/B10*100**. The result is 35.07167.

8. In cell H11, enter the formula **=(F11-B11)/B11*100**. The result shows that ibuprofen sales more than doubled over the five-year period, increasing 111.2212 percent.

FIGURE 2-15
Calculating percentage changes

	A	B	C	D	E	F	G	H
1	Alpha Pharmaceuticals							
2	Regional Sales							
3	($ millions)							
4								
5								
6						Projected	5-year	5-year
7		1995	1996	1997	1998	1999	Total	% Change
8	Northeast							
9	Aspirin	1.112	1.082	1.053	1.024	0.9728		-12.518
10	Acetaminophen	1.465	1.592	1.73	1.94	1.9788		35.07167
11	Ibuprofen	1.085	1.36	1.704	2.225	2.29175		111.2212
12	Total	3.662	4.034					
13								

H11 =(F11-B11)/B11*100

Using the SUM Function

Keying individual cell references is a reasonable way to add two or three cells. It is not practical for adding a long column or row of values, however. Excel's SUM function greatly simplifies the process of adding many values.

In general, the formula for a function is constructed with an equal sign and the function name followed by a set of parentheses, with one or more cell references or values within the parentheses.

FIGURE 2-16
Structure of a SUM formula

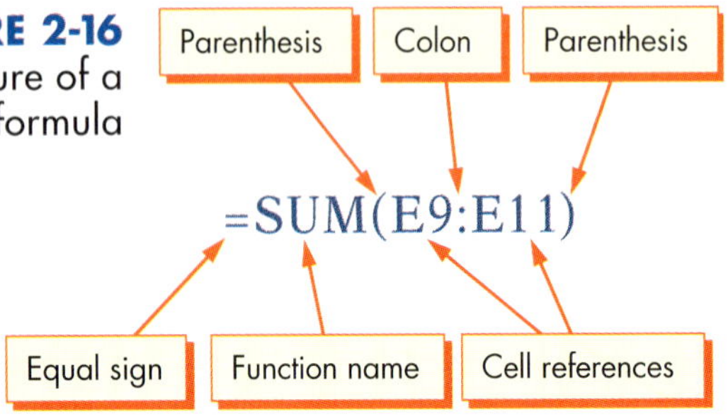

=SUM(E9:E11)

(Parenthesis, Colon, Parenthesis, Equal sign, Function name, Cell references)

In a SUM formula, the cell references can consist of a single cell or a block of cells. Excel refers to these references as a *range*. Technically, a range is any group of cells specified to be acted upon by a command. To identify a range, key the cell references for two diagonally opposite corners of a group of cells, separated by a colon.

TABLE 2-6 Examples of Ranges

RANGE	DEFINES
C4:C4	A single cell
B5:B10	A range of cells in column B
D3:G3	A range of cells in row 3
C5:F12	A rectangular range of cells in columns C through F, rows 5 through 12

EXERCISE 2-13 Key a SUM Formula

1. Move to cell D12.
2. Key **=SUM(D9:D11)** and press `Enter`. The formula adds the contents of cells D9 through D11. The result, "4.487," appears in cell D12.

> **NOTE:** Like cell references, function names are not case-sensitive, so you can key them in lowercase letters.

LESSON 2 ■ CREATING A SIMPLE WORKSHEET   EXCEL   59

EXERCISE 2-14 Enter a SUM Formula Using the Arrow Keys

1. Move to cell E12.
2. Key **=SUM(**

   NOTE: Make sure you key the parenthesis.

3. Press ↑. A moving border surrounds cell E11 and "=SUM(E11" appears in the formula bar.
4. Key a colon (:) or a period to anchor the border. The formula "=SUM(E11:E11" appears in the formula bar.
5. Press ↑ twice. The border extends the range from cell E9 through cell E11.
6. Press Enter to complete the formula. Excel inserts the closing parenthesis for you automatically. The completed formula is "=SUM(E9:E11)" and the result is 5.189. In this case, you defined the cell range from the bottom to the top. Excel can add cell contents in either direction.

EXERCISE 2-15 Use the Mouse to Enter a SUM Formula

You can create SUM formulas using the mouse to drag across cells instead of using the Arrow keys. You can also use the buttons on the formula bar to build a SUM formula.

1. In cell G9, key **=SUM(**
2. Using the mouse, click cell B9.
3. Drag across the row from cell B9 to cell F9 and release the mouse button. A moving border surrounds the selected range and the formula "=SUM(B9:F9" appears in the formula bar.
4. Click the Enter button ✓ on the formula bar or press Enter. The formula is completed and the result, "5.2438," appears in cell G9.
5. Move to cell F12.
6. Click the Edit Forumula button =. An equal sign is entered in the cell to start the formula.
7. Click the Function box on the left of the formula bar. The SUM function and a suggested range are displayed in the formula bar and the Formula Palette pop-up window is displayed under the formula bar. (If the SUM function is not shown, click the drop-down arrow and choose SUM.)

FIGURE 2-17
Formula Palette pop-up window

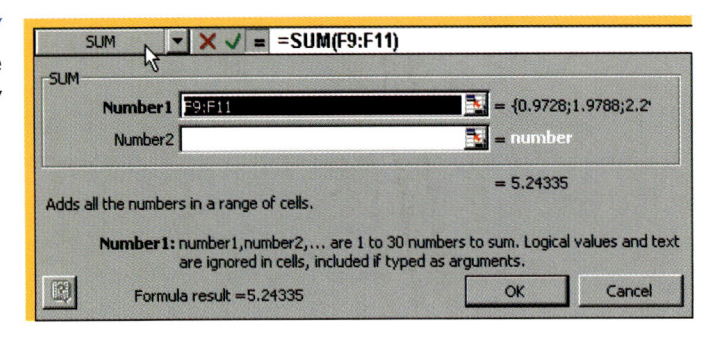

8. Click OK. The formula is completed and the result, "5.24335," appears in cell F12.

EXERCISE 2-16 Use the AutoSum Button to Enter a SUM Formula

The AutoSum button ∑ is a shortcut for entering the SUM formula, similar to the Function box. It enters **=SUM(** and suggests a range to total. At the bottom of a column of values, AutoSum totals the column. At the right of a row of values, AutoSum totals the row.

1. Move to cell G10.

2. Click the AutoSum button ∑ on the Standard toolbar. (You may need to click the More Buttons button to find it.) The formula "=SUM(B10:F10)" appears in the formula bar and in the cell and a moving border surrounds cells B10 through F10 on the worksheet.

   TIP: You can also press Alt + = to use the AutoSum function.

3. Click the Enter button ✓ on the formula bar or press Enter. The result, "8.7058," appears in cell G10.

4. With cell G11 selected, double-click the AutoSum button ∑. The SUM formula is entered with the result "13.9496." Notice that the formula range is G9:G10 (for the column) rather than B11:F11 (for the row). The AutoSum feature automatically adds column numbers above a cell before adding row numbers to the left of the cell. Because two values appeared above cell G11, Excel assumed a column SUM formula.

5. To correct the range, click the AutoSum button ∑ again. Notice the moving border surrounds the incorrect range.

6. Drag across cells B11 to F11 and press Enter. The correct result, "8.66575," appears in cell G11.

LESSON 2 ■ CREATING A SIMPLE WORKSHEET   EXCEL   **61**

    7. Enter a SUM formula in cell G12, using any method. (Try double-clicking the AutoSum button Σ now, for instance.) Check that the formulas contain the correct ranges, then press Ctrl + Home to return to cell A1.

FIGURE 2-18
Completed worksheet

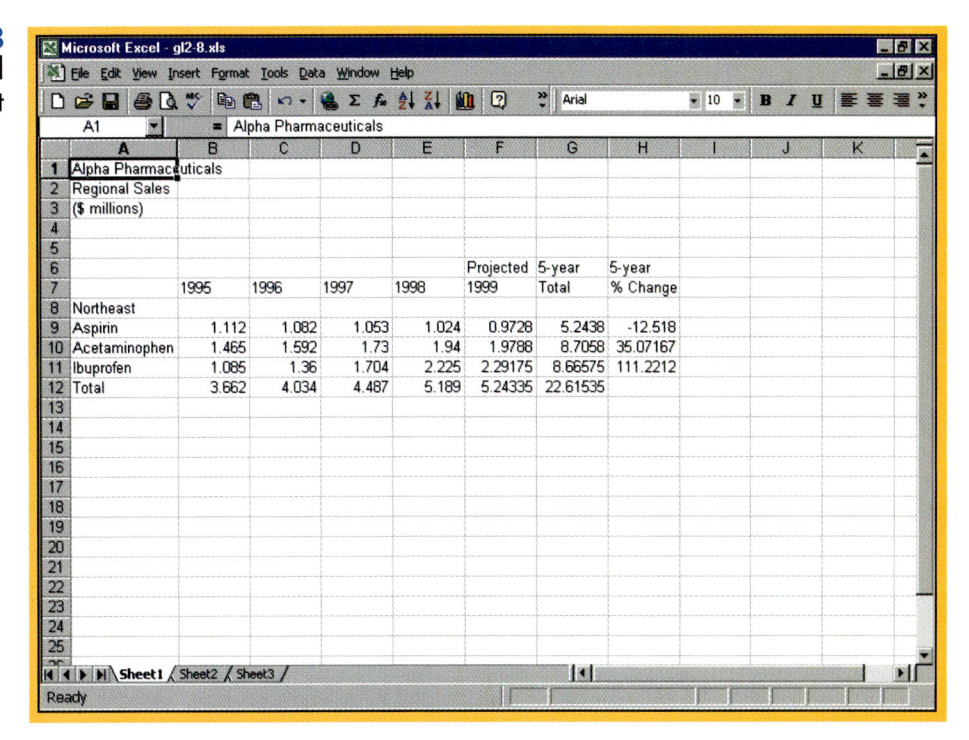

(screenshot of completed worksheet "Microsoft Excel - gl2-8.xls" showing Alpha Pharmaceuticals Regional Sales ($ millions) with columns for 1995, 1996, 1997, 1998, Projected 1999, 5-year Total, 5-year % Change; rows Northeast, Aspirin, Acetaminophen, Ibuprofen, Total)

	A	B	C	D	E	F	G	H
1	Alpha Pharmaceuticals							
2	Regional Sales							
3	($ millions)							
6						Projected	5-year	5-year
7		1995	1996	1997	1998	1999	Total	% Change
8	Northeast							
9	Aspirin	1.112	1.082	1.053	1.024	0.9728	5.2438	-12.518
10	Acetaminophen	1.465	1.592	1.73	1.94	1.9788	8.7058	35.07167
11	Ibuprofen	1.085	1.36	1.704	2.225	2.29175	8.66575	111.2212
12	Total	3.662	4.034	4.487	5.189	5.24335	22.61535	

    8. Save the workbook as *[your initials]***2-16.xls**.
    9. Print the worksheet.

> **NOTE:** Cell H9 displays three decimal places on screen, but may print showing five.

Using AutoCalculate

Excel includes an easy-to-use calculator. You can use this calculator, which is called AutoCalculate, to perform simple calculations without entering a formula. For example, if you select a range of cells, AutoCalculate displays the sum of the cells in the status bar.

> **NOTE:** In addition to the SUM function, AutoCalculate can perform other functions, such as AVERAGE, MIN, and MAX. You can consult Excel's Help for more information on these functions.

EXERCISE 2-17 Use AutoCalculate to Find a Sum

1. Select cells D12 and E12, which contain the total sales for the years 1997 and 1998.
2. Right-click the status bar to display the AutoCalculate menu. Notice the various function names.

> **NOTE:** Functions are shown in uppercase letters in this text. When you key a function in Excel, it does not matter whether you use uppercase or lowercase.

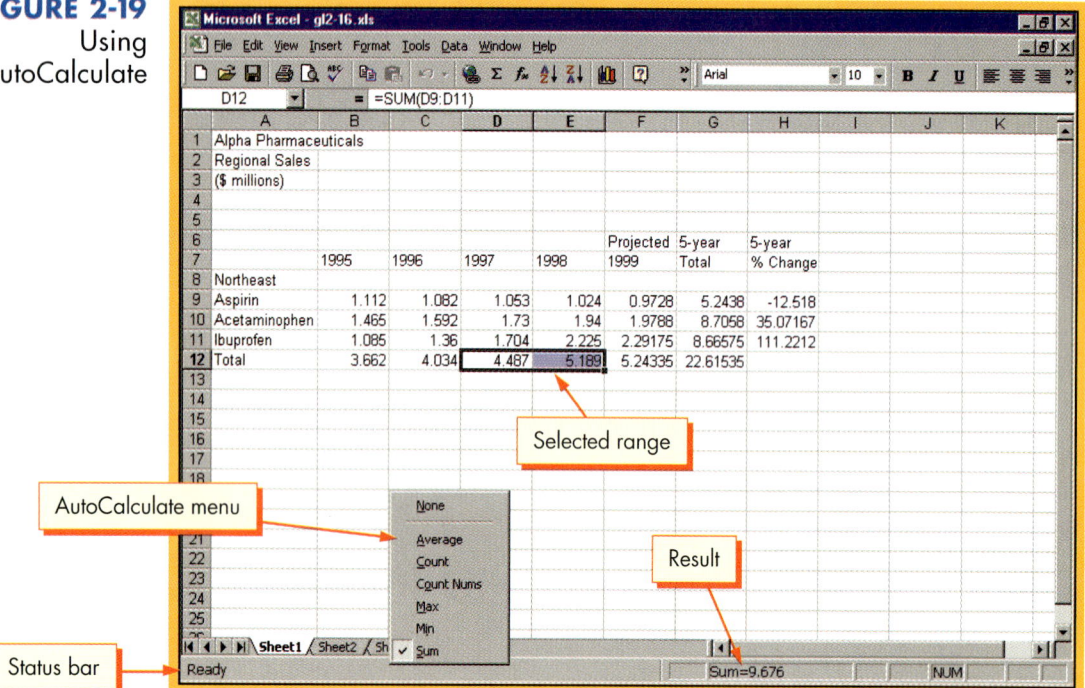

FIGURE 2-19
Using AutoCalculate

3. Choose SUM from the menu. The status bar displays "Sum=9.676."

> **NOTE:** AutoCalculate uses the last function chosen to calculate the current selection. If SUM was the last function chosen, for example, the sum of D12 and E12 is displayed as soon as the cells are selected.

4. Select another range of cells containing values. This time use the AVERAGE function. Notice the average displayed on the status bar.
5. Change back to the SUM function.
6. Close the workbook without saving it.

LESSON 2 ■ CREATING A SIMPLE WORKSHEET EXCEL **63**

COMMAND SUMMARY

FEATURE	BUTTON	MENU	KEYBOARD
Delete cell contents		Edit, Clear, Contents	Delete
Cancel current entry	✕		Esc
Enter	✓		Enter
Edit Formula	=		
AutoSum	Σ		Alt + =

USING HELP

The previous lesson introduced you to the Office Assistant. You can also display ScreenTips without using the Office Assistant. Descriptive ScreenTips are available for menu commands, dialog box options, and parts of the Excel screen.

Display descriptive ScreenTips:

1. Open a new workbook. (Click the Open button on the Standard toolbar.)
2. Click Help to open the Help menu. Click the menu item What's This? (Notice that you can also press Shift + F1.) The pointer now has a question mark attached to it.

FIGURE 2-20 Help menu

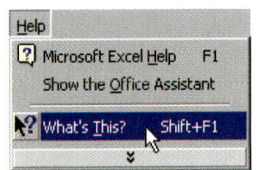

3. Click one of the tab scrolling buttons. Review the ScreenTip and click anywhere in the worksheet to close it.
4. Press Shift + F1 to display the question mark pointer again. Choose Save As from the File menu. Review the description of this command and click to close it.
5. Choose Properties from the File menu and click the Summary tab, if necessary. In the upper right corner of the dialog box, click the Help button to display the question mark pointer. Click Subject (the word or the blank text box), review the description, and close it. You can repeat this process to see as many descriptions as you like.
6. Close the dialog box and close the workbook without saving it.

Concepts Review

TRUE/FALSE QUESTIONS

Each of the following statements is either true or false. Indicate your choice by circling **T** or **F**.

T F 1. The Delete key has the same effect as choosing Clear from the Edit menu and then choosing Contents.

T F 2. If a cell containing a formula is included in another formula, the value of the first formula is included in the calculation.

T F 3. In Excel, formulas begin with an asterisk (*).

T F 4. You can use parentheses () in a formula to control the order of mathematical operations.

T F 5. The formula **=SUM(A6:D6)** adds the contents of the cells in row 6, from column A to column D.

T F 6. In formulas, function names must be entered in uppercase letters only.

T F 7. You can use the AutoSum button Σ to enter a SUM formula.

T F 8. You can use the SUM function to add the contents of both columns and rows.

SHORT ANSWER QUESTIONS

Write the correct answer in the space provided.

1. Which mode must be displayed in the status bar before you begin keying information into a worksheet?

2. When you key information into a cell, where else does the information appear on the screen?

3. In Edit mode, which key moves you to the beginning of selected cell contents (as well as the first character in the formula bar)?

4. Which mathematical operation is indicated by an asterisk (*)?

LESSON 2 ■ CREATING A SIMPLE WORKSHEET   EXCEL **65**

    5. Which mathematical operations are given last priority in the order of precedence?

    _____

    6. Which function adds columns or rows?

    _____

    7. What is the result given by the following formula =(10-4)/2?

    _____

    8. What is the result given by the following formula =10-4/2?

    _____

CRITICAL THINKING

Answer these questions on a separate piece of paper. There are no right or wrong answers. Support your answers with examples from your own experience, if possible.

1. Your boss asks you to proofread a complex worksheet and its printed sources of data. How might AutoCalculate help you verify that data was entered accurately?

2. Last month's sales report worksheet lists products in rows and sales representatives in columns. Your boss asks you to update this report with new data. How can you select cells to speed your work? If your data came from the sales reports of individual sales representatives, would you press [Enter] or [Tab] after each entry? Why?

Skills Review

EXERCISE 2-18

Enter data, edit data, and enter labels using the Pick From List and AutoComplete features.

1. Click the New button [D] to start a new workbook, if necessary.
2. Key **Alpha Pharmaceuticals** in cell A1 and press [Enter].
3. Key **1998 Sales - Northeast Region** in cell A2 and press [Enter].
4. Key **(in thousands)** in cell A3 and press [Enter].
5. Key **Region** in cell B5 and press [Enter].

6. Label columns for regional data by following these steps:
   a. In cell B6, key **NE** and press Tab.
   b. In cell C6, key **SE** and press Tab.
   c. In cell D6, key **NW** and press Tab.
   d. In cell E6, key **SW** and click the Enter button ✓ on the formula bar.
7. In cells A7 through A11, key the labels shown in Figure 2-21.

FIGURE 2-21

	A
7	Q1
8	Aspirin
9	Acetaminophen
10	Ibuprofen
11	Subtotal

8. In cell A12, enter **Q2** (for "second quarter").
9. In cell A13, use the Pick From List feature by following these steps:
   a. Right-click in cell A13 to display the shortcut menu.
   b. Choose Pic_k_ From List.
   c. Click "Aspirin" in the list.
10. Use AutoComplete to complete the labels for the second quarter by following these steps:
    a. In cell A14, key **Ac** and press Enter to enter "Acetaminophen."
    b. In cell A15, key **I** and press Enter to enter "Ibuprofen."
    c. In cell A16, key **S** and press Enter to enter "Subtotal."
11. To fit the 13-character row label "Acetaminophen," make sure any cell in column A is active and choose _C_olumn from the F_o_rmat menu. Choose _W_idth, key **13**, and click OK. (Enter a larger number if necessary.)
12. Edit cell A2 to read "1998 Sales" by following these steps:
    a. Double-click cell A2 to switch to Edit mode.
    b. Click the I-beam in the text to the right of "Sales" to position the insertion point.
    c. Press Shift + End to select the text to the end of the line.
    d. Press Delete.
    e. Click the Enter button ✓ or press Enter.

LESSON 2 ■ CREATING A SIMPLE WORKSHEET   EXCEL   **67**

13. Enter the data shown in Figure 2-22.

FIGURE 2-22

	A	B	C	D	E
6		NE	SE	NW	SW
7	Q1				
8	Aspirin	250	175	150	200
9	Acetaminophen	500	485	390	450
10	Ibuprofen	600	500	480	510
11	Subtotal				
12	Q2				
13	Aspirin	240	180	160	210
14	Acetaminophen	520	470	400	460
15	Ibuprofen	610	640	490	520
16	Subtotal				

14. Clear the word "Subtotal" from cells A11 and A16 by selecting each cell and pressing Delete.

15. Make cell A1 active and save the workbook as *[your initials]*2-18.xls in your Lesson 2 folder.

16. Print the worksheet and close the workbook.

EXERCISE 2-19

Enter and edit data, enter data in selected cells, and construct basic formulas.

1. Start a new workbook.
2. Create a heading for the worksheet by keying **Alpha Pharmaceuticals** in cell A1 and **Quality Control Payroll** in cell A2.
3. Create column headings by keying the following text in cells A4 through D4, pressing Tab to move across columns:

   Name   Salary   Years   Bonus

4. Practice selecting cell ranges by following these steps:
   a. Click column-heading B to select that column.
   b. Click row-heading 4 to select that row.
   c. Drag from cell A6 to cell A13 to select the range A6:A13.
   d. Click cell A6, hold down Shift, and click cell C13 to select the range A6:C13.
   e. Hold down Ctrl and drag across the range D6:D13 to add it to the selection.
   f. Click anywhere in the worksheet to deselect the block.
5. Select a cell range and then enter data for eight employees by following these steps:
   a. Select the range A6:C13.
   b. Enter the data shown in Figure 2-23, pressing Enter to move down each column. Begin with the name "Berenson."

FIGURE 2-23

	A	B	C
6	Berenson	28,000	2
7	Alvarez	33,000	6
8	Czerny	42,000	5
9	Teij	54,100	11
10	Silvers	22,200	3
11	Patino	57,000	9
12	Wang	35,300	2
13	Golden	41,000	6

6. Bonuses are calculated as 2% of salary multiplied by years of service (or 0.02 × Salary × Years). Enter the appropriate bonus formulas by following these steps:
   a. In cell D6, key =.02*B6*C6 and press Enter. Berenson's bonus is 1120, or 2% of 28,000 salary × 2 years of service.
   b. In cell D7, key =.02*, click cell B7, key *, and click cell C7. Press Enter. Alvarez's bonus is 3960.
   c. Using either step a or step b as your entry method, enter bonus formulas for the rest of the employees.

LESSON 2 ■ CREATING A SIMPLE WORKSHEET										EXCEL **69**

7. Make cell A1 active and save the workbook as *[your initials]***2-19.xls** in your Lesson 2 folder.
8. Print the worksheet and close the workbook.

EXERCISE 2-20

Use the SUM function, construct formulas, and use AutoCalculate.

1. Open the file **QCBonus.xls**.
2. In cell A14, key **TOTALS**
3. Key a formula that uses the SUM function to calculate the Salary total by following these steps:
   a. Make B14 the active cell.
   b. Key **=SUM(B6:B13)** and press Tab.
4. Use the mouse to build a SUM formula that calculates the total years by following these steps:
   a. In cell C14, enter **=SUM(**

   NOTE: Don't forget the parenthesis.

   b. Click cell C6, hold down Shift, and click cell C13.
   c. Press Tab. The total years is 44.
5. Use the AutoSum button Σ to calculate the total of the bonuses by following these steps:
   a. In cell D14, click the AutoSum button Σ.
   b. Press Enter. The total for bonuses is 39,106.
6. Clear the contents of cell B14.
7. Use AutoCalculate to calculate the salary total by following these steps:
   a. Select cells B6 through B13.
   b. Jot down the number displayed in the status bar. (The number in the status bar should be preceded by "SUM=." If it is not, right-click the status bar and choose Sum from the AutoCalculate menu.)
   c. Select cell B14 and use the AutoSum button Σ to enter the total. This number should be the same as the number you just jotted down.
8. Make cell A1 active and save the workbook as *[your initials]***2-20.xls** in your Lesson 2 folder.
9. Print the worksheet and close the workbook.

EXERCISE 2-21

Create and interpret formulas.

1. Open the file **Stock.xls**.
2. In cell A21, key **Totals**
3. In cell B21, create a formula that totals years.
4. In cell C21, create a formula that totals shares of stock.
5. Save the workbook as *[your initials]***2-21.xls** in your Lesson 2 folder.
6. Print the worksheet.
7. Examine the formulas in cells C6:C19 to see how shares of stock were calculated for each person. On the printout, write an explanation of how the number of shares is calculated. Do not just write the formula, but explain the logic behind the formula.
8. Close the workbook.

LESSON 2 ■ CREATING A SIMPLE WORKSHEET   EXCEL **71**

Lesson Applications

EXERCISE 2-22

Enter data in selected cells and use the SUM function.

The Quality Control director at Alpha Pharmaceuticals asked you to create a worksheet that calculates the weekly pay for Quality Control employees.

1. Open the file **QCPay1.xls**.
2. Select cells B6:C13 and delete their contents.
3. Key the data as shown in Figure 2-24, including the corrections.

FIGURE 2-24

	A	B	C	D
5	Name	Rate	Hours	Pay
6	Berenson	9.25 ~~2.95~~	40	
7	Alvarez	9.46	40	
8	Czerny	10.45	38	
9	Teij	10.64	40	
10	Silvers	37.5 →	← 9.50	
11	Patino	10.00	40	
12	Wang	9.88 ~~2~~	40	
13	Golden	9.96	40	

> **NOTE:** When you key 9.50 and 10.00, the zeros drop off after they are entered. This is because the cells are not formatted to show decimal places. You learn more about this in Lesson 3.

4. Create formulas that calculate the pay for each employee (rate × hours).
5. Key **Total** in cell A15.
6. In cell C15, use the SUM function to calculate the total hours.

7. In cell D15, calculate the total pay using the AutoSum button ∑.
8. Make cell A1 active and save the workbook as *[your initials]*2-22.xls in your Lesson 2 folder.
9. Print the worksheet and close the workbook.

EXERCISE 2-23

Enter data, construct formulas, use the SUM function, and use AutoCalculate.

The Quality Control Director now needs to add overtime hours to the Quality Control employee payroll worksheet.

1. Open the file **QCPay2.xls**.
2. Key the headings and data shown in Figure 2-25.

FIGURE 2-25

	E	F
5	Overtime	O.T. Pay
6	2	
7	3	
8	0	
9	1.5	
10	0	
11	4.25	
12	2.5	
13	3	

3. Use AutoCalculate to total the hours in column C and enter this number in cell C15. Use the same method to enter the pay total in cell D15.
4. In cell E15, use the SUM function to calculate the total overtime hours.

NOTE: If you use the AutoSum button ∑, remember to adjust the suggested cell range.

LESSON 2 ■ CREATING A SIMPLE WORKSHEET   EXCEL **73**

5. In cells F6:F13, create a formula for each employee to calculate his or her overtime pay. Use the formula "rate × overtime × 1.5." (Overtime pay is typically calculated as "time and a half"—that is, a rate of 1.5 hours.)

6. In cell F15, use the SUM function to calculate the total amount of overtime pay for all employees combined.

7. Make cell A1 active and save your workbook as *[your initials]***2-23.xls** in your Lesson 2 folder.

8. Print the worksheet and close the workbook.

EXERCISE 2-24

Enter data, use AutoComplete and Pick From List, construct formulas, use the SUM function, and use AutoCalculate.

The Research and Development manager wants to see the vacation data of the R&D staff. She feels this department needs more vacation time and wants to show the worksheet to the president.

1. Open the file **R&DStaf.xls**.

2. Key the information shown in Figure 2-26, using AutoComplete and Pick From List where possible. Note that when cells are not consecutive, the features are not available.

FIGURE 2-26

	B	C	D	E	F
5	Clearance	Level	Years	Vacation Days	Manager
6					
7	None	D15	2		Tang
8	Mid	B23	2		Richards
9	Top	A43	3		Tang
10	Mid	B23	3		Tang
11	Top	A43	5		Stevens
12	Mid	B23	5		Stevens

continues

FIGURE 2-26 continued

	B	C	D	E	F
13					
14	Top	A43	6		Richards
15	Mid	B23	6		Stevens
16	None	D15	8		Tang
17					
18	None	B23	14		Stevens
19	None	C15	15		Richards
20	Mid	D15	19		Tang

3. Calculate the number of vacation days for each employee using the following information:

   TIP: Blank lines separate employees into the following categories.

   - For 1 to 5 years: Years*0.1+5
   - For 6 to 10 years: Years*0.1+10
   - For more than 10 years: Years*0.15+15

4. Use AutoCalculate to calculate the total vacation days and enter this number in the appropriate cell.
5. Use the SUM function to calculate the total years.
6. Make cell A1 active and save your workbook as *[your initials]*2-24.xls in your Lesson 2 folder.
7. Print the worksheet and close the workbook.

EXERCISE 2-25

Enter data, construct formulas, and use AutoSum.

Alpha Pharmaceuticals' Marketing director wants to calculate the company's market share. You are to prepare a worksheet that shows market share as a percentage of national sales.

LESSON 2 ■ CREATING A SIMPLE WORKSHEET EXCEL **75**

1. Open the file **MktShare.xls**.
2. Key **1998 Market Share** in cell A2.
3. Select the cell range B8:C10 and key the data shown in Figure 2-27.

FIGURE 2-27

	B	C
8	19.671	4.085
9	25.093	7.314
10	29.384	7.457

4. In cell D8, calculate Alpha's market share for aspirin. Use the formula Alpha Sales/National Sales*100.
5. Create formulas to calculate the market share in cells D9 and D10.
6. Using either AutoCalculate or the SUM function, calculate the total pain reliever sales for National Sales and Alpha sales in cells B12 and C12, respectively.
7. Calculate Alpha's total market share for pain relievers in cell D12. (*Hint:* This is calculated the same way the market shares for cells D8:D10 are calculated.)
8. Make cell A1 active and save the workbook as *[your initials]***2-25.xls** in your Lesson 2 folder.
9. Print the worksheet and close the workbook.

EXERCISE 2-26 Challenge Yourself

Enter data, construct formulas, and use AutoSum.

To prepare for an annual financial planning meeting, the Marketing director of Alpha Pharmaceuticals asked you to create a worksheet that calculates projected national sales for aspirin, acetaminophen, and ibuprofen for 1999 and 2000. These projected sales are based on 1998 sales information.

1. Open a new workbook and create an appropriate heading for the worksheet, with an indicator that the sales figures are expressed in millions.

2. Enter the information in Figure 2-28 as 1998 data. Be sure to widen column A so the characters in "Acetaminophen" fit.

3. Make sure the text "1998" is entered as a label, so it is excluded from calculations. (This step also applies to other cells in the worksheet containing years.)

FIGURE 2-28

```
Product          1998

Aspirin          4.085

Acetaminophen    7.314

Ibuprofen        7.457
```

4. For 1999 and 2000 projected sales, show total sales that are a 2% increase over the previous year's sales for aspirin and acetaminophen, and a 3% increase each year for ibuprofen.

   NOTE: Remember that a 2% increase over last year is 102% of last year's sales.)

5. Calculate total sales of pain relievers for each year. (Include a "Totals" label.)

6. Make cell A1 active and save the workbook as *[your initials]***2-26.xls** in your Lesson 2 folder.

7. Print the worksheet and save the workbook as *[your initials]***2-26.htm** in your Lesson 2 folder. (Remember to use Save As Web Page.)

8. Close the workbook.

Enhancing a Simple Worksheet

LESSON 3

OBJECTIVES

After completing this lesson, you will be able to:

1. Select multiple columns and rows.
2. Insert cells, columns, and rows.
3. Delete cells, columns, and rows.
4. Use the Undo and Redo commands.
5. Use shortcut menus.
6. Move data.
7. Format numbers.
8. Apply text attributes and cell borders.

MOUS ACTIVITIES

In this lesson:
XL2000 **1.1**
XL2000 **1.3**
XL2000 **1.4**
XL2000 **1.6**
XL2000 **1.7**
XL2000 **3.2**
XL2000 **3.5**
XL2000 **3.6**
XL2000 **3.8**
XL2000 **5.1**

See Appendix F.

Estimated Time: 1¼ hours

This lesson teaches easy ways to modify a worksheet by inserting and deleting cells, columns, and rows; changing the number of decimal places displayed; and applying basic text, alignment attributes, and cell borders.

Selecting Multiple Columns and Rows

As you learned in Lesson 2, clicking a row or column heading selects that row or column. You can also select several columns and rows at the same time.

EXERCISE 3-1 Select Multiple Columns and Rows with the Mouse

1. Open the file **USSales1.xls**.
2. Click column heading A to select the column.
3. Click and drag over the row headings for rows 2, 3, and 4. The column is deselected and the three rows are selected.
4. Click column heading B, hold down [Shift], and click column heading E. Columns B through E are selected.
5. Drag over row headings 2 and 3 to select those rows.
6. Hold down [Ctrl] and click column heading B. Two rows and one column are selected.

FIGURE 3-1
Selecting columns and rows with the mouse

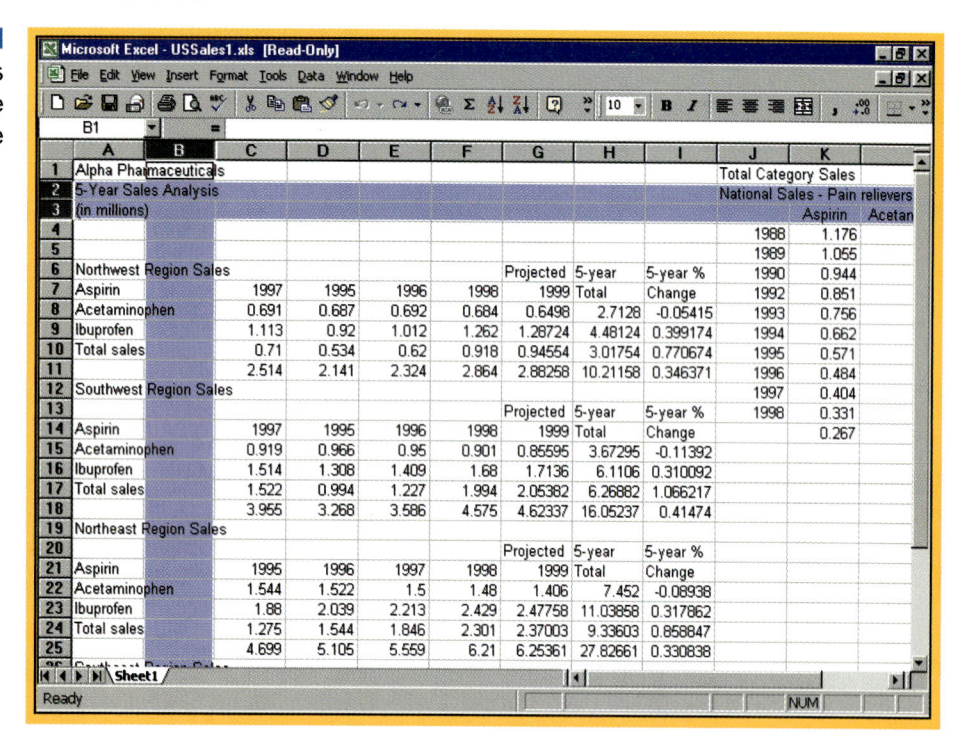

7. Click any cell in the worksheet to deselect the columns and rows.

EXERCISE 3-2 Select Multiple Columns and Rows with the Keyboard

1. In cell C7, press [Shift]+[Spacebar] to select row 7.
2. Select cell D5. Row 7 is now deselected.
3. Press [Ctrl]+[Spacebar] to select column D.

LESSON 3 ■ ENHANCING A SIMPLE WORKSHEET   EXCEL   79

4. While holding Shift, press → three times. The selection is extended through column G.
5. Select cell B7.
6. Press Shift+→ twice to select cells B7 through D7.
7. Press Ctrl+Spacebar to select columns B through D.
8. Use the keyboard to select cells C7 through E9 and then press Shift+Spacebar. Rows 7 through 9 are selected.
9. Press any arrow key to deselect the rows.

TABLE 3-1   Selecting Columns and Rows

ACTION	RESULT
Click heading	Selects a column or row.
Drag across headings	Selects multiple columns or rows.
Shift+click heading	Extends the selection to include adjacent columns or rows.
Ctrl+click heading	Extends the selection to include nonadjacent columns or rows.
Click Select All button	Selects the entire worksheet.
Shift+Spacebar	Selects the current row.
Ctrl+Spacebar	Selects the current column.
Shift+Arrow keys, PgUp or PgDn	Extends the row or column selection (first select a row or column).
Shift+Double-click	When the arrow pointer is displayed, selects the filled column or row in the direction of the vertical edge clicked.

Inserting Cells, Columns, and Rows

You can add cells, columns, and rows to a worksheet to make room for more data or to make the worksheet easier to read. You can do this using the Insert menu or the keyboard shortcut Ctrl++ (the plus key on the numeric keypad).

EXERCISE 3-3   Insert a Single Cell

A section of the **USSales1.xls** worksheet shows 10 years of national pain reliever sales, but contains some errors. When the row labels in column J were keyed, "1991" was skipped. You can insert a cell to correct this problem.

1. Scroll to bring columns J through N into view.
2. Select cell J7. Notice that cell J6 contains "1990" and cell J7 contains "1992."
3. Choose Cells from the Insert menu. The Insert dialog box opens.

FIGURE 3-2
Insert dialog box

4. Click Cancel and press Ctrl+ + on the numeric keypad. This is another way to open the Insert dialog box.

NOTE: If you are using a laptop and do not have a numeric keypad, use Insert, Cells instead of Ctrl + + or press Ctrl + Shift + + on the regular keyboard.

5. Choose Shift Cells Down and click OK. An empty cell appears at cell J7. The labels below shift down one cell.
6. Key **1991** in cell J7 and press Enter.

EXERCISE 3-4 Insert an Entire Column and Row

You can insert an entire row or column in a worksheet at the position of the active cell. Use the Insert menu or the keyboard shortcut Ctrl + + on the numeric keypad.

1. Select cell A19.

TIP: Remember, you can use the key combination Alt + PgUp to move one screen left.

2. Choose Rows from the Insert menu. A blank row appears at row 19 and all the information below this row moves down one row.
3. Select row 19 and press Ctrl + + or choose Rows from the Insert menu. Another row is inserted automatically. (You must select the entire row.)
4. Press F5 to open the Go To dialog box.
5. Key **J1** and click OK (or press Enter).
6. Click the column J heading to select the entire column.
7. Choose Columns from the Insert menu (or press Ctrl + +). A blank column appears at column J and all the information beyond column J moves right one column.

LESSON 3 ■ ENHANCING A SIMPLE WORKSHEET   EXCEL   **81**

EXERCISE 3-5 Insert Multiple Cells, Columns, and Rows

To insert several cells, columns, or rows in the same operation, select them before choosing a command. For example, if you select two rows, choosing Rows from the Insert menu (or pressing Ctrl+<kbd>+</kbd>) inserts two blank rows.

> **NOTE:** When you insert rows or columns, be careful not to separate blocks of data by mistake. Rows and columns span the entire worksheet, not just the visible portion of your screen. Rows extend 256 cells across and columns stretch 65,536 cells down.

1. Select rows 28 and 29 and press Ctrl+<kbd>+</kbd> or choose Insert, Rows. Two blank rows are inserted to separate "Northeast Region Sales" from "Southeast Region Sales."

2. Select rows 12 and 13.

3. Scroll to the right so columns K through O are visible. Notice that inserting rows here would break up data inappropriately in columns K through O.

FIGURE 3-3
Selecting to insert multiple rows

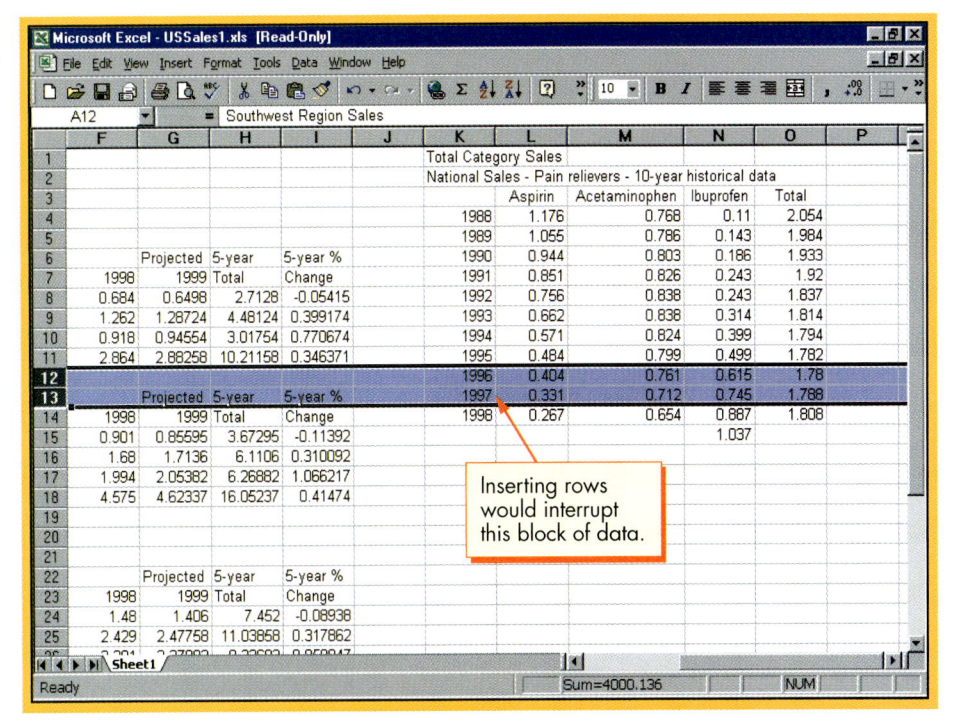

4. Deselect the rows and scroll back to view column A.

5. Select cells A12 through I13 and press Ctrl+<kbd>+</kbd> or choose Insert, Cells.

6. In the Insert dialog box, choose Shift Cells Down and click OK. Blank cells appear at cells A12 through I13 and all the data from cells A12 through I13 moves down two cells.

7. Scroll to view the 10-year historical data. Notice that no blank cells interrupt the data.

Deleting Cells, Columns, and Rows

You can delete cells, columns, and rows in much the same way that you insert them. Choose Delete from the Edit menu or press Ctrl + - (the minus sign on the numeric keypad).

When you delete cells, those cells are removed from the worksheet and the surrounding cells move to fill the space. If the deleted cells contained data, the data is also removed from the worksheet. In contrast, *clearing the contents of cells* removes the information contained in those cells, but allows the cells to remain in the worksheet.

TIP: Never clear contents by keying a blank space in a cell. Although the cell appears blank, it actually contains a label. This label may ultimately affect calculations.

EXERCISE 3-6 Delete Cells, Columns, and Rows

1. Select cell N8. This cell contains the same entry as cell N7. The data in column N extends one row below the data in the other columns.
2. Choose Delete from the Edit menu. The Delete dialog box opens.

FIGURE 3-4
Delete dialog box

3. Choose Shift Cells Up and click OK. Cell N8 is deleted and the cells move up to fill the gap.
4. Select column B and choose Delete from the Edit menu. Column B is deleted.
5. Select column B, if necessary, and press Ctrl + + or choose Insert, Columns to insert the column.
6. Press Ctrl + - or choose Delete from the Edit menu to delete column B again.
7. Select column A.
8. Adjust the width of column A to accommodate the width of the label in cell A8 by choosing Column from the Format menu, choosing Width, and

LESSON 3 ■ ENHANCING A SIMPLE WORKSHEET   EXCEL **83**

then keying **18** in the text box. Click OK. (You may need to key a larger number to fit the label.)

> **TIP:** Whenever possible remove blank columns and adjust column widths to fit text.

Using the Undo and Redo Commands

The Undo command reverses the last action you performed on the worksheet. If you deleted a column, for example, Undo brings back the column and its data. If you accidentally overwrite existing data in a cell, Undo restores the original cell contents. To use the Undo command, it is best to choose it immediately after the action you want to undo. The Redo command reverses the action of the Undo command. (You can "undo" Undo.)

You can also use these commands to undo and redo multiple actions at once. You can select Undo and Redo multiple times to step back through your last actions. Undo and Redo reverse actions sequentially. That is, to reverse a specific action, you must reverse any action that came after it first.

To use the Undo command, you can:

- Click the Undo button on the Standard toolbar.
- Press Ctrl + Z.
- Choose Undo from the Edit menu.

To use the Redo command, you can:

- Click the Redo button on the Standard toolbar.
- Press Ctrl + Y.
- Choose Redo from the Edit menu.

> **TIP:** Undo and Redo are convenient tools, but their usefulness is limited. It is always best to save your worksheet frequently. If you then make an unrecoverable error, you can simply close the worksheet without saving it and reopen the saved version.

EXERCISE 3-7 Use the Undo and Redo Commands

1. Save the worksheet as *[your initials]***3-7.xls** in a new folder for Lesson 3. Note that both the Undo and Redo buttons are shaded since there

are no actions yet to undo or redo. (You may need to click the More Buttons button on the Standard toolbar to find either of these buttons.)

2. Select column C by clicking its column heading.
3. Choose <u>D</u>elete from the <u>E</u>dit menu. The column is deleted. Notice that the shading on the Undo button is gone.
4. Choose <u>U</u>ndo Delete from the <u>E</u>dit menu (or press Ctrl + Z). The column is restored. Notice that the shading on the Redo button disappeared and the Undo button is shaded. (If Undo did not work, close the workbook without saving it and open *[your initials]*3-7.xls again.)
5. Choose <u>R</u>edo Delete from the <u>E</u>dit menu (or press Ctrl + Y). The undo is reversed and the column is deleted again.
6. Select cell B11 and press Delete . The contents of B11 are cleared.
7. Click the down arrow on the Undo button to see the drop-down list. Notice that the most recent action, which was clearing cell B11, is at the top of the list.

FIGURE 3-5
Undo drop-down list

8. Click Delete on the drop-down list. The contents of cell B11 and column C are restored.
9. Click the Redo button . This reverses the last undo, which was the column C deletion, and column C is deleted again.
10. Click the Undo button again. The column is restored.
11. Click any cell to deselect column C.

Using Shortcut Menus

Shortcut menus provide quick access to commands you use often, bypassing the menu bar. To display a shortcut menu, select a cell, a cell range, a row, or a column, and right-click the selection or press Shift + F10 . The commands you are most likely to use are listed on the shortcut menu. To choose a command, click it with the left mouse button.

EXERCISE 3-8 Use Shortcut Menus

All the row labels in column A, starting in cell A7, are positioned one cell too high. To correct this problem, you can insert a cell at cell A7.

1. Make cell A7 the active cell.
2. While pointing inside cell A7, right-click. The shortcut menu appears.

LESSON 3 ■ ENHANCING A SIMPLE WORKSHEET   EXCEL   **85**

FIGURE 3-6
Shortcut menu

3. Choose <u>I</u>nsert from the shortcut menu.
4. In the Insert dialog box, choose Shift Cells <u>D</u>own and click OK. The row labels are positioned correctly.

Moving Data to a New Location

You can easily move the contents of cells to another location without rekeying data. One way is to cut and paste the information, which is a two-step operation. First, you *cut* selected cells. You then move to a new location and *paste* the data in the cells at the new location. You can also copy a selection and paste a copy of it in a new location. You learn more about copying in Lesson 5.

To cut and paste selected data, you can use:

- The toolbar buttons Cut ✂ and Paste 📋
- Keyboard shortcuts Ctrl + X to cut and Ctrl + V to paste
- The shortcut menu

When you cut or copy data from selected cells, it is stored temporarily on the *Clipboard*, an area in the computer's active memory. The Paste command transfers the contents of the Clipboard to the location you choose.

EXERCISE 3-9   Move Data Using Cut and Paste

1. Right-click cell A3.
2. Choose Cu<u>t</u> from the shortcut menu. A moving border surrounds cell A3.
3. Click cell A4 and click the Paste button 📋 on the Standard toolbar. Cell A3 is cleared, the moving border disappears, and the contents of cell A3 appear in cell A4.
4. Click the Undo button ↶ to undo the Paste command. The moving border marks cell A3 and cell A4 remains the active cell.
5. Press Enter . The text is moved. Pressing Enter has the same effect as the Paste command when the moving border marks a range of cut cells.
6. Click the Undo button ↶ to restore the text to cell A3. Press Esc to remove the moving border.

EXERCISE 3-10 Move Data Using Insert Cut Cells

When you paste data into a cell range, any data contained in the range is overwritten by the new data. To insert data at a location that already contains data, use the Insert Cut Cells command. This command causes the existing cells to be shifted down or to the right when data is moved to that location.

1. Save the worksheet as *[your initials]*3-10.xls in your Lesson 3 folder.
2. Select cells B7 through B11.
3. Right-click the selection and choose Cut from the shortcut menu.
4. Select cell E7.
5. Press Ctrl+V, the keyboard shortcut for Paste. The "1998" data in cells E7 through E11 is overwritten by the "1997" data. Because the formulas in columns F, G, and H referenced the "1998" data, the notation #REF! appears in the cells that contain formulas, indicating a reference error.
6. Click the Undo button. The data is restored and the reference errors are no longer displayed.
7. With the moving border again surrounding cells B7 through B11, and cells E7 through E11 selected, choose Cut Cells from the Insert menu or choose Insert Cut Cells from the shortcut menu. The "1997" data is inserted between the "1996" and "1998" data.

FIGURE 3-7
Inserting cut cells

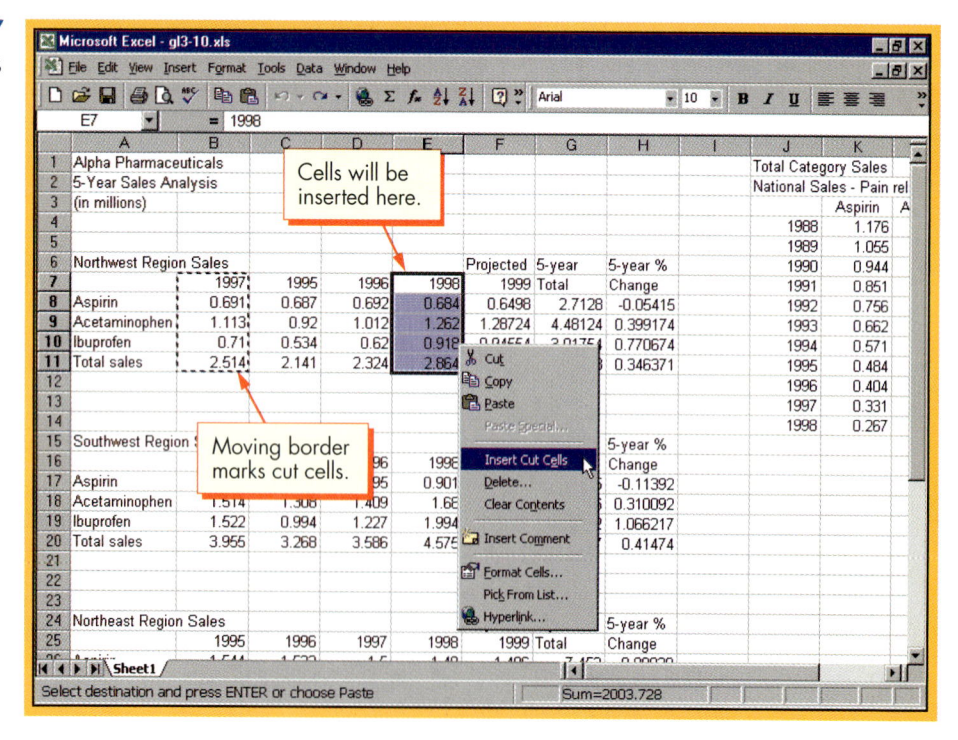

LESSON 3 ■ ENHANCING A SIMPLE WORKSHEET   EXCEL   **87**

EXERCISE 3-11   Move Data Using Drag and Drop

When you move the white-cross pointer slowly across the border of an active cell or selected cells, it changes to an arrow. This arrow is the drag-and-drop pointer, which you use to move data to a new location. Old data is replaced with moved data when you release the mouse button.

1. Select cells A1 through A3.
2. Slowly move the white-cross pointer across the selection's border until the white cross changes into an arrow.

   NOTE: If the arrow pointer does not appear, choose Options from the Tools menu, click the Edit tab, and click the Allow Cell Drag and Drop check box to select the option.

3. Press and hold the left mouse button. Notice that the status bar indicates your options.
4. Move the arrow to cell D1. A light gray border surrounds cells D1 through D3.

FIGURE 3-8
Drag-and-drop to move data

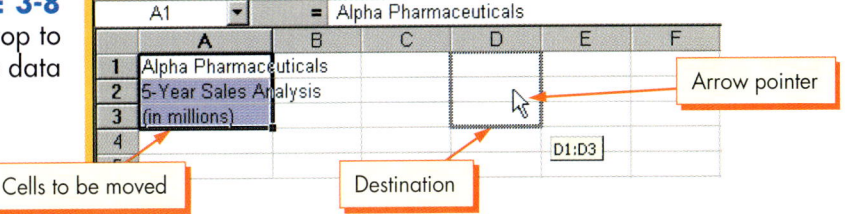

Cells to be moved
Destination
Arrow pointer

5. Release the mouse button. The data is moved and cells A1 through A3 are cleared.
6. Select cells B16 through B20.
7. Move the mouse pointer to the border of the selection until you see the arrow pointer.
8. Hold down Shift and begin to drag. An I-beam appears. Continue dragging and the I-beam alternates between vertical and horizontal. Drag it to the vertical gridline between columns D and E, with the top of the I-beam between rows 15 and 16.

FIGURE 3-9
Drag-and-drop to insert cut cells

I-beam marks destination

9. Release the mouse button and then release Shift. You inserted the cut cells. The "1997" data is inserted between the "1996" and "1998" data.

EXERCISE 3-12 Check Cell References and Formulas after Moving Data

When you move formulas, the cell references in the formulas remain the same, as do the calculations performed by those formulas. When you move cells that are referenced by formulas, Excel updates the formulas automatically so they reference the new location of the cells. For example, if a SUM function references the range C5:C10, and you move the contents of cell C10 to cell C12, the SUM function changes automatically to reference the range C5:C12. Always check formulas after moving data to ensure they are updated correctly.

1. Select cell G8. The correct formula, =SUM(B8:F8), appears on the formula bar.
2. Select cell H8. The correct formula, =(F8-B8)/B8, appears on the formula bar.
3. Check formulas throughout the worksheet.

Formatting Numbers: The Basics

You can format numbers to have a similar appearance without changing their mathematical values. For instance, the values resulting from division often have many decimal places, which may not be aligned. If you format cells to show only two decimal places, the results are neat and easy to read. Excel still stores all the undisplayed digits, however, and uses them in future computations. You can redisplay complete values at any time.

The Excel Formatting toolbar offers a convenient way to format numbers. An expanded Formatting toolbar showing all possible buttons on this toolbar appears in Figure 3-10.

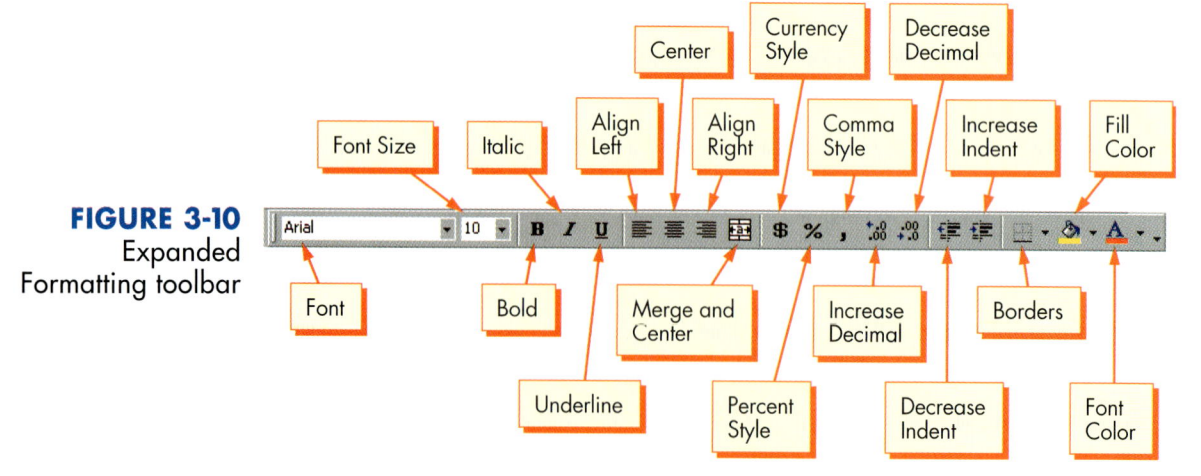

FIGURE 3-10 Expanded Formatting toolbar

LESSON 3 ■ ENHANCING A SIMPLE WORKSHEET   EXCEL   **89**

EXERCISE 3-13 Format Numbers in Comma Style and Percent Style

1. Select cell G8.
2. Click the Comma Style button on the toolbar (you may need to click the More Buttons button to locate it). Cell G8 is formatted with two decimal places. The Comma Style button inserts commas to separate thousands, if needed, and formats values to have two decimal places.
3. Select cells B8 through G11.
4. Click the Comma Style button again. All the selected cells are formatted with two decimal places and the decimals are aligned.
5. Select cells H8 through H11.
6. Click the Percent Style button. The selected cells are formatted as percentages with no decimals.

EXERCISE 3-14 Change the Number of Decimals Displayed

You can use the Increase Decimal and Decrease Decimal buttons on the Formatting toolbar to control the number of decimal places displayed in cells.

1. Select cells B17 through G20.
2. Click the Decrease Decimal button. The selected cells display two decimal places.
3. Click the Increase Decimal button. The cells display three decimal places.
4. Select cells H17 through H20.
5. Click the Percent Style button and then click the Increase Decimal button. The selected cells are displayed as percentages with one decimal place.
6. Using the Formatting toolbar, format all the sales region numbers to match the formatting of the "Southwest Region" numbers.

Applying Text Attributes and Cell Borders

You can use the buttons on the Formatting toolbar to format text as well as numbers. You can control alignment in a cell, apply bold and italic, draw lines, and change the size of text. You can also use the Format Painter button on the Standard toolbar to copy these attributes from one cell or cell range to another.

EXERCISE 3-15 Apply Text Attributes Using the Formatting Toolbar

1. Select cells D1 through D3.
2. Click the Center button on the Formatting toolbar. The text in cells D1 through D3 is centered in the cells, but spills over to cells in columns C and E.
3. Select cells D1 and D2.
4. Click the Bold button. The selected text becomes bold.
5. Select cells F6 through H7.
6. Click the Align Right button. The text is aligned with the numbers below it.

TIP: Column titles should usually be aligned with their related data.

7. Select cells A6 through H7 and cells A11 through H11.
8. Click the Bold button to make the selection bold.

FIGURE 3-11
Formatting the worksheet

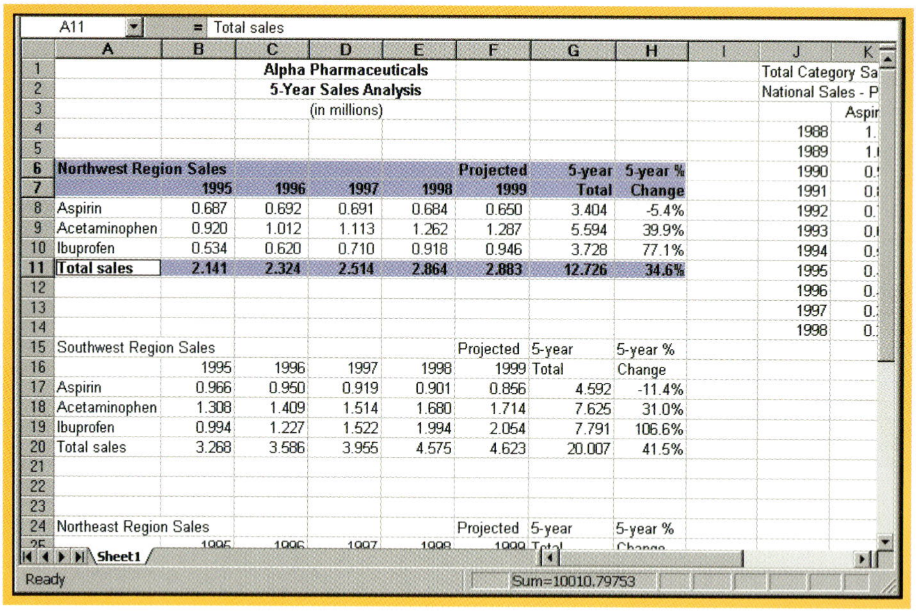

EXERCISE 3-16 Use Format Painter to Copy Attributes

Once you apply a variety of attributes to a cell range—such as bold and italic, alignment, and number styles—you can copy the attributes from one cell range to another using the Format Painter button on the Standard toolbar.

LESSON 3 ■ ENHANCING A SIMPLE WORKSHEET   EXCEL   **91**

1. Select cells A6 through H11.
2. Click the Format Painter button. A moving border surrounds the selection. You can now copy the formatting of this range to other sales region data in the worksheet.
3. Use the vertical scroll bar to display cells A15 through H20, if necessary.

   NOTE: When you use the Format Painter, use the scroll bar to navigate around the screen instead of the arrow keys to prevent the cells between the source and destination cells from being painted.

4. Using the Format Painter pointer, select cells A15 through H20, the "Southwest Region Sales" data. The formatting is applied to the data.

FIGURE 3-12
Copying attributes with Format Painter

5. With the cell range A15 through H20 still selected, double-click the Format Painter button. Double-clicking this button allows you to apply attributes to more than one consecutive selection.
6. Use the Format Painter pointer to select cells A24 through H29 and then select cells A33 through H38. All the regions now have the same formatting.
7. Press Esc to restore the normal pointer.

EXERCISE 3-17 Apply Borders to the Bottoms of Cells

You can create a line to separate data by formatting cells with a bottom border. The easiest way to apply a border is by using the Borders button on the Formatting toolbar.

1. Select cells A7 through H7.
2. Click the down arrow on the right side of the Borders button . The Borders palette appears.
3. Choose the single-line bottom border style (first row, second column) on the palette. The bottom borders of cells A7 through H7 are formatted as a single solid line. The Borders button default is now single-line bottom border.
4. Select cells A16:H16 and click the Borders button . Remember, the Borders button uses the most recently applied border style as a default.
5. Apply the same border style to separate the headings from data in the other two regions.
6. Make cell A1 active and save the file as *[your initials]*3-17.xls in your Lesson 3 folder.
7. Print the worksheet and close the workbook.

FIGURE 3-13
Borders palette

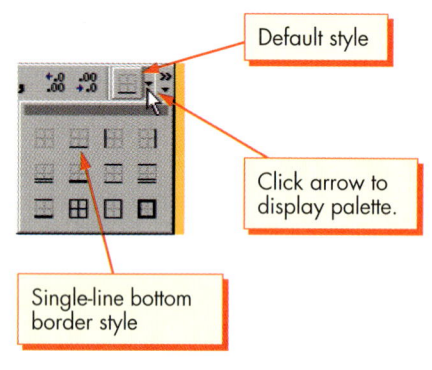

- Default style
- Click arrow to display palette.
- Single-line bottom border style

COMMAND SUMMARY

FEATURE	BUTTON	MENU	KEYBOARD
Insert Cells		Insert, Cells, Rows, or Columns	Ctrl + +
Delete Cells		Edit, Delete	Ctrl + -
Cut	✂	Edit, Cut	Ctrl + X
Paste	📋	Edit, Paste	Ctrl + V
Undo	↶	Edit, Undo	Ctrl + Z
Redo	↷	Edit, Redo	Ctrl + Y

USING HELP

Excel's online Help is extremely comprehensive. The Office Assistant can direct you to Help topics related to the work you are doing, but you can also access Help directly by browsing through the Help Contents window or using the Help Index.

LESSON 3 ■ ENHANCING A SIMPLE WORKSHEET					EXCEL **93**

Explore the range of topics available in Help Contents:

1. Press [F1] to start Help.
2. Under "What would you like to do," key **format cells** and click <u>S</u>earch.
3. Click the topic "Format cells quickly." Click the link <u>Copy formats from one cell or range to another</u>.
4. Click the Show button to expand the Help window.
5. Click the Contents tab, if necessary. Scroll the list of topics, each of which is represented by a book icon.
6. Click the plus sign to the left of the topic "Formatting Worksheets" to display subtopics.
7. Review the subtopics. Click any subtopic that interests you.

FIGURE 3-14
Exploring Help Contents

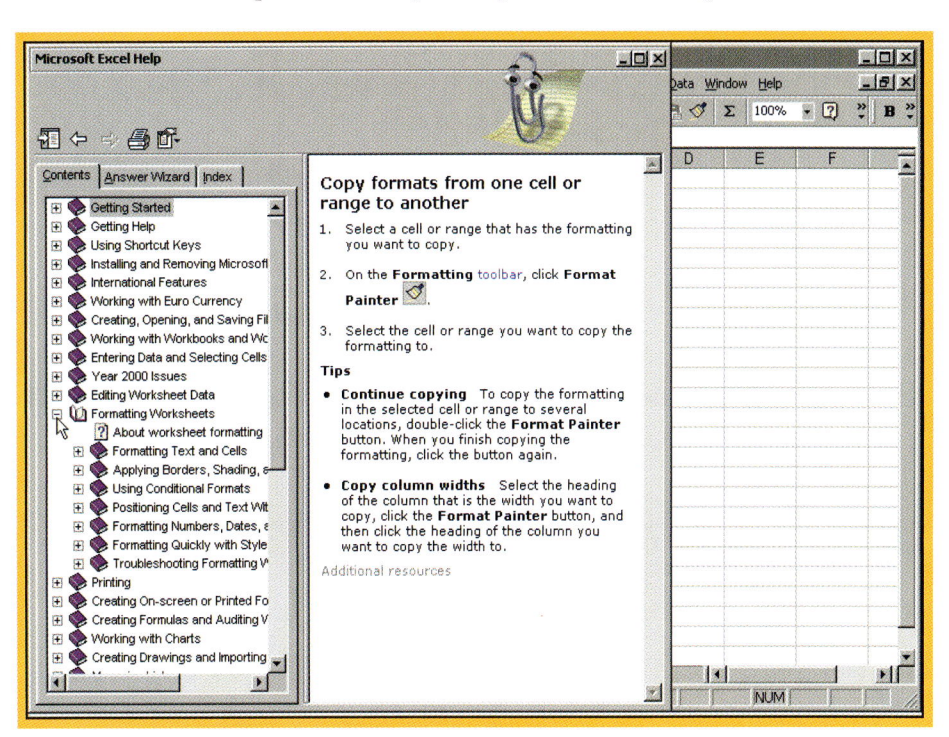

8. Click ✖ to close the Help window.

Concepts Review

TRUE/FALSE QUESTIONS

Each of the following statements is either true or false. Indicate your choice by circling **T** or **F**.

T F **1.** After selecting a column with the mouse, you can extend the selection only by using the mouse.

T F **2.** You can insert an entire row using the Insert dialog box.

T F **3.** When you delete a cell using the Delete dialog box, both the cell and its contents are removed from the worksheet.

T F **4.** Clicking the Undo button three times reverses your last three actions.

T F **5.** Double-clicking a cell displays a shortcut menu.

T F **6.** The Cut, Paste, and Copy buttons are located on the Standard toolbar.

T F **7.** The Comma Style button formats numbers to display two decimal places.

T F **8.** You can use the Format Painter button to copy both alignment and number formatting from one cell range to another.

SHORT ANSWER QUESTIONS

Write the correct answer in the space provided.

1. To extend a selection using the arrow keys, which key must you hold down?

2. To insert multiple rows, you select the number of rows to insert and then press which key combination?

3. Which menu command can restore a column you just deleted by mistake?

4. When you cut a selection, how is it marked onscreen?

LESSON 3 ■ ENHANCING A SIMPLE WORKSHEET   EXCEL   **95**

5. When you drag to insert cut cells, what symbol do you see while you drag to the new location?

_____

6. How many decimal places does the Percent Style button format numbers to display?

_____

7. On which toolbar is the Bold button **B** located?

_____

8. Which keyboard combination selects the current row?

_____

CRITICAL THINKING

Answer these questions on a separate piece of paper. There are no right or wrong answers. Support your answers with examples from your own experience, if possible.

1. You want to add a row of sales data for another product to an existing worksheet. Should you insert a row, or just selected cells? Why?

2. If Excel updates formulas automatically after you move cells, why should you check formulas?

Skills Review

EXERCISE 3-18

Select multiple columns and rows; insert and delete cells, columns, and rows; and use the Undo command.

1. Open the file **NWReps1.xls**.

2. Insert a cell to align the labels in column A with the data below by following these steps:
   a. Select cell A8.
   b. Choose Cells from the Insert menu.
   c. Choose Shift Cells Down in the Insert dialog box and click OK.

3. Insert a column by following these steps:
   a. Select any cell in column B.

96 EXCEL UNIT 1 ■ BASIC SKILLS

      b. Choose <u>C</u>olumns from the <u>I</u>nsert menu.

 4. Delete rows to close up the space between the worksheet heading and the data by following these steps:

      a. Drag over row headings 5 through 8 to select those rows.

      b. Press Ctrl + - (the minus key on the numeric keypad) or choose <u>D</u>elete from the <u>E</u>dit menu.

 5. Choose <u>U</u>ndo Delete from the <u>E</u>dit menu to restore the four rows.

 6. Delete three rows by following these steps:

      a. Click row heading 5 to select that row.

      b. Press and hold down Shift and click row heading 7.

      c. Press Ctrl + - or choose <u>D</u>elete from the <u>E</u>dit menu.

 7. Select and delete column B.

 8. Change the width of column A to 20.

 9. Save the workbook as *[your initials]*3-18.xls in your Lesson 3 folder.

10. Print the worksheet and close the workbook.

EXERCISE 3-19

Insert cells, use the shortcut menu, and move data.

 1. Open the file **NWReps2.xls**. Some data is missing and the quarterly information was keyed in the wrong order.

 2. Insert cells to make room for new data by following these steps:

      a. Select cells A14:H14.

      b. Right-click the selection and choose <u>I</u>nsert from the shortcut menu.

      c. In the Insert dialog box, choose Shift Cells <u>D</u>own and click OK.

 3. Key the data shown in Figure 3-15.

FIGURE 3-15

	Q4	Q3	Q2	Q1
Jose Garcia	73.8	72.4	77.912	75.1739

> **NOTE:** Excel has a List AutoFill feature that is turned on by default. It automatically copies formatting and formulas to new rows when they are added to a list of data. It also updates totals in total columns. For the AutoFill feature to be turned on, there must be at least five rows in the list preceding the new row(s). Formats and formulas must also appear in at least three of those five rows.

LESSON 3 ■ ENHANCING A SIMPLE WORKSHEET   EXCEL   **97**

4. Move the "Qtr 1" cells to column B by following these steps:
   a. Select cells F6:F19 and right-click the range.
   b. Choose Cut from the shortcut menu.
   c. Right-click cell B6 and choose Paste from the shortcut menu.
5. Move the "Qtr 4" cells to column F by following these steps:
   a. Select cells C6:C19.
   b. Move the mouse pointer to the border of the range until it becomes an arrow.
   c. Drag the selection to the range F6:F19 and release the mouse button.
6. Move the "Qtr 1" cells from column B to the blank column C.
7. Reverse the positions of the "Qtr 2" and "Qtr 3" information by following these steps:
   a. Select "Qtr 2" cells E6:E19.
   b. Press [Ctrl]+[X] to cut these cells.
   c. Select cell D6, which contains "Qtr 3."
   d. Choose Cut Cells from the Insert menu (or choose Insert Cut Cells from the shortcut menu).
8. Delete the blank column B.
9. Review the formulas in the "Total" column and correct them, if necessary. (They should add the sales in all four quarters for each salesperson.)
10. Review the formulas in the "% of Total" column. (They should divide the total sales for each salesperson by the total sales for all salespersons.)
11. Save the workbook as *[your initials]*3-19.xls in your Lesson 3 folder.
12. Print the worksheet and close the workbook.

EXERCISE 3-20

Move cells, format numbers, apply text attributes, and apply borders.

1. Open the file **NWReps3.xls**.
2. Format the dollar amounts in comma style and display only one decimal place by following these steps:
   a. Select cells C8:G17 and C19:G19.
   b. Click the Comma Style button [,] on the Formatting toolbar.
   c. Click the Decrease Decimal button [.oo] on the Formatting toolbar.
3. Format amounts in the "% of Total" column in percent style and displaying one decimal place by following these steps:
   a. Select cells H8:H19.
   b. Click the Percent Style button [%] and then click the Increase Decimal button [.oo].

4. Format and align the column labels by following these steps:
   a. Select cells A6:H6 and click the Bold button **B** to make the text bold.
   b. With the cells still selected, click the down arrow on the Borders button and choose the single-line bottom border.
   c. Select cells C6:G6 and click the Align Right button to right-align the text.
5. Format cells A1:A4 and A19:H19 as bold.
6. Delete the blank row 7.
7. In cells C18:H18, add a single-line top and a double-line bottom border (which is the last icon on the second row of the border palette) and delete the blank row 17.

> **TIP:** Single-line borders under numbers indicate numbers above are to be calculated. Double-line borders under numbers indicate numbers immediately above are totals.

8. Delete column B and adjust the column width of column A to fit the longest salesperson's name in the column.
9. Save the workbook as *[your initials]*3-20.xls in your Lesson 3 folder.
10. Print the worksheet and close the workbook.

EXERCISE 3-21

Move cells and rows, format numbers, apply text attributes and borders, copy formats, and use shortcut menus.

1. Open the file **USSales2.xls**.
2. Under "Northwest Region Sales," move row 8 ("Acetaminophen") below row 9 ("Aspirin") to match the sequence in the other three regions. Follow these steps:
   a. Right-click row heading 8 and click Cut on the shortcut menu.
   b. Right-click row heading 10 and click Insert Cut Cells on the shortcut menu.
3. Move "Northeast Region Sales" before "Southwest Region Sales" by following these steps:
   a. Select rows 20 through 26 by dragging with the mouse.
   b. Press Ctrl+X to cut the selected rows.
   c. Right-click row heading 13 and click Insert Cut Cells on the shortcut menu.
4. Format the title in cells A1:A3 as bold.

LESSON 3 ■ ENHANCING A SIMPLE WORKSHEET   EXCEL   **99**

5. Format text in the "Northwest Region" by following these steps:
   a. Select the row and column labels and the totals (A6:H7, A8:A11, and B11:H11), and make them bold.
   b. Right-align cells G6:H7.
   c. Apply a heavy single-line bottom border to cells A7:H7.
   d. Apply a single-line top and double-line bottom border to cells B11:H11.

6. Format numbers in the "Northwest Region" by following these steps:
   a. To the dollar amounts in cells B8:G11, apply the comma style and add one decimal place. All numbers should have three decimal places.
   b. Apply the percent style to cells H8:H11 with one decimal place.

7. Copy the formats for the "Northwest Region" to the other three regions by following these steps:
   a. Select cells A6:H11 and double-click the Format Painter button .
   b. Using the Format Painter pointer, select the "Northeast Region Sales" range (A13:H18) to copy the formatting.
   c. Select the "Southwest Region" range, and then select the "Southeast Region" range.
   d. Press Esc to end the process and restore the normal pointer.

8. Make cell A1 active and save the workbook as ***[your initials]*3-21.xls** in your Lesson 3 folder.

9. Print the worksheet and close the workbook.

Lesson Applications

EXERCISE 3-22

Select rows and columns, move cells and columns, insert and delete rows, move data, format numbers, and apply text attributes and cell borders.

The marketing director needs an attractively formatted 1998 Market Share worksheet to show to the president. You must apply text and number formatting as well as rearrange some of the data.

1. Open the file **Share1.xls**.
2. Move the information in column E to column B.
3. Check the formulas now in column B to ensure they divide "Alpha Sales" by "National Sales."
4. Widen column A to accommodate the label in A8.
5. Insert two rows at row 4.
6. Format the title cells A1 and A2 as bold.
7. Delete the blank row 12.
8. Format the column labels as centered and bold, and apply a single-line bottom border to cells B7:D7.
9. Apply a single-line top and a double-line bottom border to cells B12:D12.
10. Format the row labels and total numbers as bold, and readjust the width of column A, if necessary.
11. Format the "Market Share" numbers in percent style displaying two decimal places.
12. Format the "National Sales" and "Alpha Sales" numbers in comma style displaying two decimal places.
13. Delete the blank row 8.
14. Make cell A1 active and save the workbook as *[your initials]***3-22.xls** in your Lesson 3 folder.
15. Print the worksheet and close the workbook.

EXERCISE 3-23

Select cells, insert rows, use shortcut menus, move data, format numbers and text, and apply cell borders.

Alpha Pharmaceuticals' auditor reviewed the worksheet that calculates gross pay for the company's Quality Control Division. He noticed that overtime hours were not entered and that employee Silvers is missing from the list. These errors must be corrected and the worksheet needs to be formatted to make it easier to read.

1. Open the file **QCPay3.xls**.
2. Insert three blank rows, starting at row 3.
3. Move all the data in the "Golden" row between the data for "Czerny" and "Patino."
4. Under "Patino," insert a new row with the data for employee Silvers as shown in Figure 3-16.

FIGURE 3-16

Name	Rate	Hours
Silvers	9.50	37.5

NOTE: Excel copies the formulas to the new row automatically.

5. Check the formulas that were automatically entered by Excel in this row.
6. Format cell A1 as bold and cell A2 as bold and italic.

TIP: The Italic button *I* is on the Formatting toolbar.

7. Right-align the text in rows 6 and 7 (except for "Name" in cell A7, which should be left-aligned).
8. Format rows 6, 7, and 16 as bold.
9. Apply a single-line bottom border to cells A7 through G7 and to cells C15 through G15.
10. Apply the comma style to numbers in rows 8 through 16 and display two decimal places.

11. Key the overtime hours for all employees as shown in Figure 3-17:

FIGURE 3-17

Berenson	2
Alvarez	3
Czerny	0
Golden	3
Patino	4.25
Silvers	0
Teij	1.5
Wang	2.5

12. Use AutoSum to total regular "Hours" and "Overtime" hours.
13. Make cell A1 active and save the workbook as *[your initials]*3-23.xls in your Lesson 3 folder.
14. Print the worksheet and close the workbook.

EXERCISE 3-24

Select and insert rows and columns, move data, and format text and numbers.

Alpha Pharmaceuticals' president needs to study U.S. population trends to make sales forecasts. He is especially interested in the over-40 age group, because this group uses more pain relievers than younger people. His population worksheet should be formatted and additional data must be inserted.

1. Open the file **PopData1.xls**.
2. Insert three blank rows at row 3.
3. Move the "1991" data so it is positioned above the "1992" data.
4. Insert three blank rows below the "1987" data to make room for the "1988," "1989," and "1990" data.
5. Key the missing and additional population figures, as shown in Figure 3-18 (on the next page). Key the years as labels using an apostrophe before each year.

LESSON 3 ■ ENHANCING A SIMPLE WORKSHEET   EXCEL **103**

FIGURE 3-18

```
        Total      Over 40
1988    243.07     91.25
1989    245.35     92.61
1990    247.64     93.97


1996    263.87     105.30
1997    266.75     107.42
1998    269.65     109.55
```

> **NOTE:** Excel did not update formulas in new rows 10-12 because there are not five rows in the list (A7:D20) preceding the new rows. For automatic updating, there must be at least five rows preceding the new rows, and three out of the five must contain formulas or formatting.

6. Create formulas in cells D10:D12 to calculate the percentage of the population over age 40. (Hint: Use one of the existing formulas as a model.)
7. Edit cell A1 to read **U.S. Population**
8. Format cells A1:A2 as bold.
9. Format the column headings in row 6 as right-aligned and bold.
10. Format the numbers in columns B and C to display one decimal place.
11. Format the numbers in column D to be displayed as percentages with one decimal place.
12. Make cell A1 active and save the workbook as *[your initials]***3-24.xls** in your Lesson 3 folder.
13. Print the worksheet and close the workbook.

EXERCISE 3-25   Challenge Yourself

Select multiple columns and rows, delete columns and rows, use the Undo command, move data, apply text attributes, and format numbers.

Historical information on pain-reliever sales for the Northwest Region appears in three separate sections of a worksheet. The Marketing Director asked you to arrange the data in a single table that shows totals by year and by product.

1. Open the file **NWHist1.xls**.
2. Delete columns B and C simultaneously.
3. Delete rows 9 through 11.
4. Undo the row deletions.
5. Cut the data for "Aspirin" (B3:B14) and paste it beginning in cell D3 using the shortcut menu.
6. Cut the data for "Ibuprofen" (B29:B40) and paste it beginning in cell B3.
7. Cut the data for "Acetaminophen" (B16:B27) and paste it beginning in cell C3.
8. Clear the cells below row 15 in column A.
9. Key **Total** in E3 and create formulas in column E to total each year's sales. (*Hint:* Use AutoSum.)
10. In cell A15, key **Total**. When AutoComplete suggests "Total Category Sales," press [Delete] to restore "Total" and press [Enter].
11. Create formulas in row 15 that total individual and total product sales.
12. Clear cells A1:A2, which contain the title and key the title as shown in Figure 3-19. Insert enough rows to accommodate the title and to leave two blank lines below it.

FIGURE 3-19

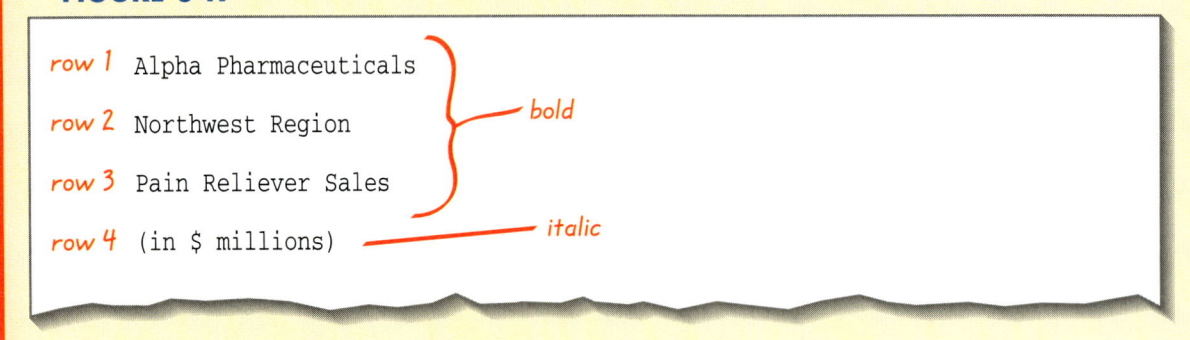

```
row 1   Alpha Pharmaceuticals  ⎫
row 2   Northwest Region       ⎬  bold
row 3   Pain Reliever Sales    ⎭
row 4   (in $ millions)    ──── italic
```

13. Insert the following data below "1998." (Be sure to enter "1999" as a label.)

    1999   0.209   0.133   0.054

> **NOTE:** Excel copies formulas to the new row automatically and updates the totals.

14. Check the formula in row 19 to make sure it does not include the year in the calculation.
15. Check the formulas in row 20 to make sure the data in row 19 is included in their calculations.
16. Delete the row containing the 1988 data, and check the formulas again.
17. Right-align the column labels and make row and column headings bold.
18. Apply a single-line heavy bottom border to the column labels (B7:E7).
19. Apply a single-line bottom border to the sales data for "1999" (B18:E18) and a double-line bottom border to the totals in cells B19:E19.
20. Format all figures in comma style displaying two decimal places.
21. Make all totals bold.
22. Make cell A1 active and save the workbook as *[your initials]*3-25.xls in your Lesson 3 folder.
23. Print the worksheet and save the workbook as *[your initials]*3-25.htm in your Lesson 3 folder.
24. Close the workbook.

Unit 1 Applications

UNIT APPLICATION 1-1

Enter and edit data, use AutoSum, create formulas, move data, and format text and numbers.

You have been asked to prepare a statement of assets for Alpha Pharmaceuticals, listing the things of value that the company owned at the end of 1998. The statement will become part of Alpha's balance sheet and be included in Alpha's annual report.

1. Open the file **Assets1.xls**.
2. Change the width of column A to accommodate the label in A6 and the width of column B to accommodate the label in B13.
3. In the cell range C7:C10, key the following data:

   2600
   5960
   4710
   600

4. In cell C11, use AutoSum to create a formula for "Total current assets."
5. In cell C13, key **4980**. In cell C14, key **1520**.
6. Cut the text in cell C15 and paste it into cell B15.
7. In cell C15, create a formula that subtracts "Depreciation" from "Property, plant, and equipment."
8. In cell C16, key **1390** for "Other Assets."
9. Italicize the amounts for "Total current assets," "Net fixed assets," and "Other Assets." Create a formula in cell C17 that totals these three amounts. Make that total bold.
10. Right-align the labels "Total current assets" and "Net fixed assets." Make both labels italic.
11. Format cells A1 and A2 as bold.
12. Format the values in column C in comma style with no decimals.
13. Apply a single-line bottom border to cells C10, C14, and C16.
14. Apply a double-line bottom border to cell C17.
15. Edit the label "(Depreciation)" so it reads **(Less depreciation)**.
16. Edit cells so only the first letter of the first word of each label is capitalized. (Do not edit the title, however.)
17. Make cell A1 active and save the workbook as *[your initials]*u1-1.xls in a new folder for Unit 1 Applications.

UNIT 1 ■ APPLICATIONS   EXCEL 107

18. Print the worksheet and close the workbook.

UNIT APPLICATION 1-2

Enter data, construct formulas, use the Sum function, and format text and numbers.

A statement of liabilities and shareholders' equity shows who has claims on the assets of a company. For instance, you can see the amounts owed to outsiders (long-term debt, current debt, accounts payable) and the amounts claimed by the owners (shareholders' equity). You have been asked to prepare such a statement for Alpha Pharmaceuticals. It will later become part of the company's balance sheet.

1. Open the file **Liablts1.xls**.
2. Change the width of column B so the label in A15 does not extend beyond the right border of column B.
3. Move the label in cell C13 to cell B13.
4. Enter the data in column C as shown in Figure U1-1, including Sum formulas in cells C8 and C13.

FIGURE U1-1

	A	B	C
5	Long-term liabilities		
6		Long-term debt	690
7		Other long-term liabilities	510
8		Total long-term liabilities	(SUM)
9	Current liabilities		
10		Debt due for repayment	1090
11		Accounts payable	1350
12		Other current liabilities	1760
13		Total current liabilities	(SUM)
14	Shareholders' equity		13320
15	Total liabilities and shareholders' equity		

5. Format cells C8, C13, and C14 as italic, add a single-line bottom border to cells C7, C12, and C14, and add a double-line bottom border to cell C15.
6. Move the current liabilities (rows 9 through 13) before the long-term liabilities (rows 5 through 8). (Hint: Cut the cells and use Cut Cells from the Insert menu to insert them in the new location.)
7. Check to make sure the formulas are still correct.
8. Create a formula in cell C15 that adds "Total current liabilities," "Total long-term liabilities," and "Shareholders' equity." Format the cell as bold.
9. Insert a new row at row 1. Make the first two lines of the title read:
   Alpha Pharmaceuticals
   Liabilities and Shareholders' Equity
10. Format the first three lines of the title as bold.
11. Format all the values in comma style with no decimals.
12. Make cell A1 active and save the workbook as *[your initials]***u1-2.xls** in your Unit 1 Applications folder.
13. Print the worksheet and close the workbook.

UNIT APPLICATION 1-3

Edit data, move data, insert and delete rows, construct formulas, use AutoCalculate, and use Save As Web Page.

A balance sheet shows that a company's total assets equal the combined sum of its liabilities and its shareholders' equity. You have been asked to construct a balance sheet for Alpha Pharmaceuticals using its asset statement and its statement of liabilities and shareholders' equity. To see the relative size of each item on the balance sheet, you should show the "asset ratio" for each item. (The asset ratio is the item divided by the total assets.)

1. Open the file **Balance1.xls**.
2. Cut the liabilities and owner's equity information in cells D6:F15.
3. Paste the material below the asset information, beginning in cell A19.
4. Edit cell A1 to read **Balance Sheet for Alpha Pharmaceuticals**
5. Insert a row at row 19, format blank cell A19 as bold, and key
   Liabilities and Owners' Equity
6. Format cell A5 (which contains the label "Assets") as bold.
7. Insert a new row at row 5.
8. Key **$** (dollar sign) in cell C5 and key **%** **Assets** in cell D5. Format both cells as bold and centered.

UNIT 1 ■ APPLICATIONS   EXCEL **109**

9. In cell D8, enter the formula **=C8/C18**. (Cell C18 contains the value for total assets. The formula gives the percentage of total assets represented by the value in cell C8—that is, the asset ratio.)
10. In column D, create asset ratio formulas for all the remaining assets in the balance sheet including total assets. Be sure to divide by total assets (C18).
11. Format the values in column D in percent style to display one decimal place.
12. Format the values in column C in comma style to display no decimals.
13. Use AutoCalculate to verify the subtotals.
14. Make cell A1 active and save your workbook as *[your initials]***u1-3.xls** in your Unit 1 Applications folder.
15. Print the worksheet and save the workbook as *[your initials]***u1-3.htm** in your Unit 1 Applications folder.
16. Close the workbook.

UNIT APPLICATION 1-4

Enter data in a selected range, construct formulas, use AutoSum, format text and numbers, and insert columns and rows.

In addition to a balance sheet, Alpha Pharmaceuticals' annual report will include an income statement. An income statement shows the revenues, expenses, and net income for a company over a period of time. You have been asked to prepare this statement and to format it attractively.

1. Open a new workbook.
2. In the cell range A1:B10, key the data shown in Figure U1-2.

FIGURE U1-2

	A	B
1	Revenue	34050
2	Cost of goods sold	20410
3	Sales expenses	2400
4	Administrative expense	5210
5	Depreciation	480

continues

FIGURE U1-2 *continued*

	A	B
6	Other expenses	200
7	Earnings before interest and taxes	
8	Interest expense	310
9	Income taxes	1930
10	Net income	

3. Change the width of column A to accommodate the label in A7.
4. Move the entire block of labels and numbers so "Revenue" appears in cell A7.
5. Starting in cell A1, key the following title:

   Income Statement
   Alpha Pharmaceuticals
   1998
   (Dollars in thousands)

6. Left-align the label in A3 if it was entered as a value.
7. Format the first three lines of the title as bold.
8. In cell B13, create a formula that subtracts cells B8:B12 (which are expenses and cost of goods sold) from "Revenue" (cell B7).
9. In cell B16, create a formula that subtracts both interest and taxes (cells B14:B15) from "Earnings before interest and taxes" (cell B13).
10. Key $ in cell B6 and % in cell C6. Format both cells as bold and centered.
11. In column C, create formulas that divide each item in column B by "Revenue" (B7). (Hint: The first three formulas are **=B7/B7**, **=B8/B7**, and **=B9/B7**.)
12. Format the values in column C in percent style to display one decimal place.
13. Format the values in column B in comma style to display no decimals.
14. Apply single-line bottom borders to cells B12:C12 and B15:C15. Apply double-line bottom borders to cells B16:C16.
15. Proofread the worksheet.

16. Make cell A1 active and save the workbook as *[your initials]***u1-4.xls** in your Unit 1 Applications folder.
17. Print the worksheet and close the workbook.

UNIT APPLICATION 1-5

Enter data; construct formulas; use AutoSum; format text and numbers; and insert and delete cells, columns, and rows, as needed.

Prepare an income statement for yourself, your household, or another individual.

1. In a new workbook, enter the income categories and data. Figure U1-3 lists suggested categories to include. (You **must** include the categories shown in bold.)

FIGURE U1-3

```
Income (include at least two subcategories)
Job1
Job2
Investments
Interest
Total income
Expenses (include at least three subcategories)
Food
Housing
Utilities
Transportation
Clothing
Insurance
Medical
Loan payments
Entertainment
Total expenses
Earnings before taxes
Taxes
Net income
```

2. Complete the worksheet by including the following information and formatting:
   - A title identifying the name of the statement and the period of time it covers.
   - Column labels for dollar amounts and for percentage of total income (not net income).
   - Bottom borders on cells before subtotals and totals.
   - Numbers and text formatted appropriately.
   - Attractive and clear layout.
3. Save your workbook as *[your initials]*u1-5.xls in your Unit 1 Applications folder.
4. Print the worksheet and close the workbook.

UNIT APPLICATION 1-6 ✓ Making It Work for You

Enter data, use Pick From List or AutoComplete, construct formulas, move data, format text and numbers, use Format Painter, and use Save As Web Page.

Now that you know how to create income statements, you can use a spreadsheet to create a future-look at your "dream" income for the years 2005, 2006, and 2007. Use labels and totals for Income, Expenses, and Net Income (no subcategories necessary), and calculate your percent of Income. Remember, this is your "dream" income; be optimistic, but realistic, too. Enter labels so you can use Pick From List and AutoComplete when possible, then use cut and paste to position data on the worksheet. Make the worksheet attractive with a meaningful title and good formatting using Format Painter when possible. Save the workbook as *[your initials]*u1-6.xls in your Unit 1 Applications folder and print the worksheet. Then save the file as a Web page, *[your initials]*u1-6.htm in your Unit 1 Applications folder.

UNIT 2

Developing a Worksheet

LESSON 4 Designing and Printing a Worksheet
LESSON 5 Copying Data and Using Toolbars
LESSON 6 Range Names and Sorting
LESSON 7 Spelling, Find/Replace, and File Management

Beautiful Belle Company

Beautiful Belle Company

Sun Soft Heats Up Skin Care Market

The Beautiful Belle Company, also known as BBC, manufactures a moderately priced line of cosmetics. BBC is currently promoting a product named "Sun Soft." It's a 100%-natural hypo-allergenic lotion that has refined almond and sesame oils as its main ingredients. Although it's not proven, and can't be used in advertising, researchers have recently claimed that these oils are beneficial in protecting against skin cancer.

BBC is test-marketing Sun Soft in its Southwest region. Renata Santo, BBC's Southwest regional-sales manager, has decided to concentrate her efforts in the Phoenix area. However, Phoenix is a challenging market for Soft Sun, because a competing product, Corn Silk Cream, has a significant market share of skin care products there.

For the test marketing, Renata will need the following:

✔ A worksheet to keep track of weekly sales of Sun Soft and the competing product, Corn Silk Cream, over a two-month period. **(Lesson 4)**

✔ Once the test is complete, a worksheet that tracks Sun Soft sales in relation to Corn Silk Cream sales for three months. **(Lesson 5)**

✔ A worksheet that shows sales of selected creams for four quarters, with sales broken down by months and by product. **(Lesson 6)**

✔ A worksheet that compares Sun Soft sales by quarter for the last three years. **(Lesson 7)**

Designing and Printing a Worksheet

LESSON 4

OBJECTIVES

After completing this lesson, you will be able to:
1. Plan a worksheet on paper.
2. Put a worksheet plan on screen.
3. Keep row and column labels in view.
4. Select display options.
5. Create user documentation.
6. Protect files.
7. Print workbooks and print areas.
8. Print formulas.

Estimated Time: 2 hours

MOUS ACTIVITIES

In this lesson:
XL2000 **4.1**
XL2000 **4.3**
XL2000 **4.4**
XL2000 **4.5**
XL2000 **4.7**
XL2000 **4.8**
XL2000 **4.9**
XL2000 **5.3**
XL2000 **5.4**
XL2000 **5.7**
XL2000 **E.10.9**
XL2000 **E.12.2**

See Appendix F.

Creating a worksheet requires careful planning. A well-designed worksheet is easy to read, the data is arranged in a logical order, and the results are readily apparent. Decide what you want to accomplish with the worksheet before you create it. Designing the worksheet with a specific purpose in mind will help you decide what you want Excel to do with the data you enter. You can then choose from a variety of print settings so the final, printed worksheet has the appearance you intended.

Planning a Worksheet on Paper

To design a worksheet that meets your goals, start your planning using pencil and paper. Even experienced users often sketch a worksheet before they key data. Your plan should include:

- Titles that indicate who the worksheet is for and what it is about
- An entry area, if necessary, for single input items that provide additional information about the worksheet in general, such as a date, or a department title
- The worksheet body, the input and output area that contains multiple entries, labels, and formulas

The procedures in this lesson generate a worksheet to help the sales manager of a small manufacturing company analyze the results of a two-month test-marketing program. The purpose of the worksheet is to compare test-market sales with those of a competing product.

EXERCISE 4-1   Sketch the Planned Worksheet

1. Write the worksheet heading **Sun Soft vs. Corn Silk Sales** at the top left corner of a blank piece of paper. The heading of the worksheet must clearly state the purpose of the worksheet and provide a concise overview of its contents. In this case, the heading names the products and promises a competitive analysis based on sales.

2. Write the subtitles **April through May, 1999** and **(Broken down by gender)** on two separate rows under the heading.

   NOTE: You do not use an entry area in this worksheet.

3. Now consider the *purpose* of your worksheet. What do you want it to do? You want it to store weekly sales information over a two-month period and make calculations that provide useful competitive information.

   TIP: Although there are no hard-and-fast rules for worksheet design, it is generally a good idea to put items that are being compared in columns and repetitive items in rows. An analysis that compares two categories usually looks better when the categories are placed side by side. This makes it easy for a user to glance back and forth to evaluate information quickly.

4. Plan the *structure* of your worksheet body by determining the placement of data in columns and rows. The first column of the body holds the date labels. The next two columns hold Sun Soft data broken down by gender. The last two columns hold Corn Silk data broken down by gender.

LESSON 4 ■ DESIGNING AND PRINTING A WORKSHEET   EXCEL   **117**

5. Define the labels that identify the rows of the worksheet. For your worksheet, the labels are the weekly dates for the two-month analysis. So, skip two rows to allow for column labels, and write the following labels in a column along the left side of the page.

April 9
April 16
April 23
April 30
Subtotal
May 7
May 14
May 21
May 28
Subtotal
Grand total

6. Consider the column headings. Remember, you are comparing products based on gender, so first you need to identify the products, then you have to identify the gender. You will need two levels of column headings.

7. Move approximately two rows above the row labels. Write **Sun Soft Lotion.** On the same row but further to the right, write **Corn Silk Cream**. This is your first-level column heading.

8. In the row beneath the column heading **Sun Soft Lotion,** write the labels **Men**, **Women**, and **Total**. In the same row beneath the heading **Corn Silk Cream,** repeat the same three labels. This is your second-level column heading. Now the preliminary design of your worksheet is complete.

FIGURE 4-1
Preliminary worksheet design

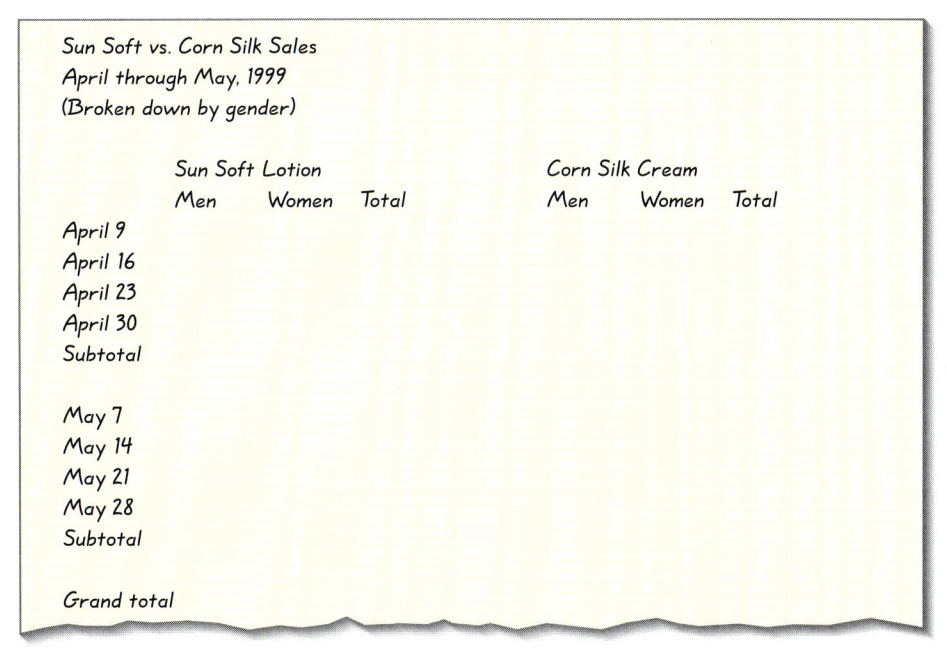

```
Sun Soft vs. Corn Silk Sales
April through May, 1999
(Broken down by gender)

              Sun Soft Lotion              Corn Silk Cream
              Men     Women    Total       Men     Women    Total
April 9
April 16
April 23
April 30
Subtotal

May 7
May 14
May 21
May 28
Subtotal

Grand total
```

9. Decide which formulas to use and where to put them on the worksheet. Your worksheet calculates monthly subtotals and a grand total of sales for both months. It also calculates total sales to men and women for both the test product and the competing product. Write an "F" (for "Formula") in all the locations where you will need to write a formula to make a calculation. (You'll use the SUM function to calculate these values.)

FIGURE 4-2
Final worksheet design

Sun Soft vs. Corn Silk Sales
April through May, 1999
(Broken down by gender)

	Sun Soft Lotion			Corn Silk Cream		
	Men	Women	Total	Men	Women	Total
April 9			F			F
April 16			F			F
April 23			F			F
April 30			F			F
Subtotal	F	F	F	F	F	F
May 7			F			F
May 14			F			F
May 21			F			F
May 28			F			F
Subtotal	F	F	F	F	F	F
Grand total	F	F	F	F	F	F

Putting the Worksheet Plan on Screen

Once you sketch the overall plan and know what data and formulas you will include, you are ready to build the worksheet in Excel.

After your worksheet is set up onscreen, you can validate the data, choose cells by content, and name the worksheet tabs.

EXERCISE 4-2 Enter Row and Column Labels

1. Open the workbook **TestMkt.xls**.

LESSON 4 ■ DESIGNING AND PRINTING A WORKSHEET   EXCEL   **119**

> **NOTE:** Usually you create a new workbook when you implement a sketch in Excel. To save class time, however, you start with an existing workbook.

2. In cell A1, edit the title to read **Sun Soft vs. Corn Silk Sales**
3. In cell A2, edit the subtitle to read **April through May, 1999**
4. In cell A3, edit the second subtitle to read **(Broken down by gender)**. This subtitle should remain bold italic.

> **TIP:** A worksheet title should not be longer than three lines and there should be some visible difference from one line of the title to the next.

5. In cell B5, key **Sun Soft Lotion**
6. In cell E5, key **Corn Silk Cream**
7. In cells B6, C6, and D6, key the following labels and center-align:

   Men   Women   Total

8. In cells E6, F6, and G6, key the same labels a second time. Center-align these labels.
9. In cell A7, key **April 9**. Notice that the date appears in the cell as "9-Apr." The date is displayed on the formula bar in the date format mm/dd/yyyy and reflects the current year.

> **TIP:** You can change the date format of selected cells. Choose Cells from the Format menu and click the Number tab. Choose Date in the Category list, select the Type of format, and click OK.

10. In cells A8 through A10, key the following dates:

    April 16

    April 23

    April 30

11. In cells A13 through A16, key the following dates:

    May 7

    May 14

    May 21

    May 28

12. To complete the worksheet design, key **Subtotal** in cells A11 and A17, and **Grand total** in cell A19. You use these rows to summarize the data. (See Figure 4-3 on the next page.)

FIGURE 4-3
Worksheet plan with labels entered

	A	B	C	D	E	F	G
1	Sun Soft vs. Corn Silk Sales						
2	April through May, 1999						
3	(Broken down by gender)						
4							
5		Sun Soft Lotion			Corn Silk Cream		
6		Men	Women	Total	Men	Women	Total
7	9-Apr						
8	16-Apr						
9	23-Apr						
10	30-Apr						
11	Subtotal						
12							
13	7-May						
14	14-May						
15	21-May						
16	28-May						
17	Subtotal						
18							
19	Grand total						

EXERCISE 4-3 Enter Test Data

The body of the worksheet consists of data. You can enter test data into the worksheet to test formula calculations. *Test data* should consist of numbers that are easy to calculate in your head so you can tell at a glance whether your formulas are correct.

1. Key the following test data for Sun Soft in columns B and C. Start with **1000** in cell B7.

April 9	1000	2000
April 16	1000	2000
April 23	1000	2000
April 30	1000	2000
May 7	1000	2000
May 14	1000	2000
May 21	1000	2000
May 28	1000	2000

2. Key the following test data for Corn Silk in columns E and F. Start with **1000** in cell E7.

April 9	1000	2000
April 16	1000	2000
April 23	1000	2000

LESSON 4 ■ DESIGNING AND PRINTING A WORKSHEET   EXCEL **121**

April 30	**1000**	**2000**
May 7	**1000**	**2000**
May 14	**1000**	**2000**
May 21	**1000**	**2000**
May 28	**1000**	**2000**

3. Select all the numbers and format them for commas and no decimal places. (Remember to press Ctrl when you click to select nonadjacent cells.) Click the Comma Style button on the Formatting toolbar, then click the Decrease Decimal button until you can see the numbers and no decimal places remain.

> **NOTE:** When there is not enough room in a cell for data, Excel inserts ### to alert you to reformat the data or widen the column.

FIGURE 4-4
Worksheet plan with data entered

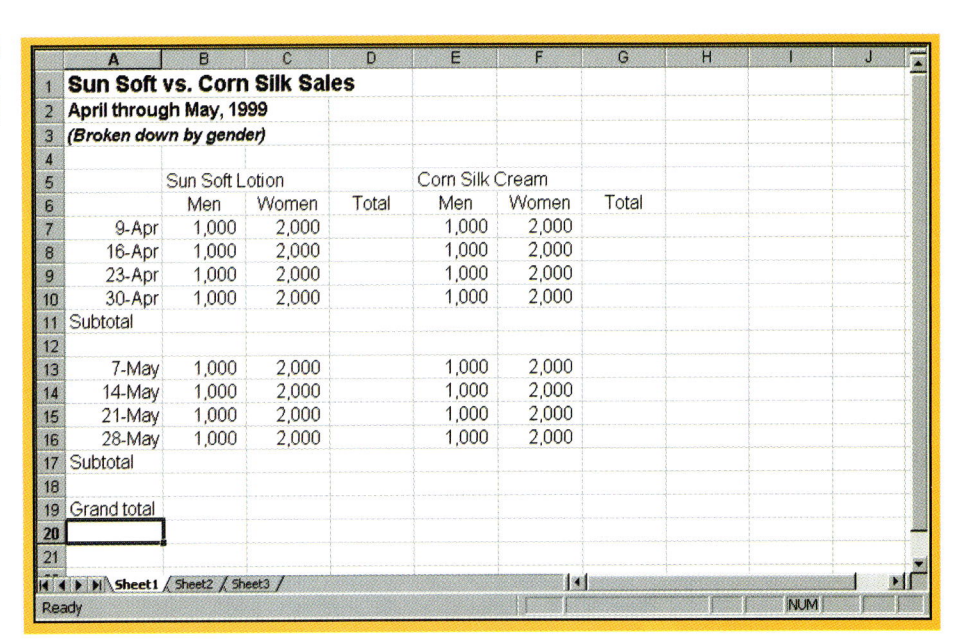

EXERCISE 4-4 Enter Formulas

Once the worksheet data is entered, you can enter formulas to automate the calculations. Since you are adding rows and columns, this is a good time to use the SUM function or the AutoSum button.

1. Select cells D7 through D10 and click the AutoSum button on the Standard toolbar. The SUM function is entered in each cell and the total values are displayed. Add the totals in your head to check the values as you go through the remaining steps.

2. Select cells B11 through D11 and click the AutoSum button ∑. This totals the three separate ranges in the same step.

3. Select cells B13 through D17 (the data cells and the cells for their totals).

4. Click the AutoSum button ∑. Excel automatically sums the rows and columns of selected data.

5. Select cells E7 through G11, hold down Ctrl, and select cells E13 through G17.

6. Release Ctrl and click the AutoSum button ∑ to enter the totals for the two cell ranges at the same time. All the totals and subtotals for Corn Silk are now entered.

7. Move to cell B19 and click the AutoSum button ∑. Excel suggests cell B17, the second subtotal to be included in the formula.

8. Hold down Ctrl and click cell B11, the first subtotal to include it in the formula.

9. Release Ctrl and press Enter. Excel totals the two subtotals. The formula =SUM(B17,B11) appears in the formula bar for cell B19.

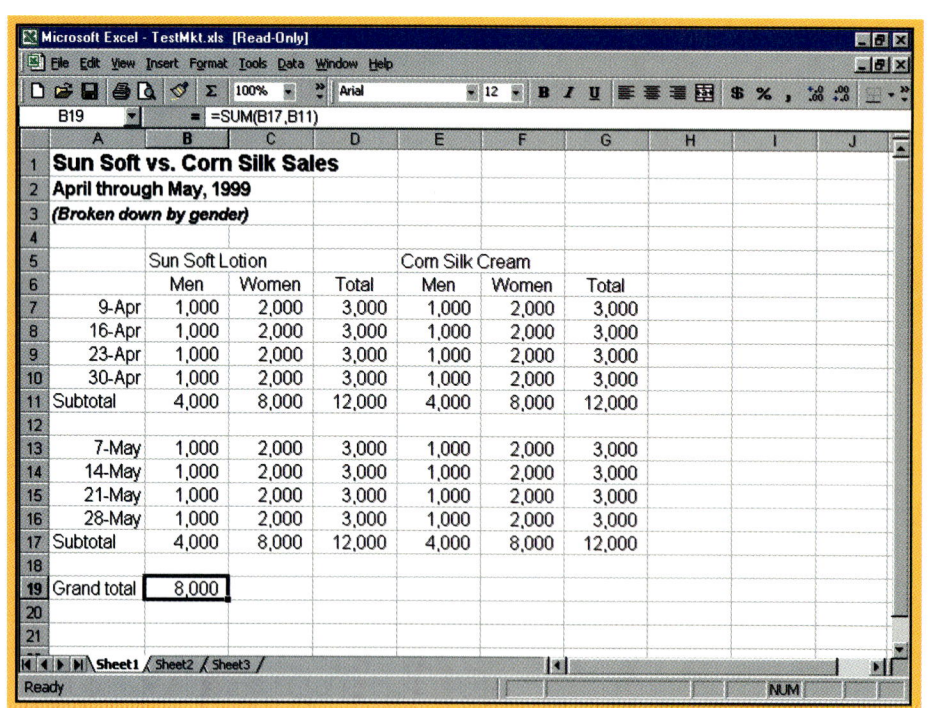

FIGURE 4-5
Worksheet with formulas

10. Select cells C7 through C19 and click the AutoSum button ∑. The formula in cell C20 adds the two subtotals in column C.

LESSON 4 ■ DESIGNING AND PRINTING A WORKSHEET   EXCEL **123**

11. Do the same for column D.

12. Select cells E7 through G19 and click the AutoSum button [Σ]. Examine the formula in cell G19. Notice that it adds the grand totals of columns E and F instead of summing the subtotals of column G (which would produce the same result).

EXERCISE 4-5 Validate Data

You can control the type of data entered in cells, such as whole numbers, date, time, and text length. If you or someone else tries to enter data into a cell that is validated, you can have Excel display a prompt specifying the type of data to enter. Excel returns an error message if incorrect data is keyed.

1. Select all the cells containing **1,000**. (Remember to press [Ctrl] and click the mouse to select nonadjacent cells.)

2. Choose Validation from the Data menu to open the Data Validation dialog box.

FIGURE 4-6
Data Validation dialog box

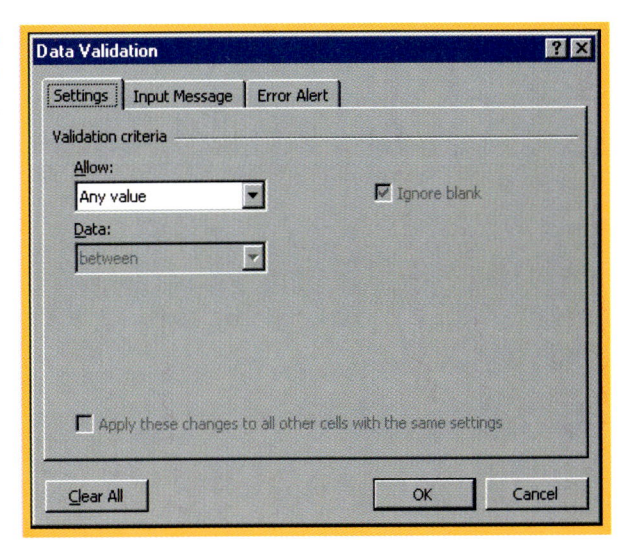

3. Click the Settings tab, if necessary, and choose "Whole number" from the Allow drop-down list.

4. Choose "greater than or equal to" from the Data drop-down list and key **0** in the Minimum text box.

5. Click the Input Message tab.

6. Under Title, key **Sales**

7. In the Input Message text box, key **Enter sales for men** and click OK. Notice the message box that appears over the last set of cells selected with the input message you created.

8. Select any cell containing **1,000**. Notice that the same message box appears.

> **NOTE:** The message reminds users what to key in that cell. If the validation message box hampers your selection, drag the box to another location on the worksheet.

9. Change the number in a cell containing 1,000 to **1,000.75**. When you try to enter the number in the cell, a message indicates the value you entered is not valid. Click Cancel.

> **TIP:** To turn off data validation, click the Clear All button at the bottom of the Data Validation dialog box. (See Figure 4-6 on the previous page.) This also clears any messages you created.

EXERCISE 4-6 Select Cells by Content

Once your worksheet is set up, you may find it useful to select cells by content. You can use this method to select a cell or group of cells that have common characteristics (such as validated data or formulas), whether they are adjacent on the worksheet or not.

1. Press Ctrl + Home to return to cell A1.
2. Choose Go To from the Edit menu. When the Go To dialog box opens, click Special to open the Go To Special dialog box.

FIGURE 4-7
Go To Special dialog box

LESSON 4 ■ DESIGNING AND PRINTING A WORKSHEET   EXCEL **125**

> **TIP:** You can also press `Ctrl`+`G` to open the Go To dialog box and then click Special to open the Go To Special dialog box.

3. Click Data Validation and click OK. All the cells with validated data are selected. Press `Ctrl`+`Home`.
4. Try this for the cells with formulas by choosing Formulas in the Go To Special dialog box. Choose Numbers under the Formulas option and deselect the others. When you are finished, press `Ctrl`+`Home` to return to cell A1.

EXERCISE 4-7 Name Worksheet Tabs

As you learned in Lesson 1, each new Excel workbook opens with three sheets that are named "Sheet1" through "Sheet3" by default. When you work with more than one worksheet, it's a good idea to name worksheet tabs so their purposes are obvious.

1. Double-click the Sheet1 tab. The tab name is highlighted.
2. Key **Sales Comparison** over the Sheet1 tab name.
3. Double-click the Sheet2 tab. Sheet2 becomes active and the tab name is highlighted.
4. Key **User Information** over Sheet2. (You use this sheet later in the lesson.)
5. Click the Sales Comparison tab to make the Sales Comparison worksheet active again.

> **TIP:** Sheet names should describe what the sheet includes using only a word or two. Sheet names can be up to 31 characters long, including spaces.

Keeping Row and Column Labels in View

Frequently, the rows and columns of a worksheet extend beyond the display screen. You can split the worksheet into multiple *panes* so you can see row and column labels as you key data or formulas. Using multiple panes you can also scroll through data to locate and select cells to be included in calculations. You do this using *split bars*. For example, when you create a grand total, you might need to scroll to the top of a large worksheet to include one or more subtotals.

EXERCISE 4-8 Split a Worksheet into Panes

1. Select cell A7 on the Sales Comparison worksheet.
2. Choose <u>S</u>plit from the <u>W</u>indow menu. The screen is split into two horizontal panes by a split bar. Each pane has its own vertical scroll bar, permitting it to be scrolled on its own.

   TIP: You can also split a worksheet horizontally by selecting an entire row first.

3. Click the down vertical scroll arrow for the bottom pane to move row 13 directly under the column labels. Splitting the screen under the column labels makes it easier to enter formulas for the May subtotal and the grand total.

FIGURE 4-8
Screen split horizontally

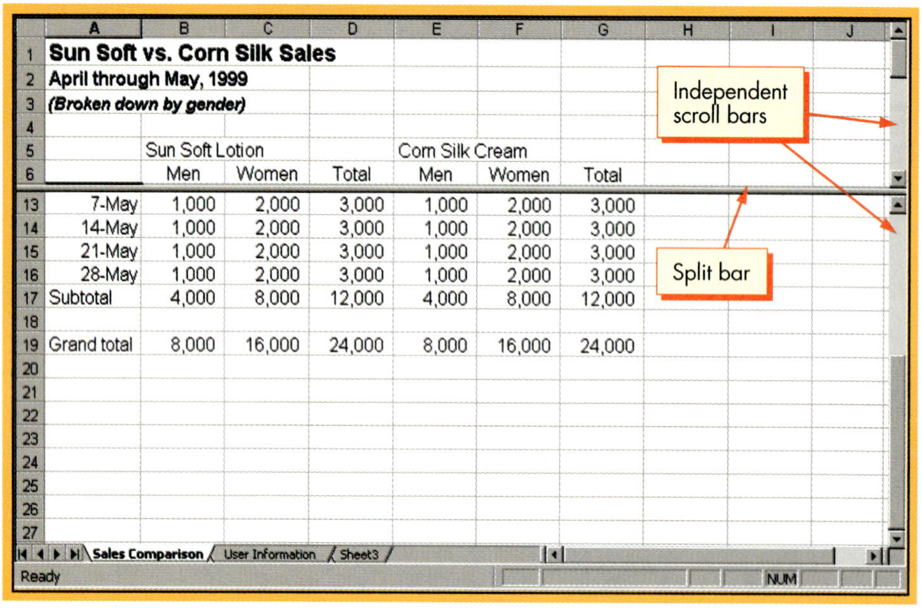

4. Experiment with the scroll buttons in both panes.
5. Choose Remove <u>S</u>plit from the <u>W</u>indow menu. The original view of the worksheet is restored.

   NOTE: The <u>S</u>plit option on the <u>W</u>indow menu changes to Remove <u>S</u>plit when a worksheet is split into panes.

6. Select cell B7. (*Hint*: You may need to drag the Validation Input Message box out of the way.)

LESSON 4 ■ DESIGNING AND PRINTING A WORKSHEET   EXCEL   **127**

7. Choose Split from the Window menu. The window splits above and to the left of the active cell. In four panes, you can see both row and column labels at the same time. Scroll to move row 13 just below column labels and select cell A1 by clicking it.

> **TIP:** To create a vertical split only, select a column other than column A (or select a cell in row 1 other than cell A1) before choosing Split from the Window menu.

FIGURE 4-9
Screen split horizontally and vertically

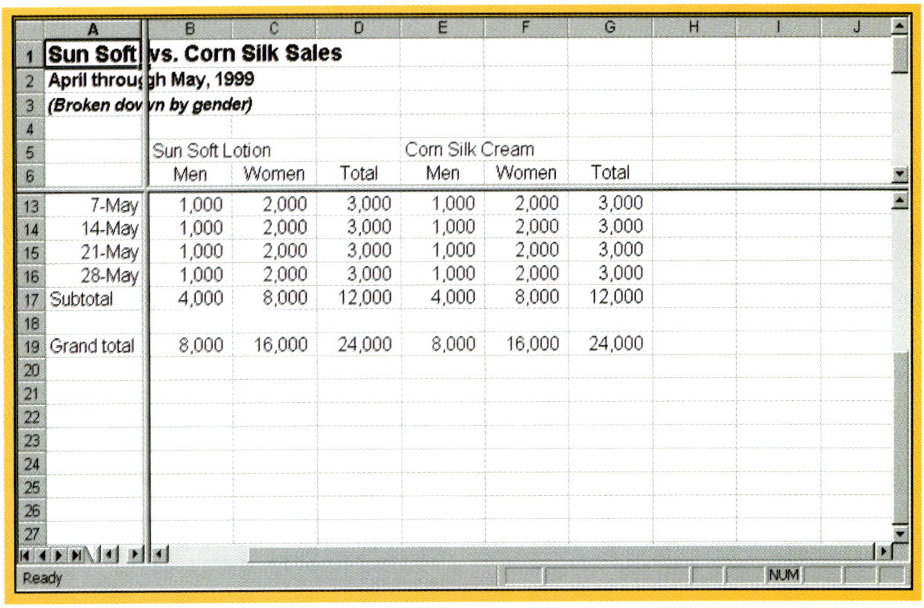

EXERCISE 4-9 Freeze Panes

You use the Freeze Panes command on the Window menu to freeze row labels, column labels, or both. A single set of scroll arrows and buttons moves data only, but leaves labels in place.

1. Choose Remove Split from the Window menu.
2. Select cell B7.
3. Choose Freeze Panes from the Window menu. Single lines divide the worksheet, marking frozen areas.
4. Experiment with the scroll buttons and the arrow keys.
5. Choose Unfreeze Panes from the Window menu to restore the original view of the worksheet.

EXERCISE 4-10   Use Split Boxes and Split Bars

Another way to split a screen into multiple panes is to use the horizontal and vertical *split boxes*. The horizontal split box appears in the upper right corner of the document window; it is the gray, rectangular box located above the vertical scroll arrow. The vertical split box is found at the far right of the horizontal scroll bar at the bottom of the document window.

Clicking a split box produces a split bar, which you can drag to the desired position on the worksheet to split the screen. Double-click a split box to position the split bar automatically.

1. Select cell B7, if necessary.

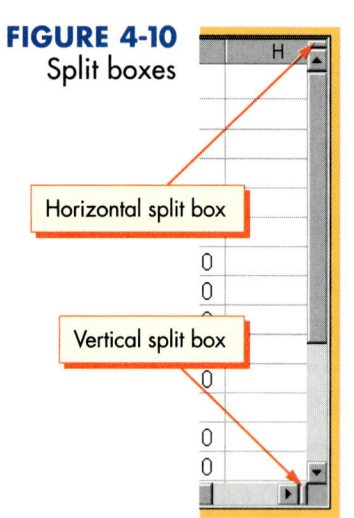

FIGURE 4-10
Split boxes

Horizontal split box

Vertical split box

2. Move the mouse pointer to the horizontal split box at the top of the vertical scroll bar. The mouse pointer changes to a split pointer.

3. Double-click the split box. A split bar appears above the active cell.

4. Move the mouse pointer to the vertical split box at the right of the horizontal scroll bar.

5. Double-click the split box and the split bar appears between column A and B.

6. Move the mouse pointer to the intersection of the two split bars. The pointer becomes a four-headed arrow.

7. Double-click the intersection of the two split bars to remove the split.

8. Press Ctrl + Home.

TIP: To adjust horizontal or vertical splits, drag the split bar to the new location. You can also change the location of a four-pane split by dragging its intersection.

Selecting Display Options

You can change how a worksheet is displayed on the screen so it is easier to work with. *Zoom* options change the magnification of the display. You can enlarge it to see more detail or reduce it to show more of the worksheet at one time.

You can also choose to display gridlines and row and column headings.

LESSON 4 ■ DESIGNING AND PRINTING A WORKSHEET   EXCEL **129**

EXERCISE 4-11 Zoom to Magnify and Reduce the Display

Zoom acts like a magnifying glass. The size of the characters displayed on the screen is expressed in terms of percentages. Higher percentages display larger characters, but less of the worksheet. Lower percentages display smaller characters, but show more of the worksheet. Zoom does not affect the size of the printed worksheet.

Excel provides two ways to use zoom:

- Choose Zoom from the View menu.
- Use the Zoom box [100%] on the Standard toolbar.

FIGURE 4-11
Zoom dialog box

1. Choose Zoom from the View menu and the Zoom dialog box opens.
2. In the Zoom dialog box, click 75% and click OK. The displayed text becomes smaller and you can see more of the worksheet. The Zoom box [75%] now displays "75%."
3. Select cell D7.
4. Choose Zoom from the View menu.
5. Click Custom, key **400**, and click OK. 400% is the largest display type you can specify.
6. Click the Zoom button (the arrow at the right of the Zoom box on the Standard toolbar) to open the drop-down list box, and click 75%.

FIGURE 4-12
Zoom box and Zoom button

Zoom button
Current display size
Zoom box
Zoom drop-down list box

EXERCISE 4-12 Remove Gridlines and Headers from the Screen

You can use other Excel options to vary the onscreen appearance of the worksheet. For example, you can choose to display cell gridlines or row and column headings.

1. Press [Ctrl]+[Home] and choose Options from the Tools menu. The Options dialog box appears.
2. Click the View tab, if necessary.

FIGURE 4-13
Options dialog box, View tab

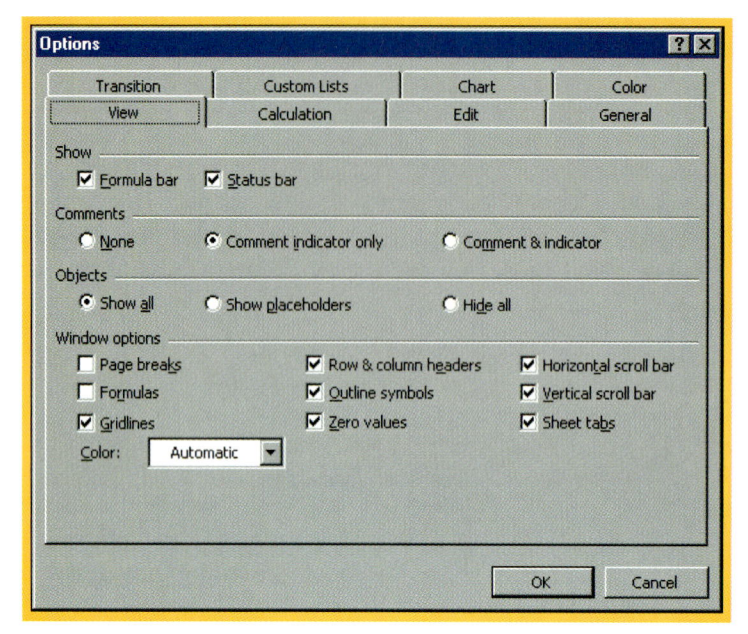

3. Under Window Options, click the Gridlines check box and the Row & Column Headers check box to clear them. Click OK. You removed gridlines and row and column headings from the worksheet display.

4. Move about the worksheet using the Arrow keys. Note that even though the gridlines are not visible, each cell is outlined when active. In addition, although the row and column headers are not visible, the address of the active cell appears in the reference area of the formula bar.

5. Select cell D19, which contains a formula. Note that the contents of the cell appear in the entry area of the formula bar.

6. Reset the options in the Options dialog box so both gridlines and row and column headings are displayed on the worksheet.

7. Press Ctrl+Home.

Creating User Documentation

Once you create a worksheet, you may want others to be able to use it. You can provide users with basic information about this worksheet or an entire workbook on a separate worksheet in the workbook. You might label this worksheet User Information or something similar. This sheet should include file information, the purpose of the worksheet, and instructions to the user. It should be easy to read.

LESSON 4 ■ DESIGNING AND PRINTING A WORKSHEET EXCEL **131**

EXERCISE 4-13   Create User Documentation

1. Click the **User Information** tab to move to the second worksheet, and change the view to 75% using the Zoom box. The varying column widths in the worksheet are already adjusted to create an easy-to-read final worksheet.

2. In cell A1, key **User Information** in bold.

3. Key the following labels as bold and right-aligned in column B, beginning in cell B3. Leave a row space between **Date created:** and **Date revised:** and a row space between **Revised by:** and **Contact for help:**

   Created by:
   Date created:
   Date revised:
   Revised by:
   Contact for help:

4. Key the following labels in bold in cells A11 and A14.

   Purpose
   User Instructions

5. In column C, starting in cell C3, key the information requested using Figure 4-14 as a reference. For example, key your name beside "Created by:" and so on down column C. Make these items left-aligned.

FIGURE 4-14
Worksheet documentation

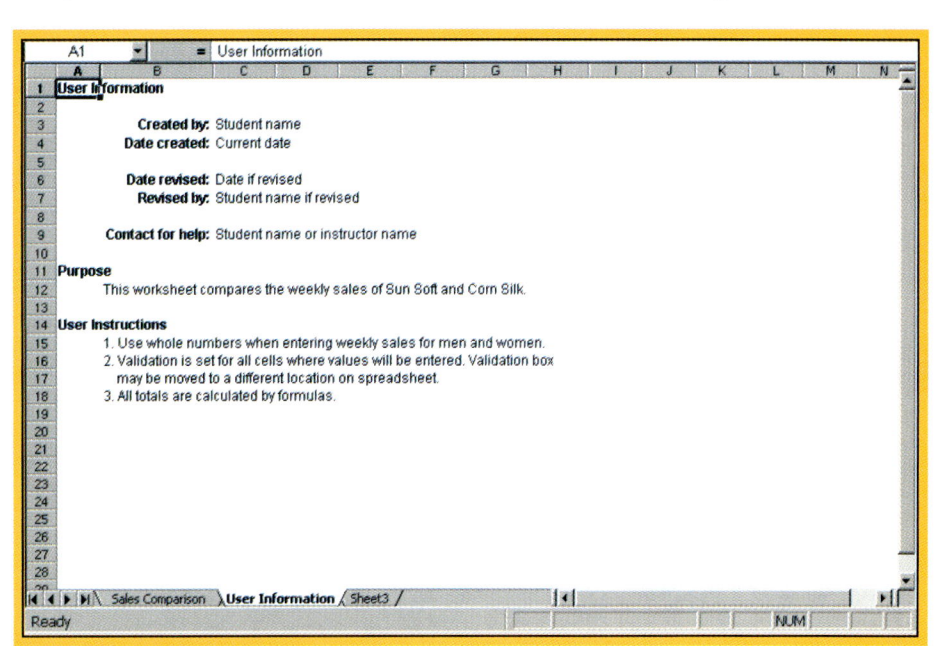

6. Using the information in Figure 4-14, in cell B12, key the purpose of this worksheet under the label **Purpose**. Below this, key user instructions for

another user or for yourself beginning in cell B15. It's a good idea to number these instructions for clarity. Put each numbered item in a separate cell. Also, put the second line of item 2 in its own cell directly below the first line of item 2.

7. Turn off gridlines for viewing using the Window Options in the Options dialog box (View tab) and return to cell A1.

8. Unused worksheets should be deleted once the workbook is complete. Right-click on Sheet3 tab. Click De̲lete and then click OK. Another way to delete a sheet is to make the sheet to be deleted active, then select De̲lete Sheet from the E̲dit menu, and click OK.

Protecting Files

Workbooks often include formats and formulas that you don't want changed. You can protect a file so users can key only in the areas you leave unlocked.

Protecting a file is a two-step process:

- Unlock areas for data entry
- Protect the file

EXERCISE 4-14 Unlock Data Entry Areas

1. Click the Sales Comparison tab and select the cells that contain test data. Do not select cells containing formulas.
2. Choose Ce̲lls from the F̲ormat menu and click the Protection tab in the Format Cells dialog box.
3. Clear the L̲ocked check box and click OK. The selected cells are unlocked. When you protect the workbook, they remain available to users.
4. Press Ctrl + Home to return to cell A1.

NOTE: By default, all cells are locked in a workbook. Locked cells become inaccessible only after you protect the worksheet.

EXERCISE 4-15 Protect a Worksheet

The P̲rotection command on the T̲ools menu offers two options:

LESSON 4 ■ DESIGNING AND PRINTING A WORKSHEET　　　　　EXCEL **133**

- Protect Workbook prevents a user from adding, deleting, renaming, or moving worksheets and from resizing or moving windows.
- Protect Sheet prevents a user from changing data in a worksheet.

1. Point to Protection on the Tools menu and choose Protect Sheet from the submenu. The Protect Sheet dialog box appears.

FIGURE 4-15
Protect Sheet dialog box

2. In the Password text box, key *[your initials]*. The text box displays asterisks instead of the characters you key to ensure the secrecy of your password. A password can be up to 255 characters long and include any combination of letters, numerals, and symbols. Passwords are case-sensitive, so you must remember whether you use uppercase or lowercase characters.

3. Click OK and the Confirm Password dialog box appears.
4. Rekey *[your initials]* in this dialog box and click OK.
5. Press Tab repeatedly to move to the cells that are available for data entry.
6. Go to cell A7 and try to key your name. The Microsoft Excel dialog box opens reminding you that the cell is protected.

Printing Workbooks and Print Areas

In Excel, you can control how your work is printed. You can:

- Preview a worksheet or an entire workbook before printing.
- Change page orientation.
- Position the print area on the page.
- Create headers and footers.
- Print with or without gridlines or row and column headings.
- Print all or part of a worksheet or workbook.

EXERCISE   4-16   Preview the Workbook before Printing

Preview a worksheet before you print it so you can see the page layout, headers and footers, print formatting, and page breaks. Although it is always a good idea to preview a worksheet, it makes particular sense if it contains graphics, drawings, or charts. After all, it takes less time to preview a complex worksheet than to print it.

1. With the Sales Comparison worksheet displayed, choose Print Preview from the File menu or click the Print Preview button on the Standard toolbar. At the top of the Print Preview screen, the Next button is dimmed. The current worksheet fits on one page and the second worksheet is not available.

FIGURE 4-16
Print Preview display

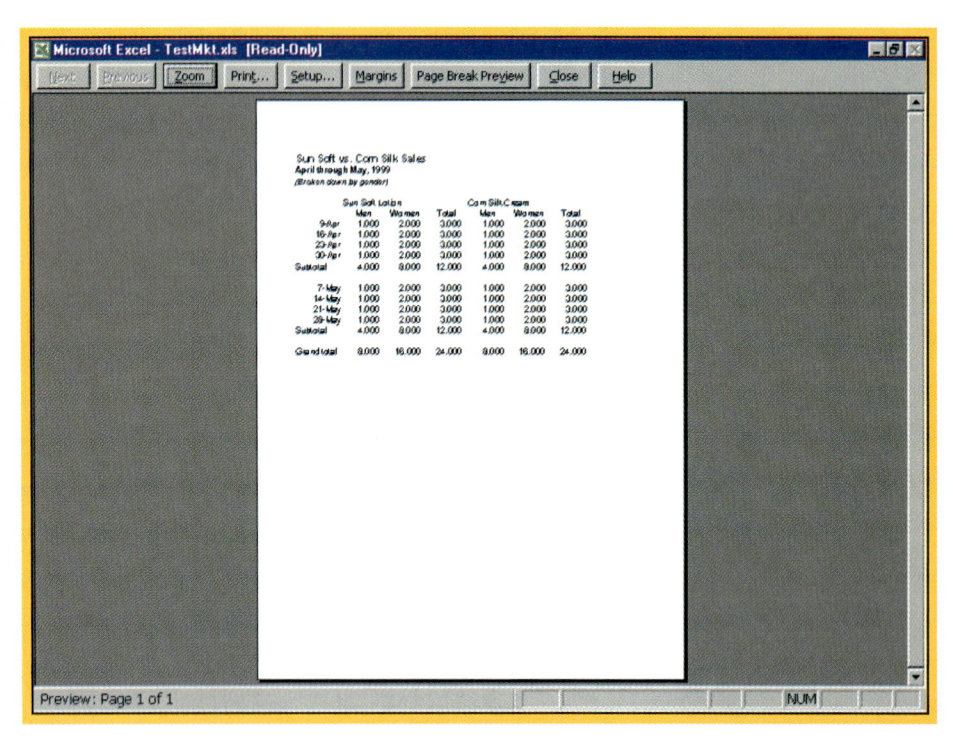

2. Click the Print button to open the Print dialog box, select Entire workbook under Print What, and click the Preview button. Preview: Page 1 of 2 appears in the Print Preview status bar, and the Next button becomes available.

3. Click Next. The User Information sheet ("Preview: Page 2 of 2") is displayed.

4. Click Zoom at the top of the preview screen (or click the reduced document). The worksheet is displayed in actual size.

> **TIP:** Click the magnifier pointer on the full-page document to Zoom to actual size. Click the arrow pointer on the enlarged document to Zoom to the reduced display.

5. Use the scroll arrows to view other parts of the worksheet in actual size.
6. Click Previous to display page 1 again.
7. Click Close to close the Preview window.

LESSON 4 ■ DESIGNING AND PRINTING A WORKSHEET   EXCEL **135**

EXERCISE 4-17 Choose a Page Orientation

One of the most useful print functions offered by Excel is *page orientation*, which you use to print worksheets in either *portrait* or *landscape* orientation. In portrait orientation, the page is vertical, 8½ inches by 11 inches. In landscape orientation, the page is horizontal, 11 inches by 8½ inches. You print worksheets with relatively few columns in portrait orientation. Wide worksheets require landscape orientation.

1. Choose Page Setup from the File menu to open the Page Setup dialog box.

   NOTE: The Setup button at the top of the Print Preview screen also opens the Page Setup dialog box.

2. Click the Page tab, if necessary.

FIGURE 4-17
Choosing page orientation

Portrait is vertical

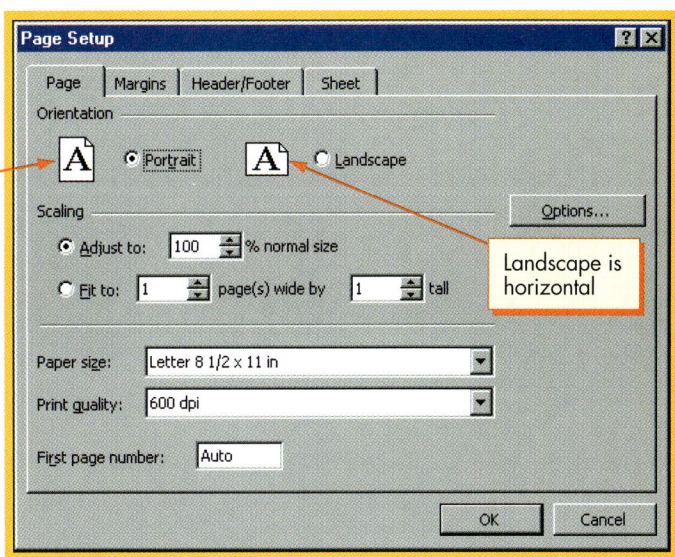

Landscape is horizontal

3. Click Landscape and click OK. The worksheet might look better in landscape orientation, especially if its width exceeds its length.
4. Click the Print Preview button.

   NOTE: Page Setup options apply only to the current worksheet.

136 EXCEL UNIT 2 ■ DEVELOPING A WORKSHEET

EXERCISE 4-18 Center the Print Area on a Page

You can center worksheets on a page to improve the page layout. This is especially useful when worksheets are relatively small or all the pages are the same size.

1. Click Setup and click the Margins tab.
2. Click the Horizontally check box under the Center On Page section. The Preview area in the dialog box displays the centered settings.

NOTE: Normally a worksheet is centered horizontally, but not vertically. You might consider vertically centering a worksheet if it contains a chart or other graphics.

FIGURE 4-18
Page Setup dialog box, Margins tab

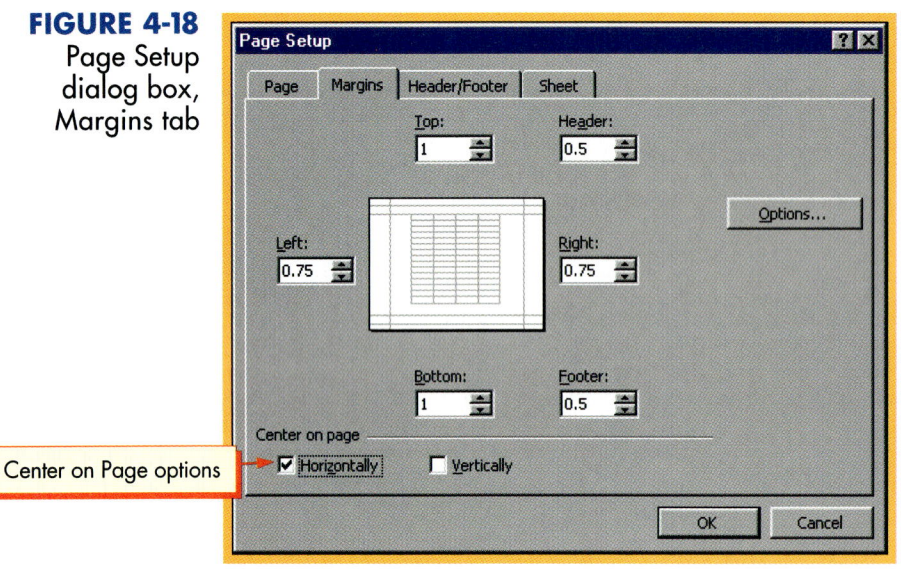

Center on Page options

EXERCISE 4-19 Enter a Header and a Footer

Headers and footers provide helpful information about a printed document. You can format these features in Excel using the Page Setup dialog box or the Setup button on the Print Preview screen.

LESSON 4 ■ DESIGNING AND PRINTING A WORKSHEET   EXCEL **137**

1. Click the Header/Footer tab.
2. Click <u>C</u>ustom Header. The insertion point is automatically positioned in the Left Section box so you can change the header.
3. Key your name in the Left Section box. This portion of the header appears in the upper left corner of the printed page.
4. Press Tab. The insertion point moves to the Center Section box.
5. Click the File Name button to show the filename in the Center Section header. The ampersand (&) and the word "File" in brackets indicate the worksheet filename will appear in the header.
6. Press Tab and click the Date button to include the current date in the <u>R</u>ight Section header.

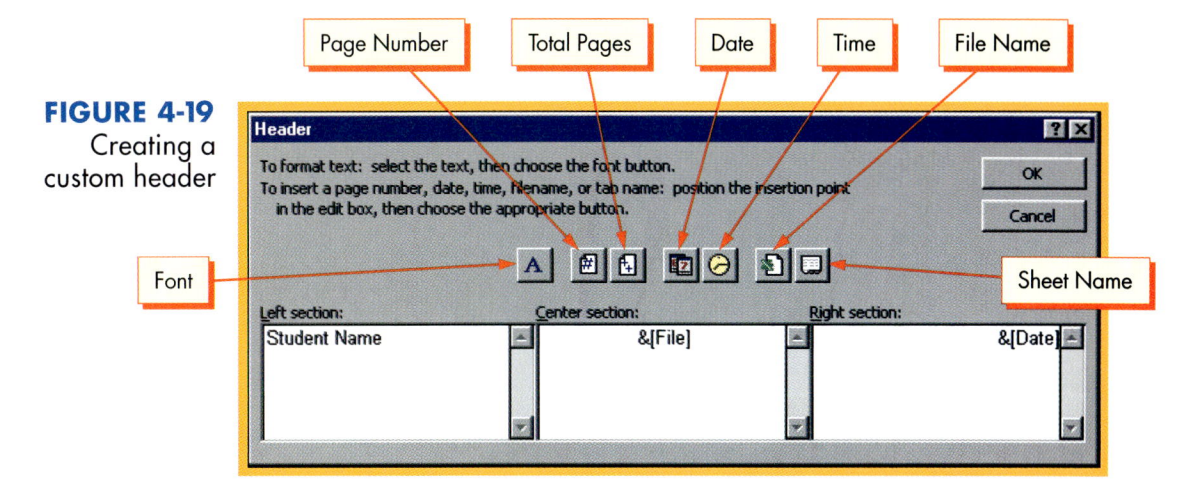

FIGURE 4-19
Creating a custom header

[Dialog box showing Header with callouts: Page Number, Total Pages, Date, Time, File Name, Font, Sheet Name. Left section: Student Name; Center section: &[File]; Right section: &[Date]]

7. Click OK. Your changes appear in the Header text box.
8. Open the drop-down list under <u>F</u>ooter and choose Page 1 of ?. This is a good footer to use when a worksheet spans more than one page.
9. Open the drop-down list again under <u>F</u>ooter and choose (none) to remove the footer.

> **TIP:** You can remove a header by choosing (none) from the drop-down list under <u>H</u>eader.

10. Click C<u>u</u>stom Footer and press Tab. The insertion point moves to the <u>C</u>enter Section box of the Footer dialog box.
11. Click the Sheet Name button to include the current sheet name in the footer, which is represented by &[Tab].
12. Click OK. Your changes appear in the Footer text box.

FIGURE 4-20
New header and footer

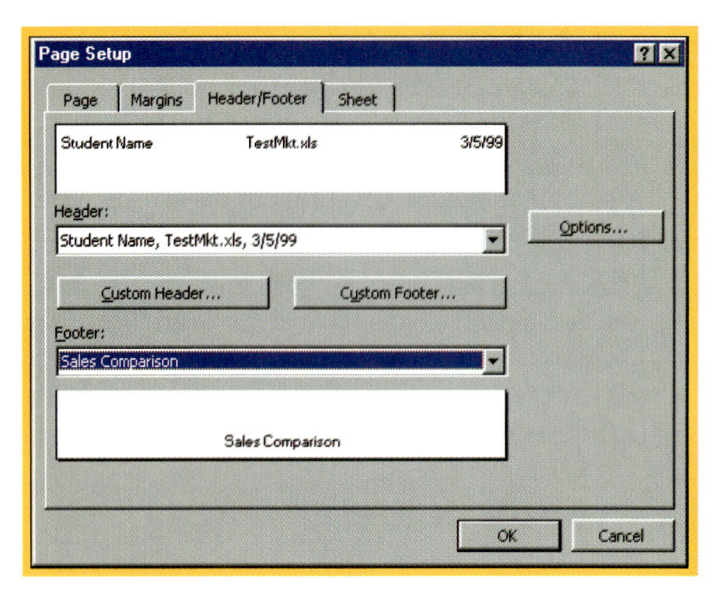

13. Click OK to close the Page Setup dialog box and notice the header and footer positioned on the page.
14. Close the Print Preview window.
15. Move to the User Information sheet. Use Page Setup to center the worksheet and to make the same changes to the header and footer of this sheet.

EXERCISE 4-20 Print a Workbook

Now that you set up the worksheet, it's time to print. You can print single sheets or multiple sheets of a workbook.

1. Move to the Sales Comparison worksheet and save the workbook as *[your initials]*4-20.xls in a new Lesson folder for Lesson 4.

   TIP: Save a workbook immediately before or after printing to preserve the current print settings.

2. Choose Print from the File menu or press Ctrl+P to open the Print dialog box. The dialog box displays Excel's default settings and identifies the designated printer. (See Figure 4-21 on the next page.)

   TIP: You can click the Print button on the Standard Toolbar to print the current worksheet automatically or choose Print from the Print Preview screen to open the Print dialog box.

LESSON 4 ■ DESIGNING AND PRINTING A WORKSHEET   EXCEL **139**

FIGURE 4-21
Print dialog box

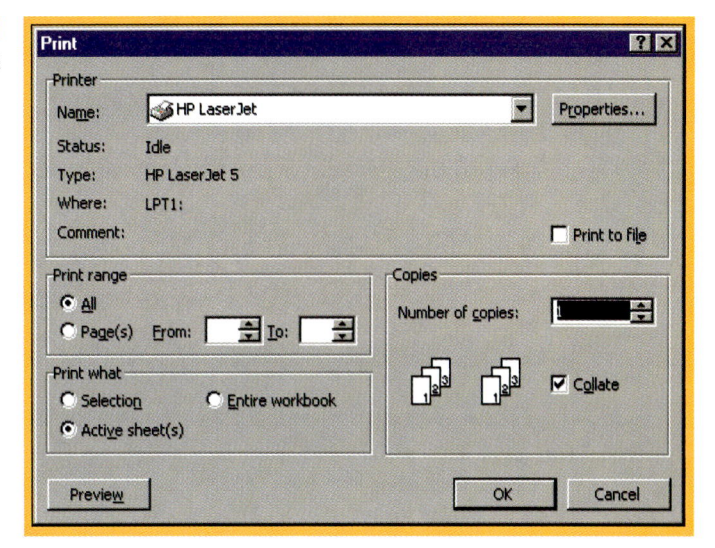

3. Click Entire Workbook and click OK to print both sheets of your workbook. The Printing dialog box appears as your workbook is sent to the printer.

EXERCISE 4-21 Change the Print Area

Excel automatically prints the entire worksheet unless you specify otherwise. Sometimes you may want to print a specific range of cells—called a *print area*. If you select multiple print areas, each area begins printing on a separate page. Headers and footers also appear when you print a print area.

1. On the Sales Comparison sheet, select cells A5 through D11.
2. Choose Print from the File menu.
3. Click Selection.
4. Click OK. Excel prints the selected portion of the worksheet.

> **TIP:** You can also define a print area by selecting a range of cells, choosing Print Area from the File menu, and choosing Set Print Area. Clicking the Print button on the Standard toolbar prints the current print area. To deselect the print area, choose File, Print Area, and then Clear Print Area.

5. Select cells A6 through D11.
6. Hold down Ctrl, select cells A13 through D17, and release Ctrl. Two areas are selected.
7. Choose Print from the File menu.
8. Click Selection and click OK. Excel prints the selected portions of the worksheet on two separate pages.

Printing Formulas

You may want to display formulas onscreen or in your printed worksheet for documentation purposes or to find and correct problems. You can either check the Formulas box on the View tab of the Options dialog box or use the keyboard shortcut `Ctrl`+`` ` ``.

EXERCISE 4-22 Set View for Formulas

1. Press `Ctrl`+`Home` and choose Options from the Tools menu.
2. Select the View tab, if necessary.

   NOTE: View options affect the onscreen appearance of your worksheet. The Formulas option, however, also affects the printed worksheet. You must control most print options—such as row and column headings and gridlines—through the Page Setup dialog box.

3. Click the Formulas check box and click OK. Excel displays all formulas entered in their appropriate worksheet cells. Note that the column widths change to accommodate the wider formulas. As a result, only a portion of the worksheet fits onscreen. Also, the dates change to serial dates and the title is not fully visible.

   NOTE: Column widths may not always be automatically widened enough to accommodate extremely wide formulas. In this case you will need to manually widen the columns so you can see the formulas onscreen and on the printed worksheet.

FIGURE 4-22
Formulas displayed in worksheet

	A	B	C	D	E	F	G
1	Sun Soft vs. Corn						
2	April through May, 199!						
3	(Broken down by gende						
4							
5		Sun Soft Lotion			Corn Silk Cream		
6		Men	Women	Total	Men	Women	To
7	36259	1000	2000	=SUM(B7:C7)	1000	2000	=SUM(E7:
8	36266	1000	2000	=SUM(B8:C8)	1000	2000	=SUM(E8:
9	36273	1000	2000	=SUM(B9:C9)	1000	2000	=SUM(E9:
10	36280	1000	2000	=SUM(B10:C10)	1000	2000	=SUM(E10
11	Subtotal	=SUM(B7:B10)	=SUM(C7:C10)	=SUM(D7:D10)	=SUM(E7:E10)	=SUM(F7:F10)	=SUM(E11
12							
13	36287	1000	2000	=SUM(B13:C13)	1000	2000	=SUM(E13
14	36294	1000	2000	=SUM(B14:C14)	1000	2000	=SUM(E14
15	36301	1000	2000	=SUM(B15:C15)	1000	2000	=SUM(E15
16	36308	1000	2000	=SUM(B16:C16)	1000	2000	=SUM(E16
17	Subtotal	=SUM(B13:B16)	=SUM(C13:C16)	=SUM(B17:C17)	=SUM(E13:E16)	=SUM(F13:F16)	=SUM(E17
18							
19	Grand total	=SUM(B17,B11)	=SUM(C17,C11)	=SUM(D17,D11)	=SUM(E17,E11)	=SUM(F17,F11)	=SUM(E19
20							

4. Press `Ctrl`+`` ` ``. The worksheet is displayed normally. (The `` ` `` key is found to the left of the `1` key.)
5. Press `Ctrl`+`` ` `` to display formulas once again.

LESSON 4 ■ DESIGNING AND PRINTING A WORKSHEET   EXCEL **141**

EXERCISE 4-23 Print with Grids and Headings

You can add gridlines and row and column headings to your worksheet printout using Page Setup. Printing a formula view with gridlines and row and column headings will help you rebuild your worksheet if needed.

1. Choose Page Setup from the File menu and click the Sheet tab, if necessary.
2. Click Gridlines and Row and Column Headings in the Print area of the dialog box.
3. Click the Print Preview command button to view the worksheet before printing. Click Next to look at the second page of the formula printout.

   NOTE: You can fit the formula printout on one page by clicking Fit on the Page tab in Page Setup. However, in some worksheets this makes the text too small to read.

4. Click the Print button at the top of the Print Preview window to open the Print dialog box and click OK.
5. Close the workbook. Don't save the changes.

   TIP: If you save settings that print formulas, you have to change settings the next time you want to print the normal worksheet.

COMMAND SUMMARY

FEATURE	BUTTON	MENU	KEYBOARD
Go To Special		Edit, Go To, Special	Ctrl + G
Split		Window, Split	
Freeze Panes		Window, Freeze Panes	
Zoom	100%	View, Zoom	
Print Preview	🔍	File, Print Preview	
Page Setup		File, Page Setup	
Protect Workbook		Tools, Protection, Protect Workbook	
Protect Worksheet		Tools, Protection, Protect Worksheet	
Print	🖨	File, Print	Ctrl + P
Display Formulas		Tools, Options	Ctrl + `
Set View		Tools, Options	

USING HELP

Another way to get help on an Excel function is to use the Help Index, where all Help topics are listed alphabetically. Simply key a subject and choose from the list of related topics. Often, one topic will lead you to several related subtopics. Some topics may provide useful information that you can print for future reference.

Use the Help Index to explore topics about troubleshooting printing:

1. Press **F1** and key **use the help index**. Click **S**earch.
2. Click the topic "Get Help without using the Office Assistant."
3. Review the explanation in the Help window, then click the Show button.
4. Click the **I**ndex tab, if necessary.
5. In the **T**ype Keywords text box, key **print**.
6. Click **S**earch. The Help Index displays a list of related topics.
7. Review the list of topics. Click the topic "Troubleshoot printing."

FIGURE 4-23
Using the Help Index

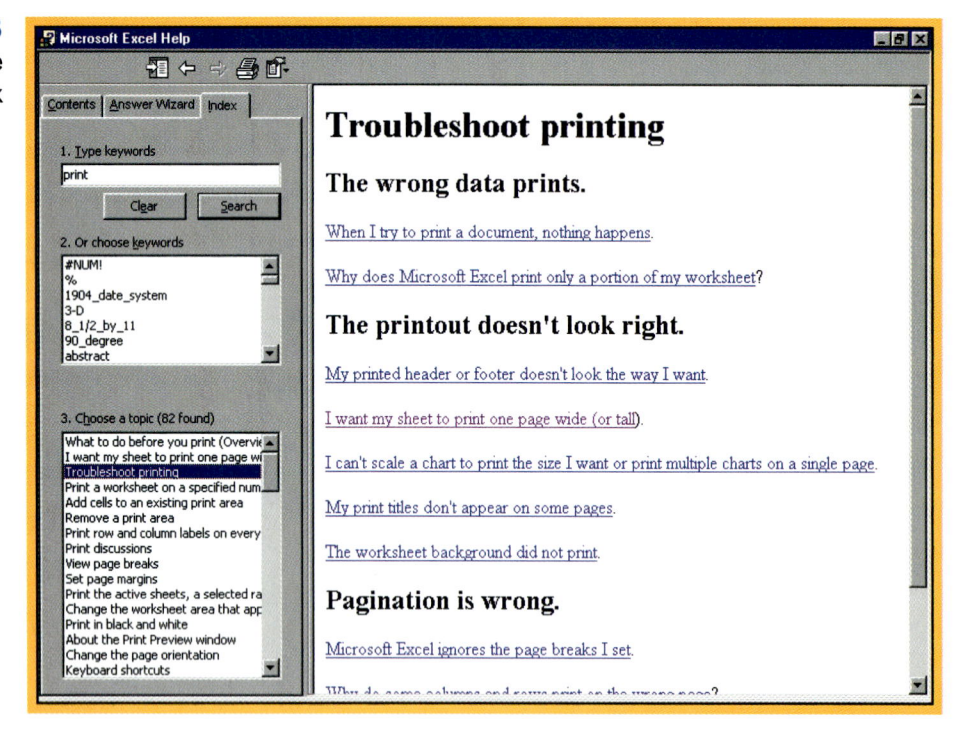

8. Review the list of topics on the right side of the Help Window, scrolling as needed. To learn more about a topic, click it. To print a topic, click the Print button in the Help Window.
9. Close the Help Window when you're done.

Concepts Review

TRUE/FALSE QUESTIONS

Each of the following statements is either true or false. Indicate your choice by circling **T** or **F**.

T F 1. It's best to begin entering data in Excel before you design a worksheet with pencil and paper.

T F 2. You should place comparative information in rows.

T F 3. The formula bar displays the current cell's contents and the name box displays the cell address.

T F 4. It's possible to select cells based on their contents, such as all cells containing formulas.

T F 5. You use Zoom to speed up the printing process.

T F 6. You can only validate data that is made up of whole numbers.

T F 7. You can select page orientation from the Page Setup dialog box.

T F 8. You can validate data using Validation on the Data menu.

SHORT ANSWER QUESTIONS

Write the correct answer in the space provided.

1. What name is given to simple numbers you can add in your head that are used to verify the accuracy of formulas?

2. Which function would you use to keep other users from changing formulas in a worksheet?

3. Which command enables you to divide a worksheet into two parts?

4. Which command enables you to keep row and column labels in one place while you scroll data?

5. What do you call a range of cells to be printed?

_____

6. Which part of the screen identifies each worksheet of an Excel workbook?

_____

7. Which dialog box enables you to enter a custom header and footer?

_____

8. Which page orientation displays the worksheet horizontally?

_____

CRITICAL THINKING

Answer these questions on a separate piece of paper. There are no right or wrong answers. Support your answer with examples from your own experience, if possible.

1. Planning and sketching a worksheet with pencil and paper might seem like a waste of time in the "computer age." What might happen if you skip the planning stage? In what types of situations would it be especially important to plan and sketch the worksheet before entering data in Excel?

2. Describe a project or work situation in which you would have liked to have documentation available. What problem were you trying to solve? How would good documentation of the project have helped you?

Skills Review

EXERCISE 4-24

Plan a worksheet in pencil, enter labels, data validation, test data, and formulas onscreen, select cells by content, name the worksheet tab, and delete unused worksheets.

1. Plan and sketch a worksheet showing sales for each month of the first quarter for five sales representatives by following these steps:
   a. Write the worksheet heading **First Quarter Sales** at the top of a blank page.
   b. Write the entry area item **Report date: [current date]** two rows below the heading in the first column and use the current date.
   c. Write the following labels in a column along the left side of your page two rows below the entry area item:

LESSON 4 ■ DESIGNING AND PRINTING A WORKSHEET EXCEL **145**

> Sales Rep
> Davis
> Jackson
> Miller
> Pierce
> Brown
> Total

  d. Write the labels **January**, **February**, **March**, and **Total** in the row to the right of the label **Sales Rep**.
  e. Write **F**'s in the cells that contain row and column totals.

2. Enter row and column labels onscreen by following these steps:
   a. Open a new Excel workbook.
   b. Key the heading **First Quarter Sales** in cell A1 in bold.
   c. Key **Report Date:** in cell B3 in bold and aligned right. Key the current date in cell C3.
   d. Key the row labels from your paper sketch in cells A5 through A11.
   e. Key the column labels from your paper sketch center-aligned in cells B5 through E5.

3. Enter data validation in the test data cells by following these steps:
   a. Select cells B6 through D10.
   b. Open the Data Validation dialog box (**D**ata menu, Va**l**idation) and click the Settings tab, if necessary.
   c. Allow for whole numbers greater than or equal to 0.
   d. Click the Input Message tab and key **Monthly sales amount** as the input message with no title.
   e. Click OK.

4. Enter the test data shown in Figure 4-24 in the worksheet and format it for comma style and no decimals using the Comma Style button and the Decrease Decimal button.

FIGURE 4-24

	B	C	D
6	1000	2000	3000
7	1000	2000	3000
8	1000	2000	3000
9	1000	2000	3000
10	1000	2000	3000

146 EXCEL UNIT 2 ■ DEVELOPING A WORKSHEET

5. Enter formulas onscreen using the following steps:
   a. Select cells E6 through E10 and click the AutoSum button [Σ].
   b. Select cells B11 through E11 and click the AutoSum button [Σ].
6. Select the monthly sales test data by content by following these steps:
   a. Press [Ctrl]+[Home].
   b. Press [Ctrl]+[G].
   c. Click Special.
   d. Click Data Validation.
   e. Click OK.
7. Name the worksheet tab by following these steps:
   a. Double-click the Sheet1 tab.
   b. Key **Quarter 1**.
   c. Press [Enter].
8. Delete the unused worksheets by following these steps:
   a. Right-click on Sheet2 tab.
   b. Select Delete and click OK.
   c. Repeat the above steps for Sheet3.
9. Save the workbook as *[your initials]*4-24.xls in your Lesson 4 folder.
10. Print the worksheet and close the workbook.

EXERCISE 4-25

Split a worksheet into panes, freeze panes, use Zoom, remove gridlines and headers from the screen, remove the split, and unfreeze the panes.

1. Open the file **Expense1.xls**.
2. Split the worksheet into panes by following these steps:
   a. Select cell B10.
   b. Choose Split from the Window menu.
   c. If necessary, click the down vertical scroll arrow for the bottom pane until the Total row for the Phoenix office becomes visible.
3. Freeze the worksheet panes by following these steps:
   a. Choose Freeze Panes from the Window menu.
   b. If necessary, click the horizontal scroll bar to compare data for the two offices.
4. Change the size of the worksheet onscreen by following these steps:
   a. Choose Zoom from the View menu.
   b. Choose 75%.
   c. Click OK.
5. Remove gridlines and headers from the screen by following these steps:
   a. Choose Options from the Tools menu.

LESSON 4 ■ DESIGNING AND PRINTING A WORKSHEET   EXCEL **147**

   b. When the Options dialog box appears, click the View tab, if necessary.
   c. Clear the Gridlines and Row & Column Headers check boxes and click OK.
 6. Remove splits and unfreeze panes by following these steps:
   a. Choose Unfreeze Panes from the Window menu.
   b. Choose Remove Split from the Window menu.
 7. Press Ctrl+Home and save the workbook as *[your initials]***4-25.xls** in your Lesson 4 folder.
 8. Print the worksheet and close the workbook.

EXERCISE 4-26

Create user documentation, unlock data entry areas, turn off gridlines for viewing, and protect a worksheet.

 1. Open the file **Expense2.xls**. Look at the first two sheets.
 2. Create documentation for the worksheet by following these steps:
   a. Click the Documentation tab and key **User Information** in cell A1 in bold. (Column widths are already adjusted for easy reading.)
   b. Key the labels and data in Figure 4-25. Key the labels in Column B in bold and right-align them. Key the information left-aligned in column C.

FIGURE 4-25

	B	C
3	**Created by:**	Jaime Santo
4	**Date created:**	29-Jun
5		
6	**Date revised:**	Current date
7	**Revised by:**	Student name
8		
9	**Contact for help:**	Jaime Santo

 3. Key the labels and information in Figure 4-26 in the appropriate columns and rows. Make the labels bold.

FIGURE 4-26

	A	B
11	Purpose	
12		This worksheet shows projected increases in Q1 expenses.
13		
14	User Instructions	
15		1. Use whole numbers when keying expense amounts.
16		2. Formulas are used to calculate percentages and totals.

4. Turn off gridlines for viewing by following these steps:
   a. Choose Options under the Tools menu.
   b. Click the View tab, if necessary.
   c. Clear the Gridlines check box and click OK.
5. Unlock data entry for the Quarter cells in the San Francisco Increase sheet by following these steps:
   a. Click the San Francisco Increase worksheet tab.
   b. Select cells B4 through C9.
   c. Choose Cells from the Format menu.
   d. Click the Protection tab on the Format Cells dialog box.
   e. Clear the Locked check box and click OK.
   f. Press Ctrl+Home.
6. Protect the worksheet by following these steps:
   a. Choose Protection from the Tools menu.
   b. Choose Protect Sheet.
   c. Enter *[your initials]* in the password section of the Protect Sheet dialog box and click OK.
   d. Enter *[your initials]* again in the Confirm Password dialog box and click OK.
   e. Test the protection by pressing Tab. (*Hint:* Only the cells available for data entry should be accessible.)
7. Press Ctrl+Home and save the workbook as *[your initials]*4-26.xls in your Lesson 4 folder.
8. Print the entire workbook by following these steps:
   a. Press Ctrl+P.
   b. Select Entire Workbook in the Print dialog box and click OK.
9. Close the workbook.

LESSON 4 ■ DESIGNING AND PRINTING A WORKSHEET   EXCEL **149**

EXERCISE 4-27

Choose page orientation, change the print area, change headers and footers, and print with and without gridlines, headings, and formulas.

1. Open the file **Revenue.xls**.
2. Choose landscape orientation by following these steps:
    a. Choose Page Setup from the File menu.
    b. Click the Page tab, if necessary.
    c. Click Landscape.
    d. Click Print Preview to view the entire worksheet on one page.
3. Center the print area on the page by following these steps:
    a. While still in Print Preview, click Setup.
    b. Click the Margins tab.
    c. Click the Horizontally check box under the Center on Page section.
4. Change the headers and footers by following these steps:
    a. Click the Header/Footer tab in the Page Setup dialog box and click Custom Header.
    b. Key your name in the Left section box and press Tab.
    c. Click the File Name button 🗎 in the Center section of the header and press Tab.
    d. Click the Date button 📅 in the Right section of the header and click OK.
    e. Click Custom Footer and press Tab.
    f. Click the Sheet Name button 🗐 and click OK.
    g. Click OK and then click Close.
    h. Save the workbook as *[your initials]*4-27.xls in your Lesson 4 folder.
5. Print the worksheet without gridlines by following these steps. (*Hint:* The default is that gridlines are turned off for printing. In this worksheet they are on.)
    a. Choose Page Setup from the File menu and then click the Sheet tab in the Page Setup dialog box.
    b. Clear the Gridlines check box and click Print Preview to view the worksheet in Print Preview.
    c. Click Print to open the Print dialog box and click OK to print the worksheet.
6. Change the print area and print the worksheet with headings and formulas by following these steps:
    a. Select the range A1 through D18, choose Print Area from the File menu, and choose Set Print Area.
    b. Press Ctrl+`.
    c. Choose Page Setup from the File menu and click the Sheet tab, if necessary.

    d. Check the Gridlines and Row and column headings boxes.
    e. Click Print Preview to view the worksheet before printing. Click Zoom to take a closer look.
    f. Click Print to open the Print dialog box and click OK to print.
7. Close the workbook without saving it.

Lesson Applications

EXERCISE 4-28

Enter a label and data, add formulas, change headers and footers, and print horizontally centered with and without formulas, grids, and row and column headings.

Nate Rosario, the controller for the Beautiful Belle Company, needs to prepare a forecast of profits (or net income) for the next five years.

1. Open the file **NetInc1.xls**. Gridlines for viewing are turned off in this worksheet, which is not the default setting.
2. Insert a row between the "Administration" and "Marketing" labels.
3. Label the new row **Salaries** and insert the data below.
   550   650   780   870   900
4. Insert Total Expenses formulas that sum Administration, Salaries, Marketing, and Research expenses for each year.
5. Insert Net Income formulas for each year. Calculate net income by subtracting Total Expenses from Sales.
6. Apply a single-line top border and a double-line bottom border to the Net Income values (below the total expense cells).
7. Format the labels "Sales," "Expenses," and "Net Income" in bold.
8. Center the worksheet horizontally on the page.
9. Create a new header that includes your name on the left, the filename in the center, and the date on the right.
10. Save the workbook as *[your initials]*4-28.xls in your Lesson 4 folder and print the worksheet.
11. Create a formula printout that shows all formulas with gridlines and row and column headings in landscape orientation. In Page Setup add a Page 1 of ? footer. (*Hint:* Open the drop-down list under Footer and choose Page 1 of ?)
12. Close the workbook without saving it.

EXERCISE 4-29

Enter data and labels, create and enter formulas, select cells by content, set up the worksheet to print in portrait orientation, and print it with gridlines, row and column headings, and formulas.

152 EXCEL UNIT 2 ■ DEVELOPING A WORKSHEET

The executives at Beautiful Belle want to examine third-quarter sales data by comparing the differences in male and female purchasers of Sun Soft and Corn Silk products.

1. Open the file **Totals.xls**.
2. Insert two rows between the July and Subtotals rows in the Men and Women sections shown in Figure 4-27. Then enter the data for the months of August and September making the appropriate corrections.

FIGURE 4-27

		Sun Soft	Corn Silk
Men	July *(lower case)*	11,685	9,350
	AUGUST	12,550	9,800
	September	8,794 *(7,8)*	12,810
	Subtotal	11,685	9,350
Women	July	24,0300 *(←9)*	49,400
	Augst *(u)*	22,104	38,465
	September	24,366	18,700
	Subtotal	24,030	49,400

3. Check and correct the Men and Women subtotal formulas, if necessary.
4. Insert two rows above the Grand Total row and key the labels **August** and **September** under "July" in the Total section.
5. Create formulas that calculate the August and September totals.
6. Check and correct the Grand Total formula, if necessary.
7. Select cells with formulas using select by content (Go To Special dialog box) and make them all italic.
8. Set up the worksheet to print in portrait orientation. (The default orientation is portrait; however, this worksheet's orientation is landscape.)
9. Center the worksheet horizontally on the page.
10. Create a standard header that includes your name on the left, the filename in the center, and the date on the right.
11. Make cell A1 active and save the workbook as *[your initials]*4-29.xls in your Lesson 4 folder and print the worksheet.
12. Create a formula printout that shows all formulas with gridlines and row and column headings.
13. Close the workbook without saving it.

LESSON 4 ■ DESIGNING AND PRINTING A WORKSHEET   EXCEL **153**

EXERCISE 4-30

Freeze panes, enter data and formulas, use Zoom, use set-up options, preview the worksheet, protect and unprotect the worksheet, and print it without and with formulas.

The Beautiful Belle Company wants to extend the comparative-sales worksheet to include test-marketing data for Sun Soft and Corn Silk through July.

1. Open the file **MktTest.xls**.
2. Edit the title in cell A2 to read **April through July, 1999**.
3. Add new rows to the Sales Comparison worksheet by selecting cells A20 through A32 and choosing Rows from the Insert menu.
4. Freeze panes in cell A8 so column headings remain visible.
5. Enter the data shown in Figure 4-28 beginning in row 20. Make sure the numbers are formatted to match the others.

FIGURE 4-28

	A	B	C	D	E	F	G
		Sun Soft			Corn Silk		
		Men	Women	Total	Men	Women	Total
20	4-Jun	2,300	3,400		1,250	1,050	
21	11-Jun	2,200	5,200		1,370	1,100	
22	18-Jun	1,950	4,300		1,290	1,000	
23	25-Jun	2,700	5,800		1,400	950	
24	Subtotal						
25							
26	2-Jul	2,500	4,500		1,500	1,100	
27	9-Jul	2,735	6,900		1,550	1,300	
28	16-Jul	2,800	5,430		1,650	1,550	
29	23-Jul	3,200	5,700		1,780	1,760	
30	30-Jul	3,300	5,820		1,910	1,880	
31	Subtotal						

6. Unfreeze panes and enter or revise formulas to calculate totals, subtotals, and grand totals. (Grand totals must include the two new months' data.)
7. Reduce the size of the worksheet to 50%.
8. View the worksheet in Print Preview.
9. Set the worksheet to print in landscape orientation without gridlines or row and column headings.
10. Center the worksheet horizontally on the page and create a standard header that includes your name on the left, filename in the center, and date on the right.
11. Close Print Preview. Change the display to 75% using the Zoom box on the Standard toolbar.
12. Protect the worksheet leaving only the cells containing weekly sales numbers available for entry. Make any cells containing formulas unavailable. Use your three initials as your password.
13. Make cell A1 active if it is not, save the workbook as *[your initials]*4-30.xls in your Lesson 4 folder, and print the worksheet.
14. Unprotect the worksheet.
15. Create a formula printout that shows all formulas with gridlines and row and column headings in landscape orientation. Choose the Page 1 of ? footer. Widen columns to show formulas if necessary.
16. Close the workbook without saving it.

EXERCISE 4-31   Challenge Yourself

Sketch a worksheet plan, enter the plan in a worksheet, validate data, select all formula cells, create documentation, name sheet tabs, use print preview and page set-up options, print the workbook, and print formulas.

The Beautiful Belle Company wants a worksheet that calculates the difference between monthly sales of Sun Soft and Corn Silk products to men and women for their Northeast division. The worksheet should also calculate the difference in total sales by gender to both groups.

1. Sketch a worksheet to calculate these values. Title the worksheet **Sun Soft vs. Corn Silk Sales.** Two rows below the title enter **Division:** and in the row below Division: enter **Year:.** The report is to be divided into two sections, **Men** and **Women.** Place these section headings in column A. Each section should have the following row labels: **April**, **May**, **June**, and **July**, which should begin below "Men" and below "Women" in

LESSON 4 ■ DESIGNING AND PRINTING A WORKSHEET   EXCEL **155**

column B. The last row of each section should be a **Subtotal** row and the last row in the worksheet should be a **Total** row. There should be three columns of data labeled **Sun Soft**, **Corn Silk**, and **Difference**.

2. Include formulas in this worksheet plan in the subtotal and total rows. Abbreviate using an F.
3. Key the title and labels in a new Excel worksheet. Use text formatting to distinguish the title and labels from other worksheet data.
4. Validate entry cells that contain sales data for men and women. Validate for whole numbers greater than 500.
5. Key the sales data for men from Figure 4-29 formatted in Comma style with no decimals:

FIGURE 4-29

		Sun Soft	Corn Silk	Difference
Men				
	April	3,300	6,600	
	May	6,450	8,150	
	June	9,150	5,310	
	July	11,235	6,480	

6. Key the following sales data for women formatted in Comma style with no decimals:

FIGURE 4-30

		Sun Soft	Corn Silk	Difference
Women				
	April	3,300	6,600	
	May	6,800	8,000	
	June	18,700	4,100	
	July	22,530	5,710	

7. Create the formulas to calculate the men's and women's subtotals.

8. Create the formulas to calculate differences between Sun Soft and Corn Silk subtotals only. (Subtract Corn Silk data from Sun Soft data.) Format the figures in Comma style, no decimals.
9. Create the formulas to calculate the totals for each section. Format the figures in Comma style, no decimals, if necessary.
10. Create the formula for the difference between product totals.
11. Select all cells containing formulas and make them italic.
12. Rename the Sheet1 tab **Sales by Gender** and delete Sheet3.
13. Rename the Sheet2 tab **User Information**.
14. Create user information as follows using the basic layout you learned in the lesson to place the documentation elements. (Don't worry about column width when placing these elements, but follow the basic design you learned in the lesson.) Use the information from Figure 4-31.

FIGURE 4-31

```
User Information

Created by:           Jane Doe

Date created:         8/13/99

Date revised:         [current date]

Revised by:           [your name]

Contact for Help:     Jane Doe

Purpose               This worksheet compares Sun Soft and Corn Silk
                      sales data by gender.

User Instructions     1. The worksheet is protected. To move to
                      unprotected entry cells, press the Tab key.

                      2. All totals, subtotals, and differences are
                      calculated by formulas.
```

15. Turn off gridlines for viewing.
16. Center the Sales by Gender sheet horizontally.
17. Create the standard header that shows your name on the left, the filename in the center, and the date at the right on both sheets.
18. Preview the workbook.

19. Save the workbook as *[your initials]***4-31.xls** in your Lesson 4 folder and print the entire workbook.

20. Create a formula printout of the Sales by Gender worksheet. Print the sheet in landscape orientation, showing gridlines and row and column headings. Use a Page 1 of ? footer, if there is more than one page of formulas to print. If not, use the Sheet tab as the footer center at the bottom.

21. Close the workbook without saving it. Submit the plan, the Sales by Gender worksheet, the User Information worksheet, and the Formula view.

LESSON 5

Copying Data and Using Toolbars

OBJECTIVES

After completing this lesson, you will be able to:
1. Build a worksheet with copy and paste.
2. Copy using drag and drop.
3. Copy using Fill and AutoFill.
4. Use Excel's toolbars.

MOUS ACTIVITIES

In this lesson:
XL2000 1.7
XL2000 1.10
XL2000 E.7.1
XL2000 E.7.2

See Appendix F.

Estimated Time: 1 hour

Designing and developing worksheets in Excel often involves repeating basic elements, including cells, formulas, and formatting. You can copy these elements to build a worksheet quickly and easily. This lesson also demonstrates the versatility of Excel's toolbars and different ways to display them.

Building a Worksheet with Copy and Paste

You can copy, move, and cut cell contents in Excel. A copy is an exact duplicate of the element you select. The copy can be pasted or inserted into other locations of a worksheet or the document area of other Windows applications. Unlike moving or cutting, you don't affect the original element when you copy it. The data remains in the original location, but is also on the Clipboard (which is a temporary computer memory location). Information is erased from the Clipboard when you initiate a new Copy or Cut command.

LESSON 5 ■ COPYING DATA AND USING TOOLBARS   EXCEL   **159**

You can choose the Copy and Paste commands three ways:
- Use the Edit menu.
- Use the keyboard shortcuts Ctrl+C for Copy and Ctrl+V for Paste.
- Click the Copy and Paste buttons on the Standard toolbar.

EXERCISE   5-1   Copy and Paste Using the Edit Menu

In this Exercise you construct a worksheet with both detail and summary comparisons of 1999 second-quarter sales for the test product, Sun Soft Lotion, and its competing product, Corn Silk Cream.

1. Open the file **Compare.xls**.
2. Select cells A6 through B9 as the *source range*. The source range is the area of the worksheet from which you copy or remove data.
3. Choose Copy from the Edit menu. A moving border surrounds the selected cells. The contents of the cells you just copied are now on the Clipboard. (The clipboard's contents don't appear on the screen.)

FIGURE 5-1
Source range selected

Moving border

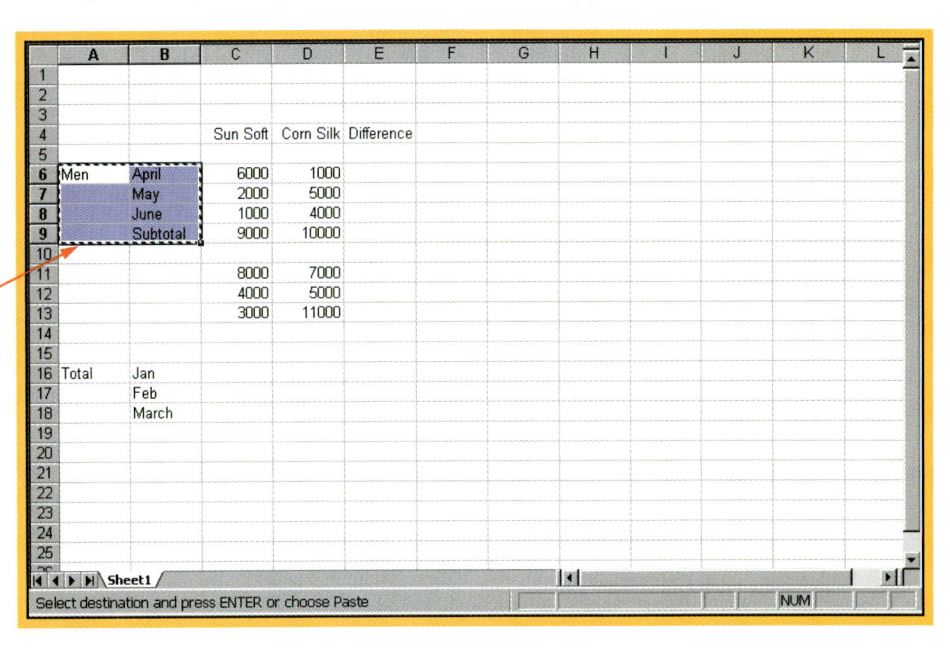

4. Select cell A11. This cell is in the upper left corner of the *target range*. The target range is the new location for the data you want to copy or move.
5. Choose Paste from the Edit menu. A copy of the data from the source range appears in the target range. A copy of the data also remains on the Clipboard. To show this, Excel still displays a moving border around the source range.

FIGURE 5-2
Source range copied to target range

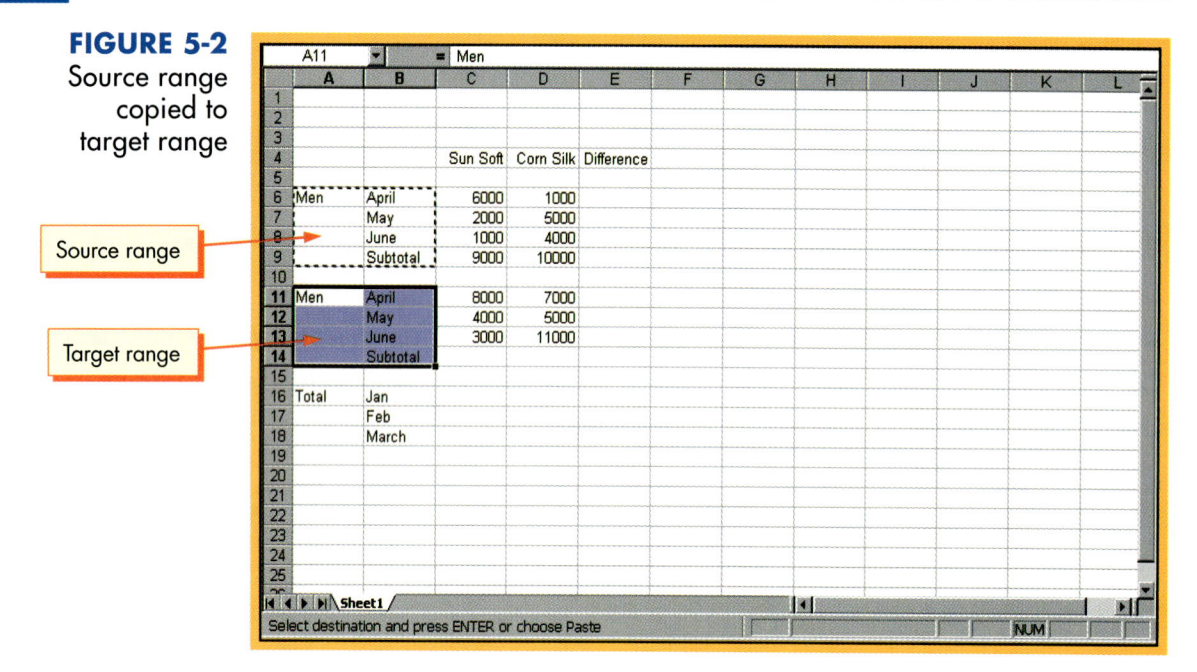

Source range → [A6:D9]
Target range → [A11:D14]

TIP: Copy and Paste are available from the shortcut menu. To see this, right-click the selected source or target, but don't choose a command. Press Esc to close the shortcut menu.

6. Press Esc to remove the moving border around the source range.

NOTE: When the moving border is no longer displayed, you cannot paste the data from the Clipboard.

7. Edit cell A11 to read **Women**.

EXERCISE 5-2 Overwrite and Insert with Copy and Paste

The Copy and Paste commands overwrite existing cell data. You can also use Copy to insert new cells and data between existing cells.

1. Select cells B11 to B13 and press Ctrl+C (the Copy keyboard shortcut).

2. Select cells B16 to B18 and press Ctrl+V (the Paste keyboard shortcut). The months "Jan" through "March" are replaced by "April" through "June."

3. Press Esc to exit Copy mode.

LESSON 5 ■ COPYING DATA AND USING TOOLBARS   EXCEL **161**

> **TIP:** You can simply select cell B16 and press Enter. The contents are pasted in cells B16 to B18 and the moving border is removed from the copied cells automatically. You do not have to press Esc.

4. Select cell A16 and choose Copy from the Edit menu.
5. Select cell E4 and choose Copied Cells from the Insert menu. The Insert Paste dialog box opens.

FIGURE 5-3
Insert Paste dialog box

6. Select Shift Cells Right and click OK. The copy of "Total" appears in cell E4 and the word "Difference" shifts one cell to the right.
7. Press Esc to exit Copy mode.
8. Delete the label "Difference" in cell F4.

EXERCISE 5-3 Copy and Paste Using the Toolbar

Like the Copy and Paste commands on the Edit menu, you can use the Copy button and the Paste button to copy cell values, formulas, and formatting.

1. Select all cells with numbers and format them for Comma style with no decimals.
2. Use the AutoSum button Σ to total April sales for Sun Soft and Corn Silk in cell E6.
3. With cell E6 selected, click the Copy button.
4. Select cell E7 and click the Paste button. Excel copies the formula and the formatting; it also adjusts the cell references so the formula is =SUM(C7:D7). This change in cells is called a *relative cell reference*. With relative referencing, Excel knows that if you copy a formula to a new row, you intend to add the numbers in the new row rather than the numbers in the original row. This type of referencing occurs with any method of copying and pasting formulas.
5. Select cell E8 and click the Paste button.
6. Select cell E9 and press Enter. Excel pastes the contents and completes the copy action, erasing the Clipboard. All the copied formulas are adjusted with relative cell references and the cell formatting is also copied.

> **TIP:** You can use the Paste Special command on the Edit menu to paste certain aspects of a cell's contents, including its formatting, values only, validation, or everything except borders. This is a handy tool if you need to be specific about what you are pasting.

Copying Using Drag and Drop

You can also copy data and formulas using drag-and-drop. This is an easy way to copy information using the mouse. You can make only a single copy using this method, however.

EXERCISE 5-4 Copy Using Drag and Drop

1. Select cells E6 through E8.
2. Move the mouse pointer across the border of the selection until it becomes an arrow.

   TIP: Avoid the lower right corner of the selection.

3. Press and hold down Ctrl. The pointer becomes the drag-and-drop pointer, with a tiny cross appearing to the right of the arrow. When the cross is present, you're copying data, not moving it.
4. Drag the selected cells to cells E11 through E13. Note the gray outline in the shape of the source range and the yellow message box containing the cell addresses as you move the mouse. When the selected cells are positioned at the target range, release the mouse button and the Ctrl key.

   TIP: You must hold down the Ctrl key to copy while dragging. Notice the + sign that appears to the right of the arrow pointer.

5. Select cells C9 to E9.
6. Drag and drop this information into cells C14 to E14. Excel copies both the formula and its formatting, and adjusts the cell references accordingly.

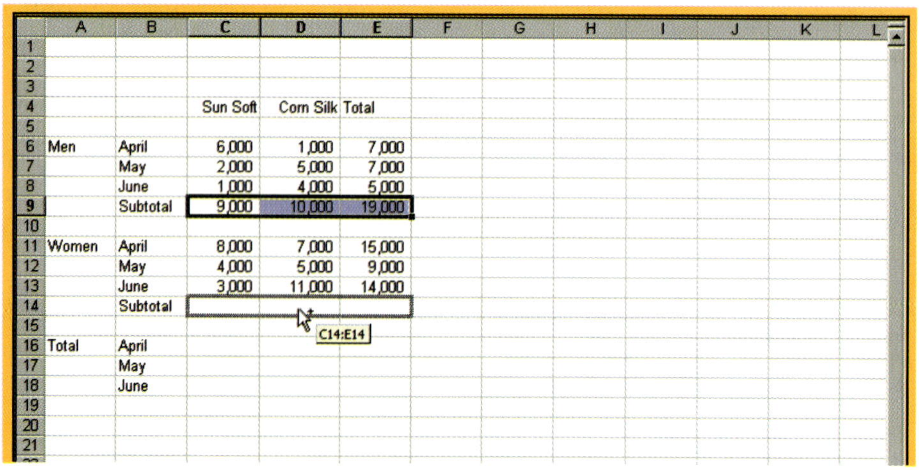

FIGURE 5-4
Copying using the drag-and-drop method

LESSON 5 ■ COPYING DATA AND USING TOOLBARS   EXCEL   **163**

7. Verify that the formulas are correct for the new location.

Copying Using Fill and AutoFill

Worksheets frequently contain repetitive formulas. Instead of copying each formula using Copy and Paste, the Fill and AutoFill commands are often a quicker technique.

EXERCISE 5-5 Copy Using the Fill Command

1. Enter the formula **=C6+C11** in cell C16.
2. Select cells C16 through C18. Be sure to select the cell that contains the desired formula and all cells to which that formula is to be copied. These cells must be adjacent to one another to use the Fill command.
3. Choose the Fill command from the Edit menu and choose Down from the submenu (or press Ctrl+D). Excel copies the formula to the selected cells and adjusts the cell references.

FIGURE 5-5
Using Fill to copy formulas (with formulas displayed)

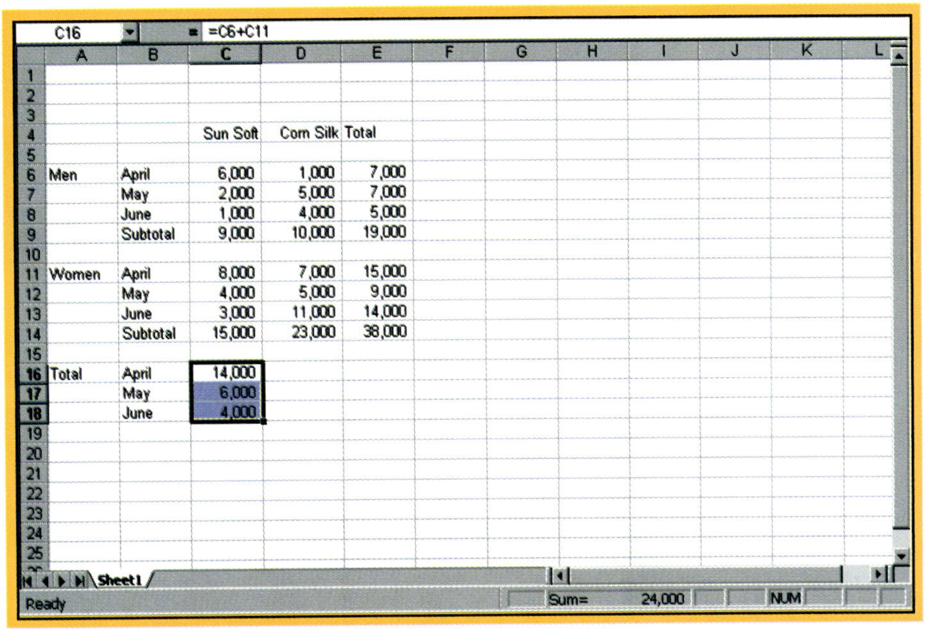

4. Click outside the selection.
5. Select cells C16 through E16.
6. Choose Fill from the Edit menu and choose Right from the submenu (or press Ctrl+R).

7. Click outside the selection.

8. To view the formulas you copied, press `Ctrl`+`` ` `` (or choose Options from the Tools menu, click Formulas, and click OK).

> **NOTE:** It's a good idea to check the formulas in cells that are copied to ensure they have the correct relative references. If possible, enter test data before keying in actual data or turn on formulas for viewing.

EXERCISE 5-6 Copy Using the AutoFill Command

Using AutoFill, you can copy a formula in a single cell to multiple cells in a single step. Drag and drop is a good way to copy when the source area and the target area are not adjacent but both are the same size. AutoFill, on the other hand, should be used for copying to adjacent cells.

1. Press `Ctrl`+`` ` `` to clear the formulas from the screen.

> **TIP:** You can also choose Options from the Tools menu and click to clear the Formulas checkbox.

2. Select cell D16 and position the mouse pointer on the *fill handle*, which is the small box in the lower right corner of the cell. The mouse pointer changes to a black cross.

FIGURE 5-6
Using AutoFill to copy formulas

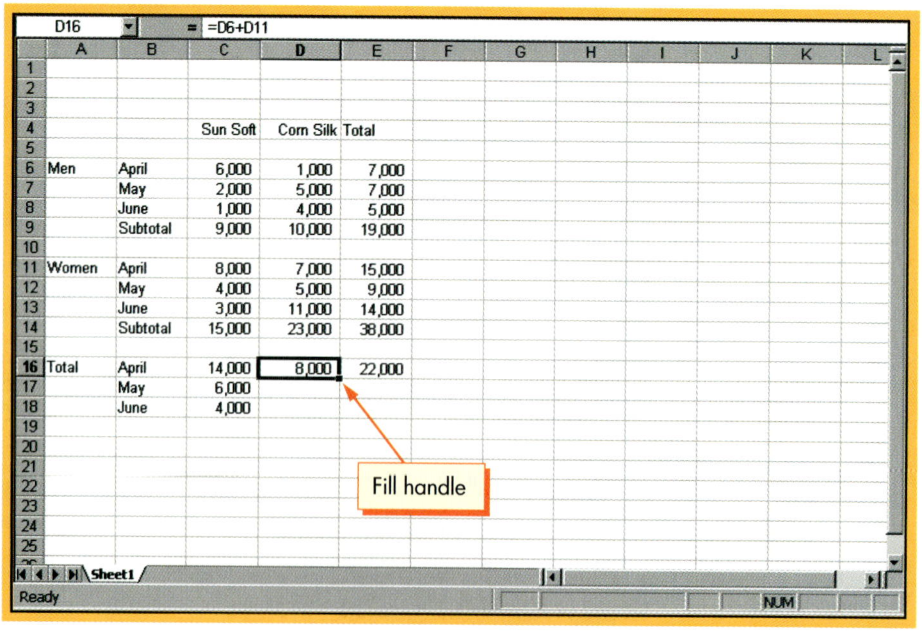

LESSON 5 ■ COPYING DATA AND USING TOOLBARS   EXCEL **165**

   3. Drag the fill handle until cells D17 and D18 are both selected. The cells are bordered in gray.

   4. Release the mouse button. Excel copies the formula from cell D16 to cells D17 and D18.

   5. Copy the formula in cell E16 to cells E17 and E18 using the same method.

   6. In cells A1 and A2, key the following title in bold:

     Sun Soft/Corn Silk Sales Comparison
     Quarter 2, 1999

   7. Create a header that includes your name in the left section, the filename in the center section, and the date in the right section.

   8. Center the worksheet horizontally on the page.

   9. Save the workbook as *[your initials]***5-6.xls** in a new folder for Lesson 5 and print the worksheet.

  10. Create a formula printout with gridlines and row and column headings in landscape orientation.

  11. Turn off formulas for viewing.

Using Toolbars in Excel

To this point, you used Excel's predefined Standard and Formatting toolbars to make your work easier. Excel provides many other predefined toolbars that make chart construction, drawing, accessing the World Wide Web, moving and copying text, and other functions faster and more convenient. You can control how toolbars appear on the screen and what functions they perform.

TABLE 5-1 **Predefined Toolbars in Excel**

TOOLBAR NAME	FUNCTION
PivotTable	Retrieve and analyze data from databases.
Chart	Create and modify charts. It automatically displays when you work on a chart.
Reviewing	Create and edit comments in files that can be sent as e-mail.
Forms	Create custom forms.
Clipboard	Keep track of copies, cut and paste in any Office program.
Stop Recording	Stop recording a macro.

continues

TABLE 5-1 **Predefined Toolbars in Excel** *continued*

TOOLBAR NAME	FUNCTION
External Data	Work with data imported from an external database.
Auditing	Trace precedents, dependents, and errors within formulas.
Full Screen	Return to Normal view after displaying the full screen.
Circular Reference	Identify circular references in cells.
Visual Basic	Work with macros.
Web	Access the World Wide Web.
Control Toolbox	Create controls to run macros.
Drawing	Create graphic objects. It contains standard drawing tools such as line, arc, and rectangle.
WordArt	Create attractive text.
Picture	Control the look of images imported into Excel.
Shadow Settings	Place shadows behind graphics.
3-D Settings	Create a 3-D effect with graphics.

EXERCISE 5-7 Display Multiple Toolbars

Sometimes it's useful to display several toolbars simultaneously. For example, your worksheet may contain multiple formulas and be targeted to someone outside your company. In that case, the Auditing toolbar helps you trace multiple calculations and the Clipboard toolbar is handy to collect and store up to 12 separate cut or copied items without erasing previous items. This toolbar acts as up to 12 separate Clipboards.

FIGURE 5-7
Toolbars submenu

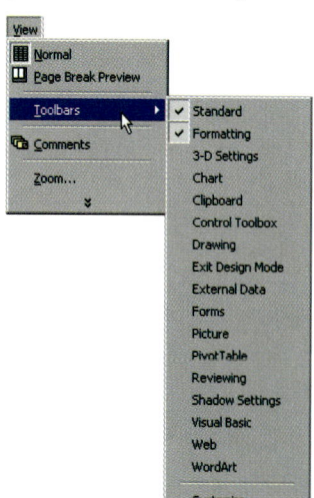

> **NOTE:** Remember, a Clipboard is a temporary storage space.

1. Choose <u>T</u>oolbars from the <u>V</u>iew menu. The Toolbars submenu opens.

LESSON 5 ■ COPYING DATA AND USING TOOLBARS   EXCEL   **167**

2. Choose <u>C</u>ustomize. In the Customize dialog box, click Tool<u>b</u>ars, if necessary, to see the complete list of existing toolbars. The Office Assistant may open to see if you want help. If it does, it closes when you close the dialog box.

FIGURE 5-8
Customize dialog box

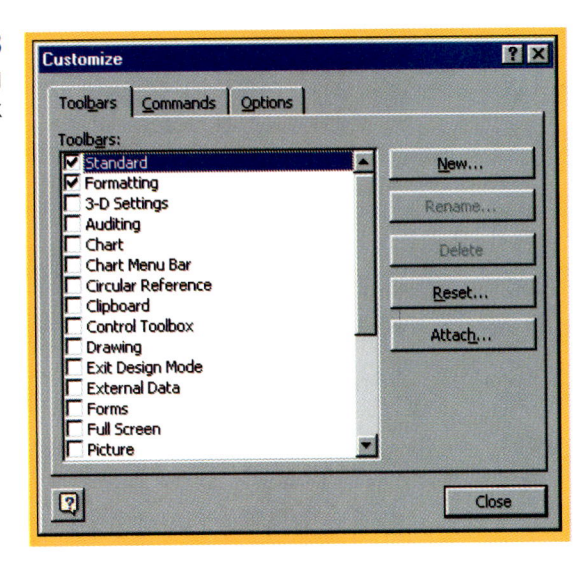

3. Click next to Auditing to display the Auditing toolbar. Click Close in the Customize dialog box.

4. Move the pointer across each button on the Auditing toolbar to identify its name and function.

> **TIP:** Remember, to identify a toolbar button, point to the button and pause for a few seconds. A small box containing the name of the button appears under the button.

5. Change the view of the document to 75%, select cell C14, and click the Trace Precedents button. An arrow appears onscreen, tracing the precedents for cell C14 (the cells to which the formula in cell C14 refers).

> **NOTE:** If the toolbar is in the way, click and hold the left mouse button in the toolbar title bar and drag it over slightly.

6. With the same cell selected, click the Trace Dependents button. An arrow appears onscreen tracing the cells that are dependent upon the value in cell C14. (See Figure 5-9 on the next page.)

> **NOTE:** Audit arrows are removed automatically when you save a workbook, but you can redisplay them at any time.

168 EXCEL UNIT 2 ■ DEVELOPING A WORKSHEET

FIGURE 5-9
Using the Auditing toolbar

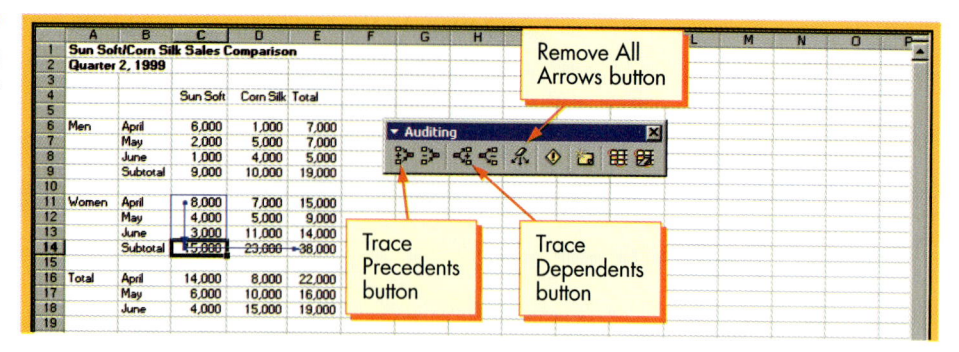

7. Click the Remove All Arrows button [icon].

8. Position the mouse on any toolbar and right-click. The Toolbar shortcut menu appears. It looks just like the Toolbars submenu.

9. Click next to Clipboard on the Toolbars submenu. The Clipboard toolbar appears.

10. If the Clear Clipboard button [icon] is visible (not grayed out) on the toolbar, click it now to clear any Clipboards. If not, move to the next step.

11. Select cells A6:E9 and click the Copy button [icon] on the Clipboard toolbar. The data is stored on a new Clipboard visible on the toolbar.

12. Select cells A11:E14 and press [Ctrl]+[C] to copy the data. The data is stored on a new Clipboard.

13. Select cells A16:E18 and press [Ctrl]+[X] to cut the data. The data is stored on a new Clipboard. Notice that the Clipboard toolbar title bar reflects the number of items available for pasting from the Clipboard.

14. Point to the first Clipboard to display its contents.

FIGURE 5-10
Clipboard toolbar with three Clipboards filled

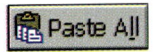

LESSON 5 ■ COPYING DATA AND USING TOOLBARS   EXCEL **169**

15. Select cell G6 and click the third Clipboard. The cut data is pasted in cells G6:K8.
16. Select cell G11 and click the Paste All button [Paste All] on the Clipboard toolbar.
17. Click the Undo button four times to remove each pasted Clipboard.
18. Click the Clear Clipboard button to clear all the Clipboards.
19. Press Ctrl + Home to return to cell A1.

> **NOTE:** You can customize toolbars in the Customize dialog box. Just click the Commands to add buttons to other toolbars. Let the Office Assistant help you learn how to customize toolbars.

EXERCISE 5-8   Move and Reshape Toolbars

Toolbars can appear either "docked" or "floating." A *docked toolbar* appears in a fixed position outside the work area (like the Standard and Formatting toolbars). A *floating toolbar* appears over the work area. You can dock a floating toolbar by dragging it out of the work area. You can float a docked toolbar by dragging it into the work area. You can also reshape a floating toolbar.

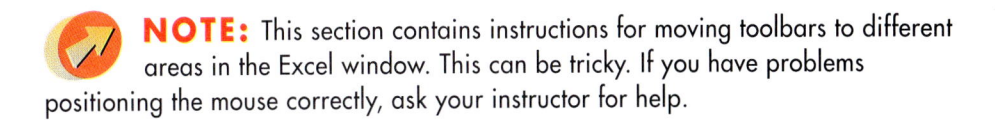

> **NOTE:** This section contains instructions for moving toolbars to different areas in the Excel window. This can be tricky. If you have problems positioning the mouse correctly, ask your instructor for help.

1. Position the pointer on the thick horizontal separator line between the Standard toolbar and the Formatting toolbar. The pointer changes to a four-headed arrow.
2. Click the left mouse button, and with the four-headed arrow, drag the Formatting toolbar just below the Standard toolbar. Release the mouse button. If the Formatting toolbar is not flush left under the Standard toolbar, drag it to the left using the four-headed arrow on the thick horizontal line.

> **NOTE:** Moving the Formatting toolbar below the Standard toolbar expands both toolbars.

3. Position the pointer on the title bar of the Auditing toolbar (not on a toolbar button), click the left mouse button, and drag the toolbar to a

position on the formula bar. The Auditing toolbar is now docked below the Standard and Formatting toolbars.

4. Position the pointer on a thin separator line between two buttons on the docked Auditing toolbar (not on a button) and hold down the left mouse button.

5. Drag the toolbar into the work area and release the left mouse button. The Auditing toolbar is now floating.

6. Drag the Clipboard toolbar to the far right side of the screen, until it is vertically positioned over the scroll bar. Excel docks the toolbar on this side of the screen and the worksheet window is resized to accommodate it.

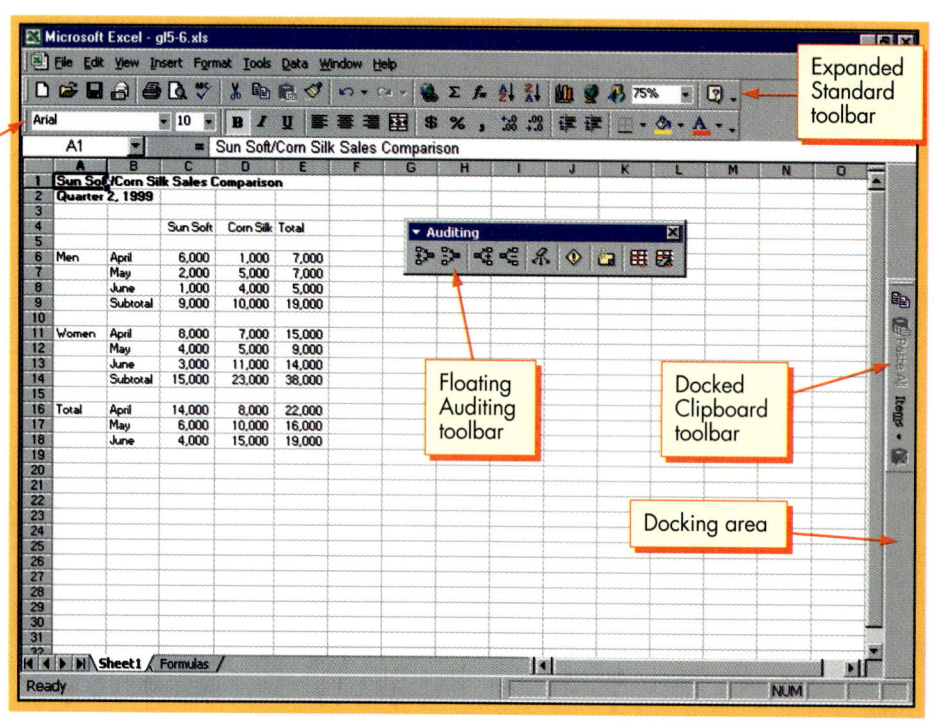

FIGURE 5-11
Docked and floating toolbars

> **NOTE:** Double-clicking a docking area displays the Customize dialog box.

7. Double-click the title bar on the Auditing toolbar (not a button) to dock it again. Notice that it docks where you previously docked it.

8. Double-click a thin separator line (between two buttons) in the gray area of the docked Auditing toolbar to undock it.

9. Position the pointer on the left side of the bottom border of the Auditing toolbar, so the pointer changes to a double-headed arrow.

10. Drag the bottom border down about half an inch and release the mouse button. The toolbar buttons are grouped in rows.

LESSON 5 ■ COPYING DATA AND USING TOOLBARS EXCEL **171**

11. Drag the bottom border down even further, until the toolbar becomes a column of buttons. Reshape it again into a more rectangular arrangement and then back to its original shape, a single row of buttons.

12. Using the four-headed arrow ✥, float the Clipboard toolbar. (Remember to point to the thick gray line at the top of the toolbar and drag the toolbar to the work area.)

EXERCISE 5-9 Close Toolbars

There's no restriction on the number of toolbars you can display in Excel, but it may be hard to read the worksheet if too many are open.

1. Position the mouse on a toolbar and click the right mouse button. The Toolbar shortcut menu appears. Notice the check mark located next to the open Clipboard toolbar. (Remember, the Auditing toolbar is listed in the Customize dialog box.)

2. Click Clipboard to deselect it. Excel closes the Clipboard toolbar. Be sure the Standard and Formatting toolbars remain checked.

3. Click the Close button ☒ in the upper right corner of the Auditing toolbar to close it.

4. Close the workbook without saving it.

COMMAND SUMMARY

FEATURE	BUTTON	MENU	KEYBOARD
Copy	🗇	Edit, Copy	Ctrl + C
Fill right		Edit, Fill	Ctrl + R
Fill down		Edit, Fill	Ctrl + D
Trace Precedents	🠒		
Trace Dependents	🠔		
Remove All Arrows	⚙		

USING HELP

This lesson showed you how to use Excel's AutoFill feature to copy data into adjacent cells. AutoFill is a powerful tool you can also use to create a data series such as numbers, dates, or text.

For example, you can start with the month Jan-97 in a cell and build a series that places Feb-97, Mar-97, and so on in adjacent cells. You can also create custom AutoFill series to build complex worksheets quickly.

To find out how AutoFill can create a series of data, use the Office Assistant:

1. Choose Show the Office Assistant from the Help menu.
2. Click the Office Assistant, key **autofill** in the Office Assistant text box, and click Search.
3. Select "Automatically fill in data based on adjacent cells." Notice that a Microsoft Excel Help window opens with the same title.

FIGURE 5-12
Using AutoFill to fill in data

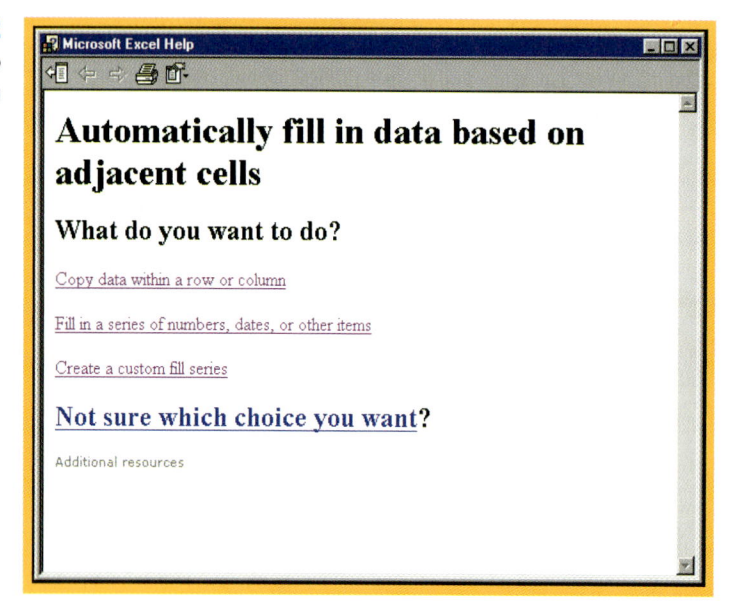

4. Select "Fill in a series of numbers, dates, or other items" and read the information, paying attention to the Fill Months series that you can generate.
5. Close the dialog box when you finish and close the Office Assistant.

LESSON 5 ■ COPYING DATA AND USING TOOLBARS   EXCEL   173

Concepts Review

TRUE/FALSE QUESTIONS

Each of the following statements is either true or false. Indicate your choice by circling **T** or **F**.

T F   **1.** Copying a cell moves its data to a new location in the worksheet.

T F   **2.** You can paste cells using keyboard shortcuts, menu commands, or toolbar buttons.

T F   **3.** When you copy cells, you must first indicate the source range.

T F   **4.** The target range is the new location for data that you copy, cut, or move.

T F   **5.** A relative cell reference is automatically adjusted in any formula you copy.

T F   **6.** To copy cells using the drag-and-drop method, use the mouse pointer and the [Alt] key.

T F   **7.** You should use AutoFill to copy only to adjacent cells.

T F   **8.** A docked toolbar appears in a position outside the work area.

SHORT ANSWER QUESTIONS

Write the correct answer in the space provided.

1. Which keyboard command copies the active cell?

_____

2. Which button copies the active cell?

_____

3. When you copy data, the information remains in the original location and is also copied to what location? (*Hint:* It's not in the worksheet.)

_____

4. What appears around selected cells to highlight them after you choose the Copy command?

_____

5. Which key do you use with the mouse to copy data when using the drag-and-drop method?

6. Which keyboard shortcut copies and fills cells to the right?

7. Which part of the cell do you drag to copy data using AutoFill?

8. Name the two predefined toolbars that appear on screen by default when you first open Excel.

CRITICAL THINKING

Answer these questions on a separate piece of paper. There are no right or wrong answers. Support your answer with examples from your own experience, if possible.

1. What are some of the potential dangers posed by relative cell references when you build a worksheet? What are the advantages? How can you effectively manage this feature?
2. Think of some other ways you might be able to use the Copy, Fill, and AutoFill features. Name at least one new way that you might use these powerful tools.

Skills Review

EXERCISE 5-10

Copy and paste using the Edit menu and the toolbar.

1. Open the file **Bonus.xls**.
2. Key the following data in cells B7 through B10:
   1500
   1800
   1800
   1500
3. Format cells B7 through B10 in Comma style with no decimal places.

LESSON 5 ■ COPYING DATA AND USING TOOLBARS   EXCEL **175**

4. Enter the formula **=B7*C7** in cell D7.
5. Copy and paste the formula in cell D7 using the Copy and Paste commands from the Edit menu by following these steps:
   a. Select cell D7.
   b. Choose Copy from the Edit menu.
   c. Select cells D8 through D10 and choose Paste from the Edit menu.
   d. Press Esc to remove the moving border from the source range.
6. Select cells B11 and D11 and click the AutoSum button Σ.
7. Copy and paste data and formulas using the toolbar by following these steps:
   a. Select cells B7 through D7 as the source range.
   b. Click the Copy button.
   c. Select cell B12 as the first cell of the target range.
   d. Click the Paste button.
   e. Press Esc to remove the moving border from the source range.
8. Copy data and formulas using a variety of methods by following these steps:
   a. Select cells B8 through D8 and choose Copy from the Edit menu.
   b. Select cell B13 and press Ctrl+V.
   c. Select cell B14 and click the Paste button.
   d. Select cells B15 through D16 and press Enter.
9. Key the following data in cells B12 through B16, overwriting the data you previously copied:

   2800

   1800

   1700

   2750

   4200

10. Use AutoSum to total the May revenues in cell B17 and the May commissions in cell D17.
11. Key **Total** in cell A18 in bold and use AutoSum to total all revenues in cell B18 and all commissions in cell D18.
12. Format the unlabeled subtotals (cells B11, B17, D11, and D17) as italic.
13. Format the totals (cells B18 and D18) as bold.
14. Add a header with your name in the left section, the filename in the center section, and the date in the right section.
15. Save the workbook as *[your initials]*5-10.xls in your Lesson 5 folder and print the worksheet.
16. Create a formula printout with gridlines and row and column headings, and close the workbook without saving it.

EXERCISE 5-11

Copy and paste using the menus, the toolbar, keyboard shortcuts, and drag and drop.

1. Open the file **SalesUp.xls**.
2. In cell C7, enter the formula **=B7*1.015**.
3. Copy this formula into cells C8 through C16 using Copy and Paste from the Edit menu by following these steps:
   a. Select cell C7 and choose Copy from the Edit menu.
   b. Select cells C8 through C16 and choose Paste from the Edit menu.
   c. Press [Esc] to remove the moving border from the source range.
   d. Format cells C7 through C16 in Comma style with no decimal places.
4. Copy formulas using drag and drop by following these steps:
   a. Select cells C7 through C16.
   b. Move the mouse pointer across the border of the selection until it becomes an arrow.
   c. Press and hold down [Ctrl] to change the pointer to the drag-and-drop pointer.
   d. Drag the source range to the target range, cells D7 through D16, and release the mouse button and [Ctrl].
5. In cell E7, enter the formula **=B7*1.22**.
6. Copy this formula into cells E8 through E16 using a keyboard shortcut by following these steps:
   a. Select cell E7 and press [Ctrl]+[C].
   b. Select cells E8 through E16 and press [Enter].
   c. Format cells E7 through E16 in Comma style with no decimal places.
7. Copy formulas using the toolbar by following these steps:
   a. Select cells C7 through D16 as the source range.
   b. Click the Copy button.
   c. Select cell F7.
   d. Click the Paste button.
   e. Press [Esc].
8. Create a "Total" row by following these steps:
   a. Key **Total** in cell A17. Format the text as bold.
   b. Select cells B17:G17 and click the AutoSum button.
   c. Format the totals as bold and currency style with no decimal places.
9. Add a header with your name in the left section, the filename in the center section, and the date in the right section.
10. Save the workbook as *[your initials]*5-11.xls in your Lesson 5 folder and print the worksheet.

LESSON 5 ■ COPYING DATA AND USING TOOLBARS   EXCEL   **177**

11. Create a formula printout in landscape orientation with gridlines and row and column headings. Use a Page 1 of ? footer if the printout exceeds more than one page.
12. Close the workbook without saving it

EXERCISE 5-12

Copy formulas using the Fill command and AutoFill.

1. Open the file **NetInc2.xls**.
2. Enter the following formulas in cells B9 through B11:

   =B6*0.2

   =B6*0.35

   =B6*0.3

3. Format cells B9 through B11 in Comma style with no decimal places.
4. Select cell B12, click the AutoSum button Σ, and press Enter.
5. Select cells B9 through F12.
6. Choose the Fill command from the Edit menu and choose Right from the submenu.
7. Enter the formula **=B6-B12** in cell B14 to calculate the net income for the year 1997 ("Sales" - "Total Expenses"). The cell is already formatted.
8. Use AutoFill to copy the formula in cell B14 to cells C14 through F14 by following these steps:
   a. With cell B14 selected, position the mouse pointer on the fill handle.
   b. Drag the fill handle to select cells C14 through F14.
   c. Release the mouse button.
9. Add bold formatting to the Total Expenses and Net Income figures.
10. Add a header with your name in the left section, the filename in the center section, and the date in the right section.
11. Save the workbook as *[your initials]***5-12.xls** in your Lesson 5 folder and print the worksheet.
12. Create a formula printout in landscape orientation with gridlines and row and column headings. Use a Page 1 of ? footer if the printout exceeds one page.
13. Close the workbook without saving it.

EXERCISE 5-13

Open multiple toolbars, move and reshape toolbars, and use the Audit toolbar.

1. Open the file **Q4.xls**.

2. Open multiple toolbars using the following steps:
   a. Choose Toolbars from the View menu to open the Toolbars submenu.
   b. Select the Chart toolbar. Repeat the steps to select the Picture toolbar.
   c. If necessary, drag one toolbar down or up to reveal the hidden toolbar.
   d. Right-click the title bar of the Chart toolbar. Select the Forms toolbar from the shortcut menu.
   e. Right-click a thin separator line between two buttons of the Forms toolbar and select Customize from the shortcut menu.
   f. Select Auditing and click Close.

3. Move and reshape toolbars by following these steps:
   a. Double-click the title bar of the Chart toolbar to dock it.
   b. Drag the Auditing toolbar onto the formula bar to dock it.
   c. Drag the Forms toolbar to the left side of the screen over the row heading to dock it.
   d. Drag the bottom border of the Picture border down until it becomes square. The toolbar should contain five rows of buttons. Drag it back to its original shape. (This toolbar may already be a square. If so, practice resizing it and return it to a long rectangular shape.)
   e. Float all the toolbars you opened in step 2, except the Auditing toolbar, by double-clicking a thin separator line between two buttons in the toolbar.

4. Close the Chart toolbar by right-clicking the Chart title bar and deselecting Chart on the Toolbar shortcut menu. Do the same for the Forms toolbar.

5. Close the Picture toolbar by clicking the Close button ☒ in the upper right corner of the title bar.

6. Add a header with your name in the left section, the filename in the center section, and the date in the right section

7. Center the worksheet horizontally.

8. Save the workbook as *[your initials]*5-13.xls in your Lesson 5 folder.

9. Use the Auditing toolbar to trace formula paths by following these steps:
   a. Select cell D14 and click the Trace Precedents button.
   b. Select cell D9 and click the Trace Dependents button.

10. Float the Auditing toolbar by double-clicking a thin separator line between two buttons in the toolbar and close it by clicking the Close button ☒.

11. Print the worksheet, including the tracing arrows.

12. Create a formula printout in landscape orientation with gridlines and row and column headings.

13. Close the workbook without saving it.

Lesson Applications

EXERCISE 5-14

Use the Copy and Paste commands, copy using drag and drop, and copy using Fill and AutoFill.

The Beautiful Belle Company needs to break down its revenues by product line and by region. The worksheet must also show product totals and subtotals, regional totals, and the grand total.

1. Open the file **Product.xls**.
2. Create a formula that totals revenues for the Monterey product line.
3. Copy the formula to cell D16 using the Copy button and the Paste button.
4. Copy the formula from cell D16 to cells D17 through D20 using the F<u>i</u>ll, <u>D</u>own command.
5. Select cells D17 through D20. Copy this range to cells D9 through D12 using the drag-and-drop method.
6. Create a formula that finds the subtotal for Creams sold in the Northwest territory.
7. Copy this formula to cells C13 and D13 using AutoFill.
8. Copy cells B13 through D13. Paste them in cells B21 through D21 using Ctrl+C and Ctrl+V.
9. Enter a formula to add the subtotals for Creams and Fragrances in cell B23.
10. Copy this formula to cells C23 and D23 using AutoFill.
11. Change the view to 100% and format the numbers in the subtotal and total rows as bold.
12. Add a header with your name in the left section, the filename in the center section, and the date in the right section.
13. Save the workbook as *[your initials]***5-14.xls** in your Lesson 5 folder and print the worksheet.
14. Create a formula printout in landscape orientation with gridlines and row and column headings.
15. Close the workbook without saving it.

EXERCISE 5-15

Copy using the Fill command, toolbar buttons, drag and drop, and AutoFill.

1. Open the file **Frgrnce.xls.**
2. Copy the labels as shown in Figure 5-13 to cells A15 through A21. (Copy the labels only. Don't copy the values.)

FIGURE 5-13

	A
6	**Fragrances**
7	Pacifica
8	Taos
9	High Sierra
10	Carmel
11	Santa Barbara
12	Total

3. Create a formula that finds the 1997 total revenues for the Pacifica product line (cell D7).
4. Copy this formula to cells D8 through D11 using the F<u>i</u>ll, <u>D</u>own command.
5. Enter the formula **=B7*1.1** in cell B16 (Pacifica 1998 sales in the Northwest).
6. Copy and paste this formula to cell C16 using the toolbar buttons.
7. Select cells B16 through C20 and copy the formulas using the F<u>i</u>ll, <u>D</u>own command.
8. Copy the formulas from cells D7 through D11 to cells D16 through D20 using drag and drop.
9. Format all the numbers in row 16 in Currency style with no decimals. Format numbers in cells B17 through D20 and B8 through D11 in Comma style with no decimals.
10. Create a formula in cell B21 that finds the projected total revenues for the Northwest territory in 1998.

LESSON 5 ■ COPYING DATA AND USING TOOLBARS   EXCEL 181

11. Copy this formula to cells C21 and D21 using AutoFill.
12. Copy cells B21 through D21 and create total formulas for 1997 using the drag-and-drop method.
13. Format the numbers in the total rows in bold.
14. Add a header with your name in the left section, the filename in the center section, and the date in the right section.
15. Save the workbook as *[your initials]*5-15.xls in your Lesson 5 folder and print the worksheet.
16. Create a formula printout in landscape orientation with gridlines and row and column headings.
17. Close the workbook without saving it.

EXERCISE 5-16

Copy using Fill, AutoFill, and drag and drop.

Build a worksheet to compare sales by quarter for Sun Soft for the years 1996 through 1998. Create formulas that calculate total sales for each year. Include a percentage change for 1996 to 1997 and 1997 to 1998.

1. Open the file **Change%.xls**.
2. Make corrections and entries as shown in Figure 5-14. Format the numbers as Comma style with no decimals as shown in the figure.

FIGURE 5-14

	A	B	C	D
4		1996	1997	1998
5	Qtr 3 [Qtr 1]	64,955	96,500	80,530	(tr)
6	~~Quarter 3~~ [Qtr 2]	70,130	90,130	100,540
7	Qtr 3	110,140	*150,350*	180,020
8	Qtr 3 [Qtr 4]	95,600	120,040	135,060

3. Create a formula that totals the four quarters for 1996 in cell B10.
4. Copy the formula to total 1997 and 1998 sales using AutoFill.

5. In cell E5, enter a formula that calculates the 1996 to 1997 change in sales as a percentage of 1996 sales. (*Hint:* Subtract 1996 sales from 1997 sales and divide the difference by 1996 sales.)

> **NOTE:** Cell E5 and the cells used in the next few steps are already formatted for Percent with one decimal place.

6. Copy the formula to Qtr2 through Qtr4 for 1997 using the F<u>i</u>ll, <u>D</u>own command.
7. Copy the formula to Qtr1 through Qtr4 for 1998 using the F<u>i</u>ll, <u>R</u>ight command.
8. Create totals for the 1997 and 1998 percentage changes by copying the Qtr4 formulas (cells E8 and F8) to row 10 using drag and drop.
9. Key the row label **Total** in row 10 in bold.
10. Change the page orientation to portrait. (This worksheet's default orientation was previously changed to landscape.) Center the page horizontally.
11. Add a header with your name in the left section, the filename in the center section, and the date in the right section.
12. Save the workbook as *[your initials]*5-16.xls in your Lesson 5 folder and print the worksheet.
13. Create a formula printout in landscape orientation with gridlines and row and column headings. Use a Page 1 of ? footer if the printout extends past one page.
14. Close the workbook without saving it.

EXERCISE 5-17   Challenge Yourself

Copy and paste formulas, use Fill or AutoFill, copy using drag and drop, and use toolbars.

Construct a worksheet comparing second-quarter sales for Sun Soft and Corn Silk for 1997, 1998, and 1999.

1. Plan the worksheet on a sheet of paper in landscape orientation. Create a two-line title that explains the worksheet, and in the body of the worksheet include labels for Sun Soft and Corn Silk sales comparisons for 1997, 1998, and 1999. Also include labels for a calculated percentage of Sun Soft as a Percent of Corn Silk for 1997, 1998, and 1999. (These should be the column labels, nine columns altogether.)

2. Include labels for the second quarter months plus a total line with a blank row before the total line. (These should be the row labels, four rows altogether.)
3. Use F for formula locations.
4. Transfer the design to the computer by keying titles and labels. Format them attractively.
5. Input test data in the Sun Soft months for 1997, 1998, and 1999. Format the data for commas with no decimals.
6. Copy and paste the test data to the Corn Silk months for 1997, 1998, and 1999.
7. Calculate the three-month total for Sun Soft in 1997. Copy that formula to the appropriate cells for Sun Soft and Corn Silk.
8. Calculate Sun Soft's sales as a percentage of Corn Silk sales for April 1997. (*Hint:* Divide Sun Soft sales by Corn Silk sales.)
9. Format the percentage formula in percent style with no decimal places.
10. Use Fill or AutoFill to copy the percentage change to the rest of the months for 1997 through 1999.
11. Use drag and drop to copy the formula to the Percent Total.
12. Check your formulas for accuracy and enter the data in Figure 5-15 into the monthly quarter cells for 1997, 1998, and 1999.

FIGURE 5-15

	Sun Soft			Corn Silk		
	1997	1998	1999	1997	1998	1999
April	19,650	24,800	36,540	33,550	28,150	26,540
May	22,630	31,300	24,000	23,260	18,440	16,500
June	27,850	34,030	31,250	29,360	25,040	21,350

13. Reduce the view to 75% and set up the worksheet to print in landscape orientation centered horizontally on one page.
14. Name the worksheet tab **Comparison**.
15. Name the Sheet2 tab **User Information** and create documentation that includes the following: File Information (Created by, Date created, Date revised, Revised by, Contact for help); Purpose of worksheet (paragraph form); and Instructions to User (special instructions needed by user to enter data correctly). Style the documentation for easy reading.

16. Add the standard header to both sheets including your name, filename, and date.
17. Delete Sheet3.
18. Save the workbook as *[your initials]***5-17.xls** in your Lesson 5 folder.
19. Use the Auditing toolbar to trace the precedents for the April 1998 percentage change formula in the Comparison worksheet.
20. Print the workbook, including the precedent arrows. Remove the precedent arrows, and then close the Auditing toolbar.
21. Create a formula printout of the Comparison sheet in landscape orientation with grids and row and column headings. Add a Page 1 of ? footer for multiple pages, if necessary.
22. Close the workbook without saving it. Submit your plan, worksheet, user documentation, and formula printout.

LESSON 6

Range Names and Sorting

OBJECTIVES

After completing this lesson, you will be able to:
1. Name ranges and constants.
2. Use names in formulas.
3. Change and delete range names.
4. Navigate in the worksheet using range names.
5. Paste names into worksheets.
6. Sort data in the worksheet.

MOUS ACTIVITIES
In this lesson:
XL2000 **E.6.1**
XL2000 **E.6.2**

See Appendix F.

Estimated Time: 1¼ hours

Instead of trying to remember a particular cell address, such as E17, or a cell range, such as I7:J43, you can use a name to designate a location. For example, you could name a cell that contains a formula "total," and use the name "total" to refer to the cell when you create other formulas. In addition to naming cells, you can also assign names to constants. For example, you could assign the name "rate" to the constant 0.07. Naming cells also makes it easier to find a particular location in a large worksheet.

At times, you will find it necessary to rearrange the information in your worksheet. You can use the Data Sort command to sort selected information in ascending or descending order according to the contents of a key column within the worksheet.

Naming Ranges and Constants

A *range name*—the name you give to a cell or range of cells—must begin with a letter. Although range names can be from 1 to 255 characters long, it is best to keep them short, but still recognizable. Range names must *not*:

- Have the form of a cell reference, such as q1 or A13.
- Use "R" or "C" as a single-letter name.
- Contain spaces.
- Contain hyphens (-) or special characters ($, %, &, #).

To separate parts of a name such as "saleseast," you can use capital letters, a period, or an underline (for example, "SalesEast," "sales.east," or "sales_east").

TABLE 6-1 Examples of Valid and Invalid Range Names

VALID NAMES	INVALID NAMES
Total.Sales	Total Sales
East_sales	east-sales
EntertainPct	Entertain%
qt1	q1
X	R

EXERCISE 6-1   Name an Individual Cell

You can name ranges using the Define Name dialog box or by keying the name in the Name Box at the left of the formula bar.

1. Open the file **98Sales.xls**.
2. Move to cell E9.
3. Choose <u>N</u>ame from the <u>I</u>nsert menu.
4. Choose <u>D</u>efine from the submenu. The Define Name dialog box appears. (See Figure 6-1 on the next page.)
5. Key **qt1** in the Names In <u>W</u>orkbook text box and click OK. The name appears in the Name Box at the left of the formula bar.
6. Move to cell E18 and click in the Name Box at the left of the formula bar. The cell address is selected.

LESSON 6 ■ RANGE NAMES AND SORTING   EXCEL **187**

FIGURE 6-1
Define Name dialog box

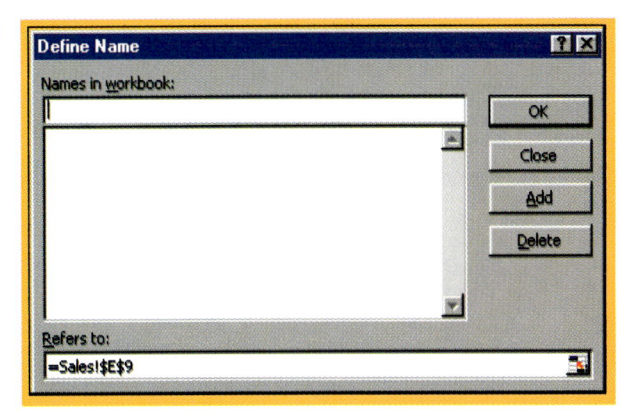

7. Key **qt2** and press Enter. The name appears in the Name Box.
8. Name cell E27 **qt3** using the Define Name dialog box.
9. Name cell E36 **qt4** by keying the text directly into the Name Box at the left of the formula bar.

EXERCISE 6-2 Name a Group of Cells

You can name any group of cells. Excel suggests a name for the range based on the title of the selected column or row. If you don't want the suggested name, you can assign a different name to the range.

1. Select all the totals for "New Century," which appear in cells E5, E14, E23, and E32.

> **TIP:** Remember, to select nonadjacent cells, press Ctrl while selecting the cells.

2. Choose **N**ame from the **I**nsert menu.
3. Choose **D**efine. The Define Name dialog box opens. Notice that Excel suggests the name Total.
4. Key **New_Century** in the Names In **W**orkbook text box and click OK.
5. Select cells E6, E15, E24, and E33.
6. Click in the Name Box at the left of the formula bar.
7. Key **Golden** and press Enter.
8. Name cells E7, E16, E25, and E34 **Monterey**, and name cells E8, E17, E26, and E35 **Herbal**.

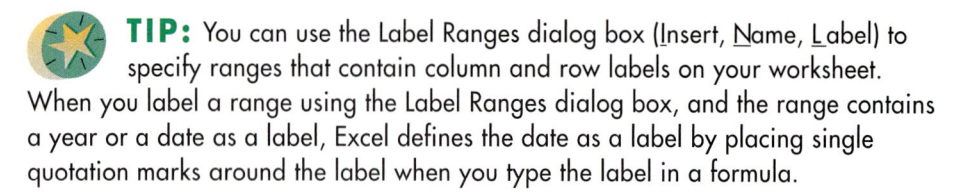

TIP: You can use the Label Ranges dialog box (<u>I</u>nsert, <u>N</u>ame, <u>L</u>abel) to specify ranges that contain column and row labels on your worksheet. When you label a range using the Label Ranges dialog box, and the range contains a year or a date as a label, Excel defines the date as a label by placing single quotation marks around the label when you type the label in a formula.

EXERCISE 6-3 Name a Constant

In addition to assigning names to cells or ranges of cells, you can assign names to *constants*. Constants are unchanging values used in formulas. Named constants don't appear in the worksheet. For example, if you assign the name "rate" to the constant .075, you could then use the name "rate" in formulas instead of the value. When you change the constant value assigned to "rate," any formula that contains "rate" automatically changes to include the new value.

1. Press [Ctrl]+[F3] to open the Define Name dialog box.
2. Key **pro** in the Names In <u>W</u>orkbook text box.
3. Edit the text to read **=.12** in the <u>R</u>efers To text box.
4. Click OK. The value 0.12 is assigned the name "pro." This name is used later in this lesson to increase the sales figures by 12%.

NOTE: You cannot name a constant in the Name Box.

Using Names in Formulas

Once you create names for cell references or constants, you can use these names in formulas. You key the formula in the normal way, but key the name instead of the cell reference. To use constants, key the name for the constant wherever you would key the constant in the formula.

EXERCISE 6-4 Create Formulas Including Names

1. In cell B41, key **=sum(new_century)** and press [Enter]. Once you enter the formula in the cell, Excel converts the name to include uppercase letters as you created it.

TIP: You can use [F3] to place a name in a formula. For instance, key **=sum(** Then, press [F3], select the name from the list, click OK, and finish the formula.

LESSON 6 ■ RANGE NAMES AND SORTING   EXCEL **189**

2. In cell B42, key **=sum(golden)**
3. In cell B43, key **=sum(monterey)**
4. In cell B44, key **=sum(herbal)**
5. In cell C41, calculate a 12% projected sales increase for 1999 by keying **=B41*(1+pro)**. (B41 is the 1998 total and "1+pro" equals 1.12, since you earlier defined "pro" to be 0.12.)
6. Copy this formula to cells C42, C43, C44, and C45. Format cell C45 as bold; it equals zero for now.
7. In cell B45, use the cell names you created by keying **=qt1+qt2+qt3+qt4**

FIGURE 6-2
Total projected
1999 sales, so far

	A	B	C
40		1998	1999
41	New Century	474,015	530,897
42	Golden Gate	328,731	368,179
43	Monterey	353,950	396,424
44	Herbal Essence	627,284	702,558
45	TOTAL:	1,783,980	1,998,058

B45 = =qt1+qt2+qt3+qt4

8. In cells D32 through D35, enter the data as shown below. When you finish, the total for 1999 in cell C45 should be 2,199,716.

	Dec
New Century	**79,658**
Golden Gate	**22,457**
Monterey	**32,568**
Herbal Essence	**45,369**

Changing and Deleting Range Names

You can change a name or delete one that you no longer need. When you change a name, Excel does not replace the old name with the new name in relevant formulas. The old formulas remain valid, however, unless you delete the old name.

EXERCISE 6-5 Change and Delete Range Names

1. Press **Ctrl**+**F3** to open the Define Name dialog box.
2. Choose **New_Century** from the Names In Workbook list box.
3. Highlight "New_" in the Names In Workbook text box and press **Delete**. "Century" remains in the text box.
4. Click OK.

5. Move to cell B41. The name New_Century is not changed in the formula bar.
6. Choose **N**ame from the **I**nsert menu and then choose **D**efine.
7. Choose "New_Century" from the Names In **W**orkbook list box.
8. Click **D**elete and click OK. The formulas that refer to New_Century display the #NAME? error message.

> **NOTE:** You can use the Undo command to reverse the deletion of a name.

9. In cell B41, double-click New_Century in the formula bar to select it and key **century** to change the formula to reflect the new range name.

> **NOTE:** You can also edit the cell by highlighting New_ and then pressing Delete, or you can use F3 to paste Century into the formula.

10. Click the check box in the formula bar. The #NAME? error message is no longer displayed in cell B41 or cell C41 and the formulas calculate correctly.

Navigating Using Range Names

Named ranges not only make calculations easier, but also enable you to move around a worksheet more quickly. For example, you can assign a name to a cell and then locate the cell by choosing **G**o To from the **E**dit menu (or pressing F5). Excel opens the Go To dialog box, which lists all named cells in the worksheet. It also lists the last four cell addresses the **G**o To command located. You can also use the Name Box drop-down list to move to named ranges.

EXERCISE 6-6 Move to Named Ranges

1. Select cells B4 through E9.
2. Choose **N**ame from the **I**nsert menu and choose **D**efine.
3. Key **one** in the Names In **W**orkbook text box and click OK.
4. Select cells B13 through E18.
5. Click in the Name Box, key **two**, and press Enter.
6. Name cells B22 through E27 **three**, cells B31 through E36 **four**, and cells B40 through C45 **grandtot**.

LESSON 6 ■ RANGE NAMES AND SORTING   EXCEL **191**

7. Choose <u>G</u>o To from the <u>E</u>dit menu or press `F5` . The Go To dialog box appears.

FIGURE 6-3
Go To dialog box

8. Double-click the named range "two." Excel moves to the selected range. (You may have to scroll down the list.)

FIGURE 6-4
Name Box drop-down list

9. Press `Ctrl`+`Home` to move to cell A1. Click the Name Box arrow. The drop-down list appears. (See Figure 6-4.)

10. Click the named range "one." Excel moves to the selected range.

11. Practice moving to named ranges using both the <u>G</u>o To command and the Name Box drop-down list.

Pasting Names into Worksheets

You can use the Define Name dialog box to display a list of named ranges and constants to see how a worksheet is set up. Using the **Paste Name dialog box**, you can paste a list of range names and references into a worksheet as documentation. You can also use this dialog box to paste range names and constants into formulas.

EXERCISE | **6-7** | **Paste Range Names into Worksheets**

Before pasting a list of range names, move to a clear area of your worksheet. Make sure the area is large enough so the paste does not overwrite existing data.

1. Move to cell A18 in the sheet named User Information.
2. Key the label **Range Names** in bold and press Enter.
3. Move to cell B19 and key **The following range names have been created in the Sales worksheet.**
4. Move to cell B21 and key **Name** in bold. In cell C21, key **Location** in bold.
5. Move to cell B22, choose Name from the Insert menu, and choose Paste. The Paste Name dialog box appears.

FIGURE 6-5 Paste Name dialog box

6. Click the Paste List button. (See Figure 6-6.) The list of named ranges is pasted into the Documentation worksheet. You can key descriptions of the named ranges into the worksheet as necessary.
7. If necessary, change the view to 75% so you can see all the range names.
8. In the documentation worksheet, key today's date for "Date revised" and key your name for "Revised by." Turn off gridlines for viewing.

FIGURE 6-6 Names pasted into a worksheet

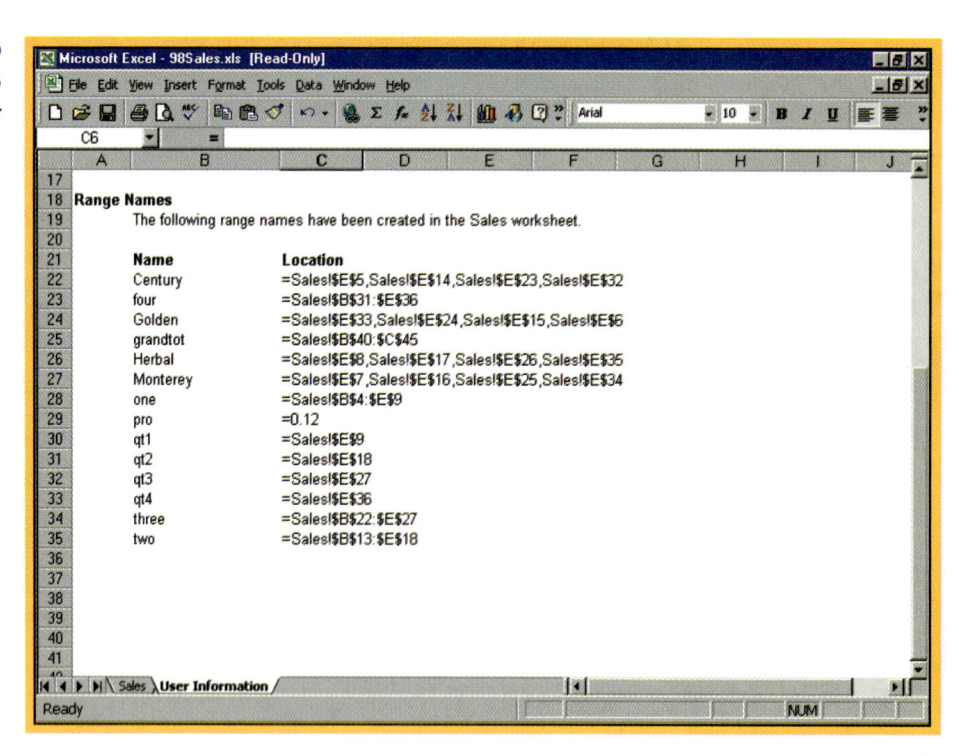

9. Save the workbook as *[your initials]*6-7.xls in a new folder for Lesson 6.

LESSON 6 ■ RANGE NAMES AND SORTING
EXCEL 193

Sorting Information in a Worksheet

You can use the Sort command from the Data menu to rearrange information in the worksheet. You sort information by first selecting the range to be sorted. Then you choose the Sort command and specify the column the information will be sorted by and the sort order.

EXERCISE 6-8 Sort Information in a Worksheet

1. Move to cell A5 in the sheet named Sales.
2. Highlight the range A5:E8.

FIGURE 6-7
Highlighted sort range

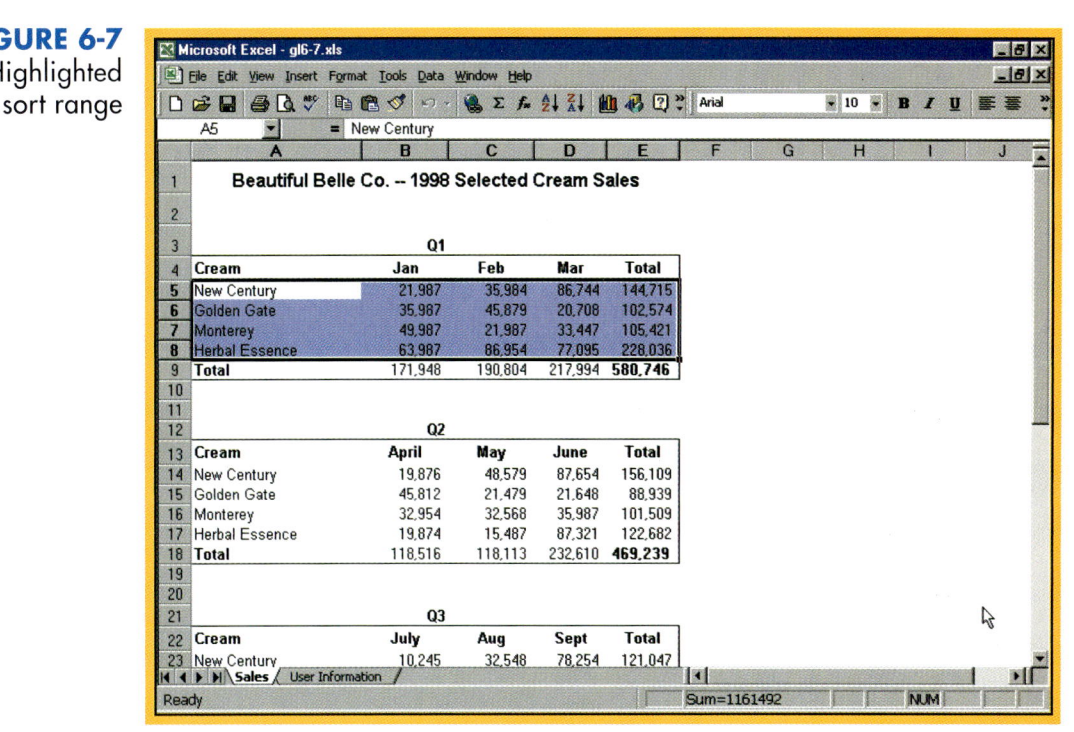

3. Choose Sort from the Data menu. The Sort dialog box appears (see Figure 6-8 on the next page.) Notice that the Sort By text box automatically matches the column label of the active cell, A5. The list will, therefore, be arranged in alphabetical order by Cream. The Ascending order of arrangement is also selected. This orders the list from smallest to largest (if they are numbers) or A to Z (if they are labels). The Descending order arranges items largest to smallest (if numbers) or Z to A (if labels).

FIGURE 6-8
Sort dialog box

NOTE: You can also use the Sort Ascending and Sort Descending buttons on the Standard toolbar to sort a selected range.

4. Click the OK button. The highlighted information is rearranged in alphabetical order by Creams.

FIGURE 6-9
Sorted information

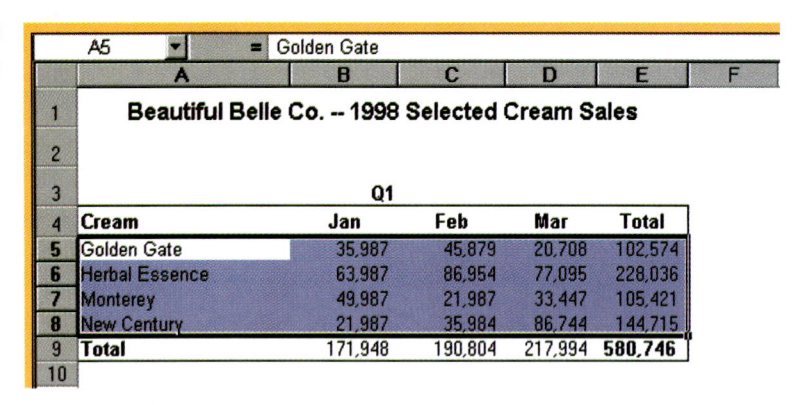

5. Move to cell A14 and highlight the range A14:E17. Click the Sort Descending button to sort the information in descending order.
6. Click the Undo button.
7. Click the Sort Ascending button to sort the information in ascending order.
8. Sort the ranges A23:E26, A32:E35, and A41:C44 in ascending order.
9. Add the standard header containing your name, filename, and date to both sheets.
10. Save the workbook as *[your initials]*6-8.xls in your Lesson 6 folder.
11. Print the entire workbook, and then create the standard formula printout for the Sales sheet with grids and row and column headings. Add a Page 1 of ? footer to the formula printout if it exceeds one page.
12. Close the workbook without saving it.

LESSON 6 ■ RANGE NAMES AND SORTING   EXCEL   **195**

COMMAND SUMMARY

FEATURE	BUTTON	MENU	KEYBOARD
Define Name		Insert, Name, Define	Ctrl + F3
Go To		Edit, Go To	F5 or Ctrl + G
Paste Name		Insert, Name, Paste	F3
Sort Ascending	⇡↓	Data, Sort	
Sort Descending	⇣↑	Data, Sort	

USING HELP

In this lesson you were given a tip on using the Label Ranges dialog box. To find out more about how and when to use this feature, ask the Office Assistant.

To find out how and when to use the Label Ranges dialog box:

1. Choose Show the Office Assistant from the Help menu. Click the Office Assistant to activate it.
2. Key **label ranges** in the text box and click Search.
3. Select "About labeling ranges using the Label Ranges dialog box." Maximize the Help window.
4. The Office Assistant displays information that shows you how to use the Label Ranges dialog box.

FIGURE 6-10
Labeling ranges using the Label Ranges dialog box

About labeling ranges by using the Label Ranges dialog box

Specifying labels When you select cells in labeled ranges to create formulas, Microsoft Excel can insert the labels in place of cell references in your formulas. Using labels can make it easier to see how a formula is constructed. You can use the **Label Ranges** dialog box (**Insert** menu, **Name** submenu, **Label** command) to specify the ranges that contain column and row labels on your worksheet.

Using dates as labels When you label a range by using the **Label Ranges** dialog box and the range contains a year or date as a label, Excel defines the date as a label by placing single quotation marks around the label when you type the label in a formula. For example, suppose your worksheet contains the labels 1996 and 1997 and you have specified these labels by using the **Label Ranges** dialog box. When you type the formula =SUM(1997), Excel automatically updates the formula to =SUM('1997').

For more information about the options in the **Label Ranges** dialog box, click the question mark ? and then click the option.

Tip If you label a list by using the **Label** command and then zoom the view of the worksheet to 39 percent or less, Excel adds a blue border around the labels you have specified with the **Label Ranges** command on the worksheet. The blue border does not print and is not displayed when you zoom the worksheet view above 39 percent.

Additional resources

5. Read the information and close the dialog box and the Office Assistant.

Concepts Review

TRUE/FALSE QUESTIONS

Each of the following statements is either true or false. Indicate your choice by circling **T** or **F**.

T F **1.** A range name can include spaces and hyphens.

T F **2.** A cell or range name can include as many as 255 characters.

T F **3.** Named cells can contain only formulas.

T F **4.** Range names can include special characters like $, &, and #.

T F **5.** Names applied to constants can later be used in formulas.

T F **6.** You can use range names to replace cell references in formulas.

T F **7.** When you change a name, Excel automatically replaces the old name with the new name in the appropriate formulas.

T F **8.** The Go To dialog box lists all named cells in the worksheet.

SHORT ANSWER QUESTIONS

Write the correct answer in the space provided.

1. Which command enables you to move to the location of a named cell in the worksheet?

2. What do you call an unchanging value in a formula?

3. Which keyboard combination do you use for the Define Name command?

4. Which keyboard combination do you use for the Paste Name command?

5. Which menu commands do you use to name a range?

6. Which dialog box is opened by pressing [F5]?

LESSON 6 ■ RANGE NAMES AND SORTING   EXCEL **197**

   7. Which menu commands do you use to paste a range name?

   _____

   8. Which menu commands do you use to sort a list?

   _____

CRITICAL THINKING

Answer these questions on a separate piece of paper. There are no right or wrong answers. Support your answer with examples from your own experience, if possible.

   1. What are some of the possible disadvantages related to using range names and cell names in formulas? How can you avoid these potential drawbacks?

   2. Describe potential uses for range names in Excel other than those described in this lesson. Explain how you would apply each use in a worksheet.

Skills Review

EXERCISE 6-9

Create names for cell ranges and constants, and use names in formulas.

   1. Open the file **Lotions.xls**.
   2. Create names for cell ranges by following these steps:
      a. Select cells B7 through D7.
      b. Choose <u>N</u>ame from the <u>I</u>nsert menu and choose <u>D</u>efine.
      c. Excel suggests the name "Cypress" in the Names In <u>W</u>orkbook text box. Click OK.
      d. Select cells B8 through D8.
      e. Choose <u>N</u>ame from the <u>I</u>nsert menu and then choose <u>D</u>efine.
      f. Excel suggests the name "Jojoba" in the Names In <u>W</u>orkbook text box. Click OK.
      g. Select cells B9 through D9.
      h. Press [Ctrl]+[F3].
      i. Excel suggests the name "Sesame" in the Names In <u>W</u>orkbook text box. Click OK.
      j. Select cells B10 through D10.
      k. Choose <u>I</u>nsert, <u>N</u>ame, and then choose <u>D</u>efine.

l. Edit the suggested name "Joshua_Tree" in the Names In <u>W</u>orkbook text to **Joshua** and click OK.

3. Create names for constants by following these steps:
   a. Choose <u>I</u>nsert, <u>N</u>ame, and then choose <u>D</u>efine.
   b. Key **slow** in the Names In <u>W</u>orkbook text box.
   c. Edit the text to read **=1.05** in the <u>R</u>efers To text box. Click <u>A</u>dd.
   d. Edit the text in the Names In <u>W</u>orkbook text box to read **moderate**
   e. Edit the text to read **=1.1** in the <u>R</u>efers To text box. Click <u>A</u>dd.
   f. Edit the text in the Names In <u>W</u>orkbook text box to read **fast**
   g. Edit the text to read **=1.15** in the <u>R</u>efers To text box. Click OK.

4. Use names in formulas by following these steps:
   a. Key **=sum(cypress)** in cell E7.
   b. Key **=sum(jojoba)** in cell E8.
   c. Key **=sum(sesame)** in cell E9.
   d. Key **=sum(joshua)** in cell E10.

5. Build formulas with range names and constant names by following these steps:
   a. Key **=cypress*slow** in cell B17.
   b. Use AutoFill to copy this formula to cells C17 and D17.
   c. Key **=jojoba*moderate** in cell B18.
   d. Use AutoFill to copy this formula to cells C18 and D18.
   e. Key **=sesame*fast** in cell B19.
   f. Use AutoFill to copy this formula to cells C19 and D19.
   g. Key **=joshua*slow** in cell B20.
   h. Key **=joshua*moderate** in cell C20.
   i. Key **=joshua*fast** in cell D20.
   j. Use AutoSum and AutoFill to enter formulas for the totals of each type of lotion in cells E17 through E20.

6. Add the standard header including your name, filename, and date.

7. Save the workbook as **[*your initials*]6-9.xls** in your Lesson 6 folder and print the worksheet.

8. Create a standard formula printout in landscape orientation with grids and row and column headings and close the workbook without saving it.

EXERCISE 6-10

Use names in formulas, change range names, and delete range names.

1. Open the file **Powders.xls**.
2. Use names in formulas by following these steps:
   a. Key **=sum(sahara)** in cell E6.
   b. Key **=sum(marin)** in cell E7.

LESSON 6 ■ RANGE NAMES AND SORTING EXCEL **199**

   c. Key **=sum(mohave)** in cell E8.
   d. Key **=sum(april_fresh)** in cell E9.
   e. Key **=sum(spring_day)** in cell E10.
   f. Key **=april_fresh+spring_day** in cell B12.
3. Use AutoFill to copy the formula from cell B12 to cells C12 and D12.
4. Use AutoSum to enter a formula that totals the new products in cell E12.
5. Change range names by following these steps:
   a. Choose Insert, Name and then choose Define.
   b. Choose "april_fresh" from the Names In Workbook list box.
   c. Delete "_fresh" from the name. Click Add.
   d. Choose "spring_day" from the Names In Workbook list box, change the name to **spring**, and click OK.
6. Delete range names by following these steps:
   a. Press Ctrl + F3.
   b. Choose "april_fresh" from the Names In Workbook list box and click Delete.
   c. Choose "spring_day" from the Names In Workbook list box, click Delete, and click OK.
7. Use the new range names in formulas by following these steps:
   a. Move to cell E9.
   b. Double-click "april_fresh" in the formula to select it and key **april**.
   c. Press Enter.
   d. In cell E10, change the name "spring_day" in the formula to **spring**.
   e. Change the formula in cell B12 to **=april+spring**.
   f. Copy the new formula in cell B12 to cells C12 and D12.
8. In cell A13, key **Grand Total**. In cells B13 through E13, calculate the totals for each month and for the three-month period. Do not include the "New Product Totals" in the "Grand Totals."
9. Add the standard header including your name, filename, and date, and center the worksheet horizontally on the page.
10. Save the workbook as *[your initials]***6-10.xls** in your Lesson 6 folder and print the worksheet.
11. Create a standard formula printout with grids and row and column headings. Use a Page 1 of ? footer.
12. Close the workbook without saving it.

EXERCISE 6-11

Name a range of cells and navigate in the worksheet using range names.

1. Open the file **Credit.xls**.

2. Add the following data for each customer into the worksheet:

Hall, Martha	240	9%
Spencer, Jon	150	10%
May, Violet	23	7%
Bernard, Frank	542	13%
Brown, JoAnne	500	11%

3. Name a range of cells by following these steps:
   a. Select cells A24 through C24.
   b. Choose Insert, Name, and then choose Define.
   c. Excel suggests the name "Hall_Martha" in the Names In Workbook text box. Click OK.

4. Use the Go To command to navigate with names in the worksheet by following these steps:
   a. Choose Go To from the Edit menu.
   b. Double-click the range "Ferrara_Joseph."
   c. Press F5.
   d. Double-click the range "fifteen." All new customers with credit at the 15% interest rate are selected.

5. Sort the list of customers by customer name in ascending order.
   a. Select cells A6 through C28.
   b. Choose Sort from the Data menu. Notice how Excel recognized the bold row as column headings and omitted them from the sort highlight. Click OK.

6. Add the standard header including your name, filename, and date.

7. Save the workbook as *[your initials]*6-11.xls in your Lesson 6 folder and print the worksheet.

8. Create a standard formula printout in landscape orientation with grids and row and column headings and close the workbook without saving it.

EXERCISE 6-12

Name constants, paste names into a formula, and paste names into a worksheet.

1. Open the file **Freight1.xls**.

2. Name constants using the following steps:
   a. Choose Insert, Name, then choose Define.
   b. Key **mileage** in the Names In Workbook text box.
   c. Edit the text to read **=4** in the Refers To text box.
   d. Click Add.
   e. Key **weight** in the Names In Workbook text box.

LESSON 6 ■ RANGE NAMES AND SORTING EXCEL 201

    f. Edit the text to read **=.0015** in the Refers To text box.
    g. Click OK.

3. Change a formula by inserting the newly named constants using these steps:

    a. Select and delete the contents of cell D7.
    b. Key **=b7/mileage*c7*weight** and press Enter.

4. Using AutoFill, copy the new formula in cell D7 to cells D8 through D16.

5. Paste names into a worksheet by following these steps:

    a. Move to cell A18 in the sheet labeled **User Information**.
    b. Key the label **Constant names** in bold and press Enter.
    c. In cell B19, key **These are the constant names used in the worksheet.**
    d. In cell B21, key **Name** in bold and in cell C21 key **Refers to** in bold.
    e. In cell B22, choose Name from the Insert menu and choose Paste. The Paste Name dialog box appears.
    f. Click the Paste List button.
    g. Change the "Date revised" to today's date and key your name for "Revised by."
    h. Turn off gridlines for viewing.

6. Add the standard header including your name, filename, and date to both worksheets, and center the first worksheet horizontally on the page.

7. Save the workbook as *[your initials]***6-12.xls** in your Lesson 6 folder and print it.

8. Create a standard formula printout in landscape orientation with grids and row and column headings, and close the workbook without saving it.

Lesson Applications

EXERCISE 6-13

Name constants, use names in formulas, define range names, change range names, and paste range names into the worksheet.

Complete and revise Beautiful Belle's fuel estimation worksheet so managers can better control the costs associated with product shipments.

1. Open the file **Freight2.xls**.
2. Enter the data shown in Figure 6-11 (making the corrections shown).

FIGURE 6-11

Seattle	*827*	Van	524
Denver	1270	Light truck	1642
Portland	652	Semi	2159
Albuquerque	1*2*7	Van	312
Los Angeles	403	Semi	*8*2493
Phoenix	800	Semi	2200
Dallas	1806	Semi	3200
Salt Lake City	759	Semi	3200
Mexico City	2419	Semi	2047
Topeka	1811	Van	750

3. Name the following constants:

   Van = 16

   Truck = 10

   Semi = 6

4. Substitute the appropriate names (**Van**, **Truck**, or **Semi**) for the name "mileage" in the Fuel Estimate formulas in column E.

LESSON 6 ■ RANGE NAMES AND SORTING   EXCEL **203**

5. Enter the following labels in cells A18 through A21. Make "Territories" bold.

   Territories

   Northwest

   Southwest

   Midwest

6. Key **Total Fuel** in cell B18 in bold.

7. Define the range name "Northwest" to include the values in the Fuel Estimate column for the following cities: Seattle, Portland, and Salt Lake City.

8. Define the range name "Southwest" to include Fuel Estimates for the following cities: Albuquerque, Los Angeles, Phoenix, and Mexico City.

9. Define the range name "Midwest" to include Fuel Estimates for the following cities: Denver, Dallas, and Topeka.

10. Create a formula using range names to calculate the total estimated fuel for each territory: "Northwest," "Southwest," and "Midwest."

11. Format cells containing formulas (Total Fuel, Fuel Estimates) as Comma style with two decimal places and all other cells containing values as Comma style, no decimals.

12. Paste the range names somewhere at the bottom of the worksheet so your instructor can check your work.

13. Add the standard header including your name, filename, and date, and center the worksheet horizontally on the page.

14. Save the workbook as *[your initials]***6-13.xls** in your Lesson 6 folder and print the worksheet.

15. Create a standard formula printout with gridlines and row and column headings in landscape orientation. (The printout may cut off range name locations. Disregard this for now.) Use a Page 1 of ? footer if the printout exceeds one page.

16. Close the workbook without saving it.

EXERCISE 6-14

Define range names, build formulas using range names, change and delete range names, navigate in a worksheet using range names, and paste range names into the worksheet.

Develop a worksheet that audits selected Beautiful Belle product sales by store.

1. Open the file **Stores.xls**.

2. Define range names for each city in the worksheet by highlighting the corresponding cells in the Amount column.

3. In cells A27 through A33, enter the labels shown below. Format the labels in bold.

   Store Totals
   Dallas
   New York
   Chicago
   San Francisco
   Boston
   Indianapolis

4. Use these range names to build formulas that calculate the total sales for each store. Enter the formulas in column B beside the appropriate label and format the results in Comma style with two decimals.

5. Change the range name "Dallas" to **Denver**.

6. Delete the range name "Dallas."

7. Change the name "Dallas" to **Denver** in the formula that calculates the store total.

8. Change the labels in the Store column and Store Totals column from "Dallas" to **Denver**.

9. Use the Go To command to highlight the Denver sales amounts.

10. Paste the range names somewhere at the bottom of the worksheet so your instructor can check your work.

11. Add the standard header including your name, filename, and date.

12. Save the workbook as *[your initials]***6-14.xls** in your Lesson 6 folder and print the worksheet.

13. Create a standard formula printout with grids and row and column headings and a Page 1 of ? footer.

14. Close the workbook without saving it.

NOTE: The formula printout may cut off range name locations. You can disregard this for now.

EXERCISE 6-15

Create range names, build formulas using range names, paste names into the worksheet, and use the Go To command to navigate in the worksheet.

Construct a worksheet for the Beautiful Belle Company that calculates the total sales and commissions paid over four quarters.

1. Open the file **Cmsions.xls**.

LESSON 6 ■ RANGE NAMES AND SORTING EXCEL **205**

2. In cell C16, use the AutoSum button Σ to add the column.
3. Use Autofill to copy the SUM formula to cells D16 through J16.
4. Create the name **rt** for the constant **.07** (7%).
5. Create formulas using the constant name "rt" in cells D4, F4, H4, and J4 that calculate the commission due for each quarter. Copy the formulas using AutoFill to complete the columns.
6. Create the names **sq1**, **sq2**, **sq3**, and **sq4** for the total sales for each quarter.
7. Create a formula in cell B17 that uses names to calculate the total sales for the year.
8. Create the names **com1**, **com2**, **com3**, and **com4** for the total commissions for each quarter.
9. Use the commission range names to create a formula in cell B18 that calculates the total commissions for the year.
10. In cell B21, paste all the names you created on the worksheet.
11. Key the following information in cells A21, A25, and A26 and make all labels bold.

    commission q1

    commsn rate

    sales q1

12. Use the <u>G</u>o To command to locate the cell named "sq4."
13. Sort the data in rows 4 through 15 in ascending order.
14. Add the standard header including your name, filename, and date and center the worksheet horizontally on the page.
15. Set up the worksheet to print without gridlines in landscape orientation on a single page.

   TIP: On the Page tab in the Page Setup dialog box, activate <u>F</u>it To under Scaling and make sure the number of pages is 1 to have the worksheet fit on one page.

16. Save the workbook as *[your initials]***6-15.xls** in your Lesson 6 folder.
17. Create a standard formula printout with grids and row and column headings and a Page 1 of ? footer.

   TIP: On the Page tab in the Page Setup dialog box, activate <u>A</u>djust To under Scaling and make sure the percentage is 100 so the printout does not fit on one page.

18. Close the workbook without saving it.

EXERCISE 6-16 — Challenge Yourself

Name cells, create formulas using named cells, and paste range names into the user documentation.

In an effort to understand its expenses by region, the Beautiful Belle Company needs to calculate quarterly, biannual, and yearly total expenses based on its 1999 expense information.

1. Create a worksheet sketch that includes a title, row and column labels, and an area for data and formulas. The worksheet should include January through December expense information (columns) for the Southeast, Northeast, and Northwest regions (rows). (*Hint:* Use abbreviations and start a new section for the second half of the year below the first section.) There should also be row labels for monthly totals, totals for each quarter, and half-year totals for each section. Use F for formula locations.

2. Transfer the sketch into Excel by keying and formatting the labels including the title. Key the data from Figure 6-12 in the worksheet formatted in Comma style, no decimals.

FIGURE 6-12

	Jan	Feb	Mar	Apr	May	Jun
S.E.	32,098	189,074	156,976	82,514	188,365	174,958
N.E.	11,098	294,651	192,634	99,254	201,648	89,254
N.W.	132,098	486,277	326,584	135,698	543,958	142,360

	Jul	Aug	Sept	Oct	Nov	Dec
S.E.	124,725	93,581	54,321	42,587	748,512	154,879
N.E.	124,521	84,516	68,954	859,641	365,894	254,369
N.W.	123,695	99,365	67,987	102,587	411,758	254,879

3. Include calculations for monthly total expenses.
4. Name each cell containing a monthly total.
5. Below the monthly data, use your range names to calculate quarterly expenses based on the monthly totals for all regions.
6. Below the quarterly totals, use cell names to calculate half-year expenses.

LESSON 6 ■ RANGE NAMES AND SORTING

7. Format all the cells containing values in Comma style with no decimal places.
8. Format the cells above monthly totals with bottom borders.
9. Rename Sheet1 **Regions,** Sheet 2 **User Information**, and delete Sheet 3.
10. On the User Information worksheet, create the following:

    File Information (with the following subheads: **Created by**, **Date created**, **Date revised**, **Revised by**, **Contact for help**)

    Purpose/Description of Worksheet *[Use a paragraph form]*

    Instructions to User *[Add special instructions needed by the user to enter data correctly]*

    Range Names *[Provide the names used in the worksheet and their location]*

11. Style the documentation for easy reading.
12. Add the standard header including your name, filename, and date to both worksheets, and center the Regions worksheet horizontally on the page.
13. Save the workbook as *[your initials]***6-16.xls** in your Lesson 6 folder.
14. Print the entire workbook, then create a standard formula printout in landscape orientation with grids and row and column headings. Use the Page 1 of ? footer for multiple pages. Do not fit the formula printout on one page.
15. Close the workbook without saving it.

LESSON 7

Spelling, Find/Replace, and File Management

OBJECTIVES

After completing this lesson, you will be able to:
1. Check spelling.
2. Use AutoCorrect.
3. Find and replace data.
4. Find files.
5. Rename, copy, and delete files.

MOUS ACTIVITIES
In this lesson:
XL2000 **1.8**
XL2000 **2.7**
XL2000 **5.6**

See Appendix F.

Estimated Time: 1 hour

Creating and building a workbook is only the beginning of effective data management and analysis. You must make your workbooks accurate and easy to use, and Excel can help. Excel provides automated dictionaries to check your spelling. It also provides a Find and Replace function you can use to make global changes and revisions.

Excel's Open dialog box lets you find files easily and offers many file management functions.

Checking Spelling

Excel's spell-checker scans the active worksheet and highlights words not found in any of its dictionaries. It also finds repeated words. A Spelling dialog

LESSON 7 ■ SPELLING, FIND/REPLACE, AND FILE MANAGEMENT   EXCEL **209**

box provides a choice of options for handling the highlighted word, as shown in Table 7-1.

TABLE 7-1 **Spell-Checking Options**

BUTTON	ACTION
Ignore	Do not take any action; do not change the spelling. If it is a repeated word, do not delete or change it.
Ignore All	Do not take any action for all occurrences of this word in the worksheet.
Change	Change the current spelling of this word to the spelling highlighted in the Change To box.
Delete	Delete a repeated word.
Change All	Change all occurrences of this word to the spelling highlighted in the Change To box.
Add	Add this word to the dictionary. Once added, Excel no longer highlights this word as "Not in Dictionary."
Suggest	Display a list of proposed suggestions.
Undo Last	Reverse the last action.
Cancel/Close	End spell-checking.
AutoCorrect	Add to the list of corrections that AutoCorrect makes as you key text in a worksheet.

You can customize the spell-checker so it works smarter for you. Adding words to a dictionary is especially useful for worksheets that contain data from specific fields, such as law, real estate, or science. You can also turn off the Suggestions list box choice and ignore words that contain numbers or all uppercase letters.

EXERCISE 7-1 Spell-Check the Entire Worksheet

Excel begins spell-checking at the active cell. If you begin spell-checking in the middle of the worksheet, a dialog box appears when the spell-checker reaches the end. You can continue spell-checking at the beginning of the worksheet.

1. Open the file **Change%2.xls**.
2. Select cell A1 to begin spell-checking from the beginning of the worksheet.

3. Choose Spelling from the Tools menu or press F7. Excel locates the first word not found in its dictionary, "Introducsion." The correct spelling appears in both the Change To text box and the Suggestions drop-down list box.

FIGURE 7-1
Spelling dialog box

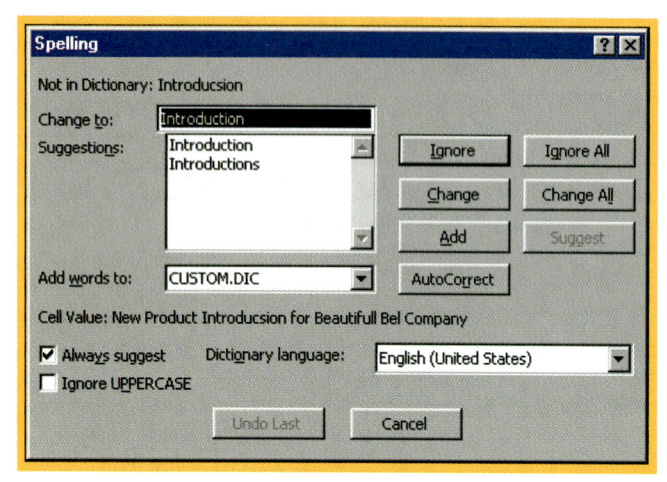

4. Click Change. Excel changes the word to "Introduction" and locates the next word not found in its dictionary.

> **TIP:** You may want to view a word in the worksheet before you change its spelling. To move the Spelling dialog box, drag its title bar.

5. Continue spell-checking until you reach the end of the worksheet. Click Ignore if no change is required. If the correct spelling appears in the Suggestions drop-down list box but not in the Change To text box, select the correct word from the list and click Change.

> **NOTE:** If the correct word does not appear in the drop-down list, key it directly into the Change To text box and click Change.

6. When the spell-check is completed, click OK in the dialog box.

EXERCISE 7-2 Spell-Check a Range in the Worksheet

To spell-check a range in a worksheet, highlight the range to be checked and choose Spelling from the Tools menu (or press F7, or click the Spelling button on the Standard toolbar). Excel checks only the highlighted range.

1. Move to the User Information sheet and select cells A1 through D7.

LESSON 7 ■ SPELLING, FIND/REPLACE, AND FILE MANAGEMENT   EXCEL **211**

2. Click the Spelling button on the Standard toolbar. The Spelling dialog box appears. Excel locates "Creted," the first word in the selected range not found in its dictionary.

3. Click "Created" in the Suggestio_n_s drop-down list box, if necessary, and click _C_hange to change the misspelled word to "Created." Excel locates "Dat," the next word not found in its dictionary.

4. Click "Date" in the Suggestio_n_s drop-down list box, if necessary, and click _C_hange.

5. Click _C_hange to correct "Revisd" to "Revised."

6. Click "by" in the Suggestions drop-down list and click _C_hange. A dialog box appears when the spell-check of the range is complete.

7. Click OK and deselect the range.

Using AutoCorrect

The AutoCorrect feature automatically corrects your spelling as you key text. You can customize AutoCorrect by adding words you commonly misspell to Excel's list. You can also turn off AutoCorrect, if desired.

EXERCISE 7-3   Use AutoCorrect to Correct Typos

1. Choose _A_utoCorrect from the _T_ools menu. (Remember, you may have to expand the menu.) The AutoCorrect dialog box appears.

FIGURE 7-2
AutoCorrect dialog box

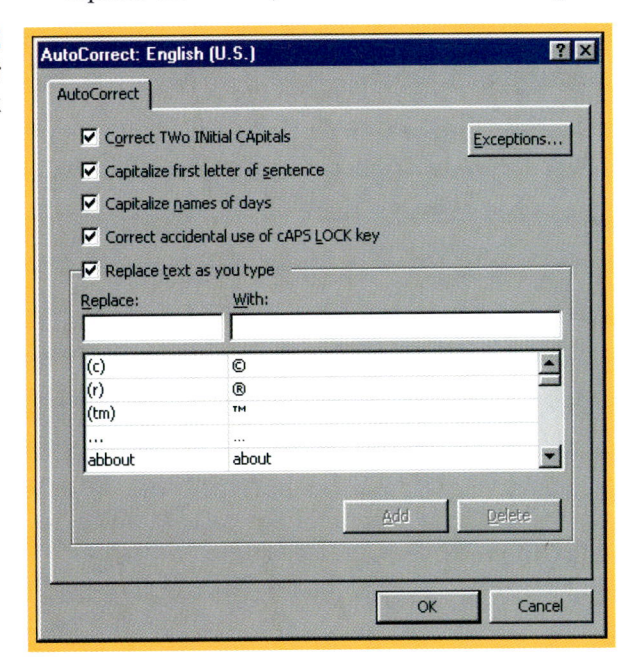

2. Clear the Replace Text As You Type check box and click OK. The AutoCorrect feature is deselected and Excel will not correct spelling automatically.

3. Key **Purpse** in bold in cell A9 and press Enter. Remember to key the word exactly as shown. With AutoCorrect deselected, the spelling error is not corrected.

4. Choose AutoCorrect from the Tools menu.

5. Click the Replace Text As You Type check box to select it and click OK. AutoCorrect becomes active again, but does not correct existing text.

6. Key the following text in cell B10 exactly as shown to see AutoCorrect at work:

   Analyze teh sale groth of new product line

   AutoCorrect changes the word "teh" to "the" as you type. Note, however, that the misspelled word "groth" was not corrected. In addition, errors in sentence syntax, such as the word "sale" in this entry, are not corrected by AutoCorrect or the spell-checker.

EXERCISE 7-4 Add AutoCorrect Entries for Your Common Typos

You can have AutoCorrect automatically correct a word you misspell often. Simply add the misspelling and its correction to AutoCorrect's list of words.

1. Select cells A9 through B10.

2. Click the Spelling button. Excel suggests "Purpose" to correct the first word in the range that does not match its dictionary.

3. Double-click "Purpose" in the Suggestions drop-down list box (another way to select a word). Excel finds "groth," the next word in the range not found in its dictionary. Select "growth" in the Suggestions drop-down list box.

4. Click AutoCorrect. Excel changes the spelling of the word and adds this correction to AutoCorrect's list of words to correct as you type. A dialog box appears when the spell-check of the range is complete.

5. Click OK.

6. Move to cell B10 and change the word "sale" to **sales**.

7. Choose AutoCorrect from the Tools menu.

8. Key the following words in the Replace and With text boxes and click Add. Be sure to type the words exactly as shown.

   produtc   product

LESSON 7 ■ SPELLING, FIND/REPLACE, AND FILE MANAGEMENT   EXCEL   **213**

FIGURE 7-3
Adding a new AutoCorrect listing

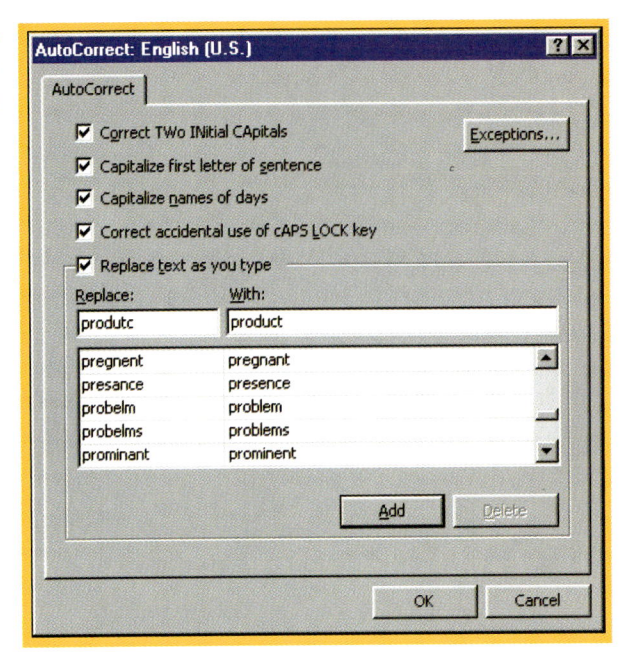

9. Scroll up the Replace and With text boxes to confirm that the word "groth" was added to the AutoCorrect list.
10. Choose "groth," and click Delete to remove it from the list.
11. Click OK, return to cell A1, and turn off gridlines for viewing.

> **TIP:** You can also use AutoCorrect to create abbreviations that speed data entry. For example, assume that you type the phrase "Pending Release" frequently in your worksheets. Just add the abbreviation "pr" to the Replace text box and the full phrase "Pending Release" to the With text box in the AutoCorrect dialog box.

Finding and Replacing Data

Find and Replace are handy tools for updating worksheets. Find locates occurrences of a *character string*—a sequence of characters in a formula or text. You can use Find to return to a particular location in a worksheet, to verify that text is consistent, or to check that a formula appears in all intended locations.

Replace locates occurrences of a character string and replaces them, either one at a time or globally. As a result, it can change a formula that occurs in multiple cells. You can also use Replace to change repeated labels, such as a category or product name.

EXERCISE 7-5 Find Data in a Worksheet

You can use the Find command in relatively long worksheets that contain too many formulas and values to check individually. Find is especially useful in locating all instances of a formula or error in a worksheet. Excel uses the asterisk (*) as a *wildcard* symbol, which instructs Excel to allow any combination of letters or numbers to replace it. If, for example, Excel was searching for 7-*, it would locate 7-1, 7-2, 7-A, 7-SOFT, and so on.

All error values begin with # (the number sign), so you can key # in the Find What text box to locate error values in a worksheet. You can also look for specific error values, such as #DIV/0!, the error value produced if you try to divide by zero.

1. Move to the Sun Soft worksheet and choose Find from the Edit menu or press Ctrl+F. The Find dialog box appears.

FIGURE 7-4
Find dialog box

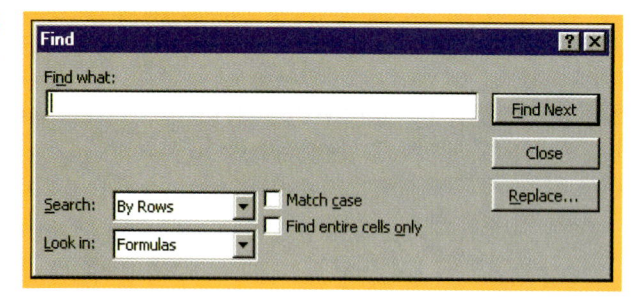

2. Key **=SUM(C7:C10)** in the Find What text box.
3. Choose Formulas from the Look In drop-down list box, if necessary. Make sure the Match Case box is not checked so Excel does not try to match the case (upper or lower) of the word you keyed.
4. Click Find Next. Excel finds the formula in cell C12 and displays the cell reference in the Name box and the formula in the Formula bar.

> **TIP:** Drag the Find dialog box out of the way so you can see the selected cell in the worksheet.

5. Edit the text in the Find What text box to read **=SUM(*7:*10)** and click Find Next. Excel selects cell D12.
6. Click Find Next to find the next occurrence of the formula. Excel selects cell B12.

> **NOTE:** You cannot edit the worksheet when the Find dialog box is open. If you close the Find dialog box, however, you can repeat the last search by pressing F4.

LESSON 7 ■ SPELLING, FIND/REPLACE, AND FILE MANAGEMENT EXCEL **215**

7. Click <u>F</u>ind Next. Excel selects cell C12 again.
8. Choose Values from the <u>L</u>ook In drop-down list.
9. Key **#** in the Fi<u>n</u>d What text box (replacing the formula) and click <u>F</u>ind Next. Excel finds cell E7, which contains a formula that attempts to perform division by zero. (The formula "C7/B7" is a division by zero, because cell B7 is empty.)
10. Close the Find dialog box.
11. In cell B7, key **57,809** to correct the error.

EXERCISE 7-6 Replace Data in a Worksheet

You can replace character strings globally or one at a time.

1. Select cell A6 and choose <u>R</u>eplace from the <u>E</u>dit menu (or press `Ctrl`+`H`). The Replace dialog box appears. The Fi<u>n</u>d What text box contains # (the number sign), which is the last entry in the Find dialog box.

FIGURE 7-5
Replace dialog box

Most recent Find string

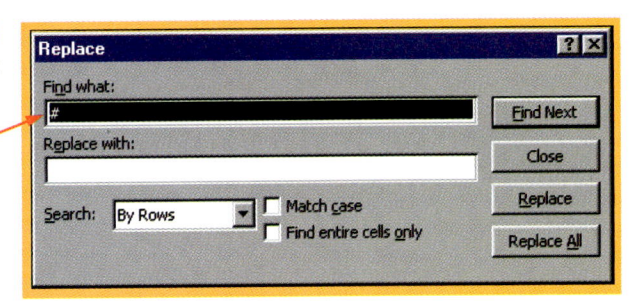

2. Key **1997** in the Fi<u>n</u>d What text box (replacing #), press `Tab`, and key **Year 1** in the <u>R</u>eplace With text box.
3. Click <u>F</u>ind Next.

TIP: Drag the Replace dialog box out of the way so you can see the selected cell in the worksheet.

4. Click <u>R</u>eplace. The worksheet displays "Year 1" in cell B6.
5. Close the Replace dialog box. Select cell B6 and right-align the label.
6. Choose <u>F</u>ind from the <u>E</u>dit menu, edit the date in the Fi<u>n</u>d What text box to read **1998**, and click <u>F</u>ind Next. Cell C6 is selected.
7. Click <u>R</u>eplace to expand the Find dialog box to the Replace dialog box.
8. Make the <u>R</u>eplace With text box read **Year 2** and choose Replace A<u>l</u>l. Both occurrences of "1998" are replaced with "Year 2."

9. Choose Replace from the Edit menu. Edit the Find What box to read **1999** and edit the Replace With box to read **Year 3**.
10. Click Find Next. Excel moves to cell D6.
11. Click Replace and Excel moves to cell F6.
12. Click Replace.
13. Close the Replace dialog box and right-align the rest of the column labels on row 6.
14. Change the title text in cell A3 to **Year 1-Year 3** and the text in cell A15 to reflect the same.

FIGURE 7-6
Revised worksheet

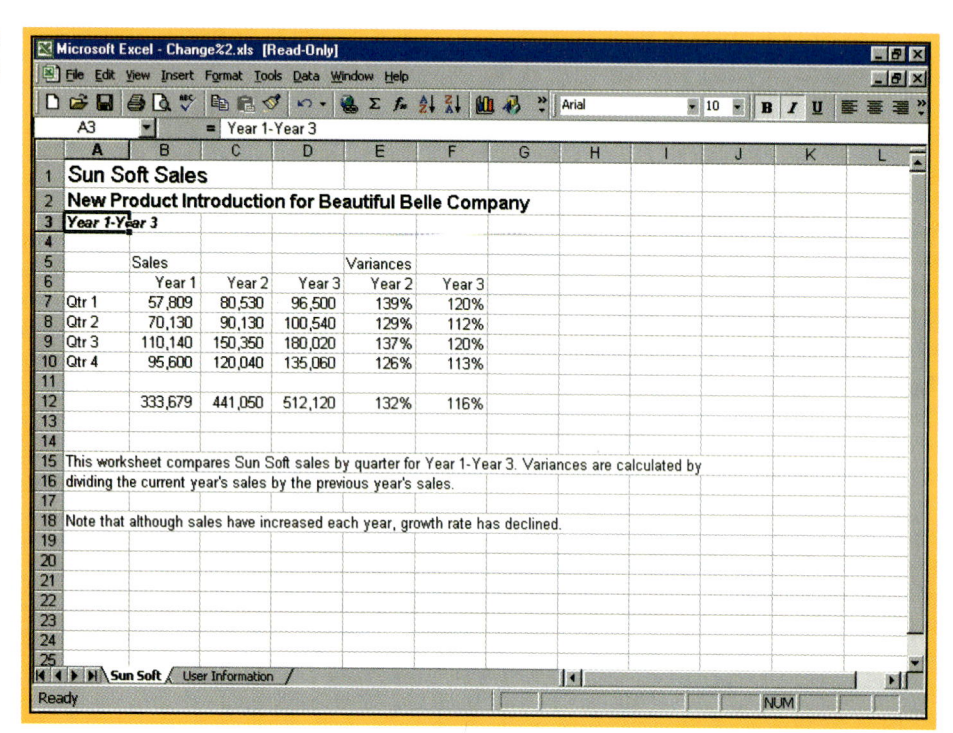

15. Add the standard header with your name, filename, and date to both worksheets and make the Sun Soft worksheet active if it is not already.
16. Save the workbook as *[your initials]***7-6.xls** in a new folder for Lesson 7.
17. Print the entire workbook and then close it.

Finding Files

You can use Excel's Open dialog box to find a file, even if you do not remember its exact name. You can also display different types of details about files to determine which file to open.

LESSON 7 ■ SPELLING, FIND/REPLACE, AND FILE MANAGEMENT   EXCEL **217**

TABLE 7-2   Open Dialog Box Buttons

BUTTON	BUTTON NAME/ACTION
⬅	*Back* changes the current location in the Look In text box to the last folder viewed.
🔼	*Up One Level* moves up the file tree shown in the Look In drop-down list.
🔍	*Search the Web* accesses the World Wide Web.
✕	*Delete* removes the selected file or files.
📁	*Create New Folder* adds a new folder to the current location.
⊞	*Views* offers a menu of viewing options for displaying filenames and folders.
Tools	*Tools* offers a menu of options.

If you choose Find from the Tools menu and check the Search Subfolders checkbox, Excel searches in the current folder and any subfolders.

You can also have Excel search for files that contain specific words or phrases. To take this approach, choose Find from the Tools menu, select "Contents" from the Property drop-down list, select "includes words" from the Condition drop-down list, key the text in the Value text box, and click Add to List before you start your search.

EXERCISE 7-7 Find a Workbook

Excel can search for specific filenames or for filenames containing a certain pattern. For example, you can search for all filenames with a specific prefix or extension.

1. Click the Open button 📂 or choose Open from the File menu or press Ctrl+O. The Open dialog box appears.
2. Specify the location of your student files in the Look In drop-down list.

> **NOTE:** If you are unsure of the location to use in the above step, ask your instructor.

3. Choose All Microsoft Excel Files from the Files of Type drop-down list, if necessary.

4. Choose Find from the Tools drop-down list to open the Find dialog box that is used specifically to find files.
5. Key **Sales*** in the Value text box. Click Add to List.

> **TIP:** The asterisk * is the wildcard character, so Sales* means any filename beginning with "Sales". You could key *[your initials]*6* to search for all your answer files in Lesson 6, for example.

FIGURE 7-7
Finding files

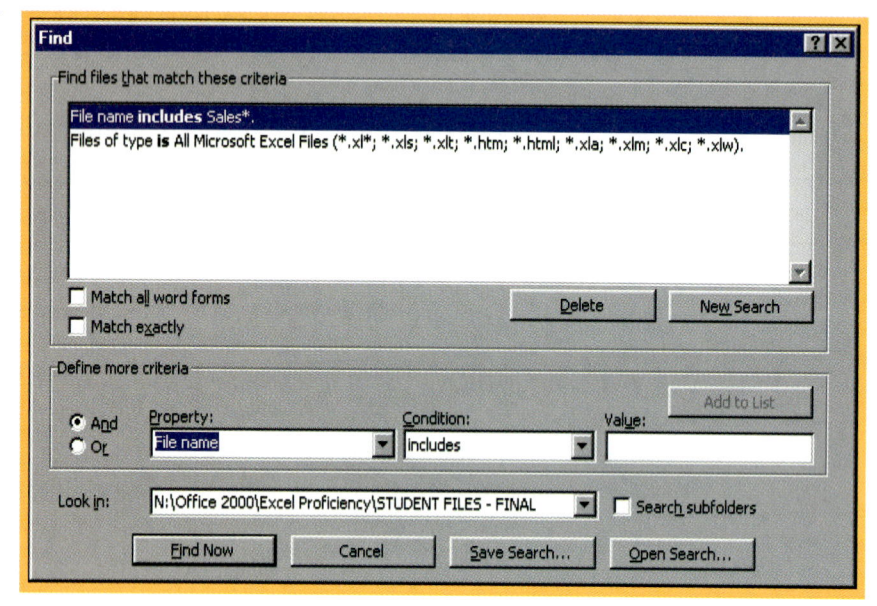

6. Click Find Now. The Open dialog box appears with a list of all Excel-type filenames that begin with "Sales."
7. Click Cancel.

> **TIP:** When you double-click the Find Fast icon in the Windows Control Panel, you open the Find Fast utility. Find Fast creates indexes to speed up file searches by content, properties, or both. For information about using Find Fast, refer to Help in the Find Fast dialog box.

Renaming, Copying, and Deleting Files

You can open, copy, print, rename, or delete files directly from the Open dialog box. However, when a file is already open, you cannot rename it.

LESSON 7 ■ SPELLING, FIND/REPLACE, AND FILE MANAGEMENT   EXCEL **219**

EXERCISE 7-8 Rename, Copy, and Delete a File Using the Open Dialog Box

1. Click the Open button 📂. In the Open dialog box, locate the file *[your initials]***7-6.xls**, which you saved earlier in this lesson. Click the file once to select it, but do not open it.

2. Choose the Preview option from the Views drop-down list 🔽. The upper left corner of the selected file appears in the Preview box.

FIGURE 7-8
File preview in the Open dialog box

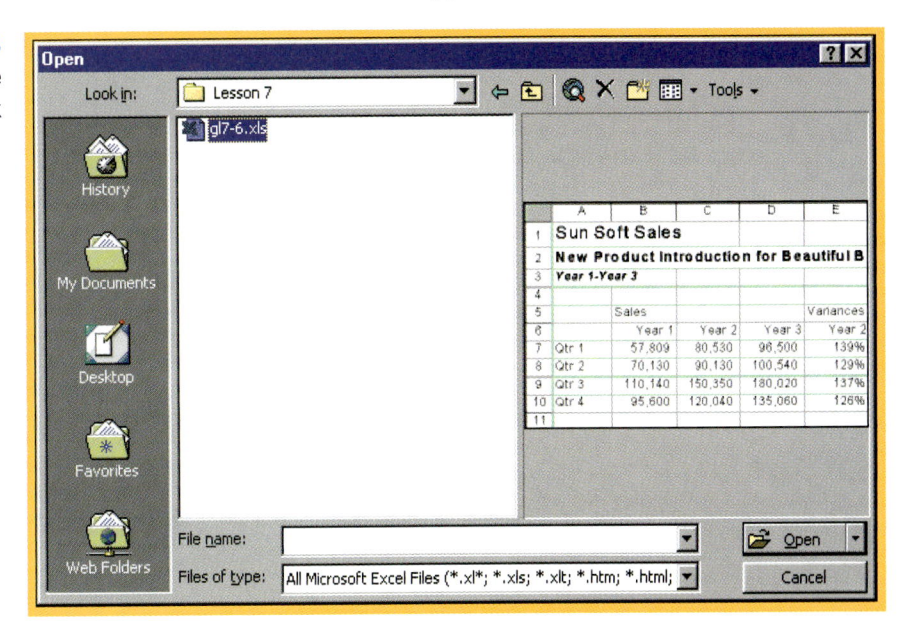

3. With the file *[your initials]***7-6.xls** still selected, press Ctrl+C. The file is copied to the Clipboard (there is no change on the screen, however).

4. Press Ctrl+V to paste a copy of the file into the current folder.

5. Click the file **Copy of *[your initials]*7-6.xls** to select it, if necessary, and choose Print from the Tools drop-down list.

6. Excel opens the file, prints the active worksheet in the workbook, and then closes the file and the Open dialog box.

TIP: You can also right-click a filename and choose Print from the shortcut menu.

7. Click the Open button 📂 to open the Open dialog box again.

8. Right-click the file **Copy of *[your initials]*7-6.xls** to open the shortcut menu.

9. Choose Rename, key *[your initials]***7-8.xls** (making sure to key the ".xls"), and press Enter. Excel changes the filename.

> **NOTE:** Be sure to key the file extension (.xls) when you rename a file. Otherwise, that file cannot be recognized as a file of its type.

10. Select the file *[your initials]*7-8.xls, if necessary.
11. Click the Delete button ⊠. A dialog box appears asking if you're sure you want to delete the file.
12. Click Yes. The file is deleted.

> **TIP:** You can also press Delete or choose Delete from the shortcut menu.

13. Open the Views drop-down list and choose List.
14. Close the Open dialog box.

> **TIP:** You may want to access other information about your files. Explore the other options available in the Tools drop-down list.

COMMAND SUMMARY

FEATURE	BUTTON	MENU	KEYBOARD
Spell-check		Tools, Spelling	F7
Find		Edit, Find	Ctrl + F
Replace		Edit, Replace	Ctrl + H
Repeat (last) Find			F4
AutoCorrect		Tools, AutoCorrect	
Find and Manage files		File, Open	Ctrl + O

USING HELP

Suppose you need to get data from an Excel worksheet to someone in another city quickly. One way to accomplish this is to send the worksheet via e-mail. To find out more about using the e-mail feature (including the system requirements for mailing workbooks and worksheets), search "e-mail" in Help. Locate the topic "Distribute workbooks and worksheets to other people."

NOTE: Before you send e-mail, consult your instructor to make sure your computer is correctly set up and that you have an appropriate e-mail address to use. Individual configurations may cause the E-Mail feature to work differently than described below.

To send a workbook via e-mail:

1. With an Excel worksheet open, click the E-Mail button on the Standard toolbar. The E-Mail toolbar appears.

FIGURE 7-9
E-Mail toolbar

2. In the "To" box, enter the recipient's name. (If there is more than one, separate them by commas). Do the same for the "Cc" box.

TIP: To select a recipient (for either the "To" box or the "Cc" box), click the icon next the "To" box or the "Cc" box. You could also use the Address button to review names in your Address book.

3. Key a Subject for the e-mail. (In some configurations, the title of the Workbook may appear on the "Subject" line. In others, the last "Subject" may appear.)

4. Set the options you want for this message. For example, you can specify the urgency of the e-mail using the Set Priority button.

NOTE: You could also attach an entire Workbook to an e-mail using the Attach File button.

5. Click Send this Sheet. Your e-mail is sent and the E-Mail toolbar closes.

6. Close the worksheet.

Concepts Review

TRUE/FALSE QUESTIONS

Each of the following statements is either true or false. Indicate your choice by circling T or F.

T F **1.** Excel's spell-checker automatically deletes repeated words.

T F **2.** You access the <u>F</u>ind and <u>O</u>pen commands from the same menu.

T F **3.** You can add words to customize Excel's spell-checking dictionaries.

T F **4.** A character string is a sequence of characters in a formula or worksheet text.

T F **5.** All error values in Excel begin with the number sign (#).

T F **6.** You can use a <u>w</u>ildcard to find and replace data or to find files.

T F **7.** AutoCorrect identifies common typos and automatically changes them to the correct spelling.

T F **8.** Using the Open dialog box, you can copy worksheets, but you can't print them.

SHORT ANSWER QUESTIONS

Write the correct answer in the space provided.

1. Which key starts Excel's spell-checker?

_____

2. Which menu commands do you use to open the Replace dialog box?

_____

3. Which keystroke combination do you use to open the Find dialog box?

_____

4. Which Excel dialog box offers file-management tools?

_____

LESSON 7 ■ SPELLING, FIND/REPLACE, AND FILE MANAGEMENT   EXCEL **223**

  5. Which keystroke combination do you use to access the Open dialog box?

  6. How do you instruct Excel to allow any combination of letters or numbers to replace a symbol in a search?

  7. How do you look at a worksheet without opening it?

  8. How do you print from the Open dialog box?

CRITICAL THINKING

Answer these questions on a separate piece of paper. There are no right or wrong answers. Support your answer with examples from your own experience, if possible.

  1. Describe a work situation in which Excel's Replace feature would be useful. Can Replace All be too much of a good thing?
  2. What are the implications of features such as AutoCorrect that seem to do the thinking for you?

Skills Review

EXERCISE 7-9

Spell-check a worksheet, spell-check a range, and correct typos with AutoCorrect.

  1. Open the file **MktExp.xls**.
  2. Spell-check the worksheet by following these steps:
   a. Move to cell A1, if necessary, and click the Spelling button.
   b. Select or key appropriate spellings in the Change To text box and click Change. Remember Excel's suggested replacement may not be the correct word for your worksheet.
   c. Click OK when the spell-check is finished.
  3. Key the text as shown in Figure 7-10 on the next page, starting at cell A16.

FIGURE 7-10

	A	B	C	D	E
16	Pacifica	9200	9800	10000	12000
17	Taos	5000	5000	7500	8500
18	High Sierra	3000	4000	6000	7500
19	Carmel	9550	9550	12500	12500
20	Santa Barbara	2300	2500	6000	9000

4. Key **Total** in cell F15.
5. Spell-check the range you just entered using these steps:
   a. Select cells A16 through E20.
   b. Choose **S**pelling from the **T**ools menu (or press F7).
   c. Change any misspelled words. If you're a good typist, the range may not include any misspelled words. Remember, Excel's suggested replacement may not be the correct word for your worksheet.
   d. Click OK when the spell-check is finished.
6. Enter formulas to find the product and quarterly totals by following these steps:
   a. Select cell F7. Click the AutoSum button Σ twice.
   b. Copy this formula to cells F8 through F12 using AutoFill.
   c. Select cell B12. Click the AutoSum button Σ twice.
   d. Copy this formula to cells C12 through E12 using AutoFill.
   e. Copy the range F7 through F12 to cells F16 through F21 by dragging the range.
   f. Use the AutoSum button Σ to calculate totals in cells B21 through E21.
7. Key **Subtotal** in cell A21.
8. Use AutoCorrect to correct typos by keying the following text, exactly as shown, in cell A24:
   Acn we acheive any ohter cost savings in teh third quater?
9. Format the individual product expenses in Comma style with no decimal places.
10. Format the totals in Currency style with no decimal places.
11. Add the standard header with your name, filename, and date, and center the worksheet horizontally on the page.

LESSON 7 ■ SPELLING, FIND/REPLACE, AND FILE MANAGEMENT   EXCEL   **225**

12. Save the workbook as *[your initials]***7-9.xls** in your Lesson 7 folder and print the worksheet.
13. Create a formula printout that fits on one page in landscape orientation with grids and row and column headings. (*Hint:* Use the Fit To feature in the Page Setup dialog box.)
14. Close the workbook without saving it.

EXERCISE 7-10

Use AutoCorrect to correct common typos, and find and replace values in a formula.

1. Open the workbook **AdCosts.xls**.
2. Use AutoCorrect for common typos by following these steps:
   a. Choose AutoCorrect from the Tools menu.
   b. Key the following words in the Replace and With text boxes and click Add. Be sure to type the words exactly as shown.

   diretc   **direct**

   mial   **mail**

   c. Click OK.
3. Key the following misspelling in cell A10 and watch AutoCorrect at work:

   Diretc Mial
4. Key the following amounts in the cells indicated:

   B10: **1000**   D10: **1500**   E10: **2000**
5. Copy the formula from cell F9 to cells F10 and F11 using AutoFill.
6. Find and replace data in the worksheet using these steps:
   a. Select cell A1 and choose Find from the Edit menu.
   b. Key **=SUM(*7:*9)** in the Find What text box.
   c. Choose Formulas from the Look in drop-down list box, if necessary. Make sure the Match Case box is not checked.
   d. Click Find Next. Excel finds the formula in cell C11.
   e. Click Replace.
   f. In the Replace With text box key **=SUM(C7:C10)** and then click Replace.
   g. Click Close.
7. Format all values in Comma style with no decimal places.
8. Delete the AutoCorrect entries you made in this exercise by following these steps:
   a. Choose AutoCorrect from the Tools menu.
   b. Select "diretc" in the scroll box and click Delete.

c. Select "mial" in the scroll box and click Delete.
   d. Click OK.
9. Add the standard header with your name, filename, and date, and center the worksheet horizontally on the page.
10. Save the workbook as *[your initials]*7-10.xls in your Lesson 7 folder and print the worksheet.
11. Create a formula printout in landscape orientation with grids and row and column headings that fits on one page. (*Hint:* Use the Fit To feature in the Page Setup dialog box.)
12. Close the workbook without saving it.

EXERCISE 7-11

Find and open a file, and find and replace data.

1. Find a file containing the word "inventory" and open it by following these steps:
   a. Click the Open button.
   b. Choose the drive containing your student files (if necessary) from the Look in drop-down list box or key the location directly in the text box.
   c. Click Tools and click Find.
   d. Key **Inv** in the Value text box and click Add to List. Click Find Now.
   e. Open the file **InvntyQ1.xls**.
2. Find and replace data in the worksheet using these steps:
   a. In cell A1, choose Replace from the Edit menu.
   b. Key **subtotal** in the Find What text box.
   c. Key **Monthly subtotal** in the Replace With text box.
   d. Select By Columns from the Search drop-down list box.
   e. Click Find Next. Excel selects cell A13.
   f. Click Replace. Excel selects cell A22.
   g. Move the Replace dialog box out of the way to see the selected cell, if necessary.
   h. Click Replace again. Excel selects cell E6.
3. Change the text to be replaced by following these steps:
   a. Key **Product subtotal** in the Replace With text box.
   b. With cell E6 selected, click Replace. Excel selects cell E16.
   c. Click Replace again.
   d. Click Close.
4. Add the standard header with your name, filename, and date.
5. Save the workbook as *[your initials]*7-11.xls in your Lesson 7 folder and print the worksheet.

LESSON 7 ■ SPELLING, FIND/REPLACE, AND FILE MANAGEMENT   EXCEL   **227**

   6. Create a formula printout in landscape orientation with grids and row and column headings.
   7. Close the workbook without saving it.

EXERCISE 7-12

Use the Open dialog box to copy, rename, and delete a file; use the Open dialog box to print a file.

   1. Open the file **COGS.xls** and save it as *[your initials]***7-cogs.xls** in your Lesson 7 folder. Close the workbook.
   2. Copy a file using the Open dialog box by following these steps:
       a. Open the Open dialog box.
       b. Open the Views drop-down list and choose List, if necessary.
       c. Click the icon for the file *[your initials]***7-cogs.xls** to select it and press Ctrl + C.
       d. Press Ctrl + V to paste a copy of the file into the same drive or folder.
   3. Rename a file using the Open dialog box by following these steps:
       a. Right-click the file **Copy of** *[your initials]***7-cogs.xls** to open the shortcut menu.
       b. Choose Rename, key *[your initials]***7-12.xls**, and press Enter.
   4. Copy this file, *[your initials]***7-12.xls**, into its current folder (see steps 1c and 1d).
   5. Print the copy of your file using the Open dialog box by following these steps:
       a. Click the file **Copy of** *[your initials]***7-12.xls** to select it, if necessary.
       b. Choose Print from the Tools drop-down list.
   6. Delete the copy of your file by following these steps:
       a. Open the Open dialog box and click the file **Copy of** *[your initials]***7-12.xls** to select it.
       b. Press Delete. A dialog box appears asking if you're sure you want to delete the file.
       c. Click Yes.
       d. Perform these steps again to delete the file *[your initials]***7-cogs.xls**.
       e. Close the Open dialog box.

Lesson Applications

EXERCISE 7-13

Find and open a file, find and replace data, and spell-check a worksheet.

Correct and complete Beautiful Belle's cost of goods sold worksheet for the second quarter.

1. Find and open **COGS2.xls**.
2. Key the values for fragrances as shown in Figure 7-11.

FIGURE 7-11

	A	B	C	D
15	Pacifica	6652	1665	9816
16	Taos	6654	4455	224
17	High Sierra	6698	4334	7358
18	Carmel	211	3669	10322
19	Santa Barbara	3983	1112	4983

3. Use AutoSum and AutoFill to enter formulas that calculate monthly and product subtotals for the new data.
4. Replace the month labels "Jan," "Feb," and "Mar" with **Apr**, **May**, and **Jun**, respectively.
5. Spell-check the entire worksheet, correcting any misspellings.
6. Add the standard header with your name, filename, and date, and center the worksheet horizontally on the page.
7. Save the workbook as *[your initials]*7-13.xls in your Lesson 7 folder and print the worksheet.
8. Create a formula printout in landscape orientation with grids and row and column headings.
9. Close the workbook without saving it.

LESSON 7 ■ SPELLING, FIND/REPLACE, AND FILE MANAGEMENT   EXCEL **229**

EXERCISE 7-14

Find and open a file, use AutoCorrect to convert abbreviations into words, and use the Open dialog box to rename and print a file.

Create a worksheet showing the sales history for the Carmel product line.

1. Find and open the file **Carmel.xls**.
2. Use AutoCorrect to convert the following abbreviations into complete words:

Abbreviation	Complete word
Qtr	**Quarter**
Tot	**Total**

3. Key the data as shown in Figure 7-12. Bold and center-align the column labels.

FIGURE 7-12

	A	B	C	D	E	F
5		Qtr 1	Qtr 2	Qtr 3	Qtr 4	Tot
6	1997	26544	25799	30124	35666	
7	1998	30118	69765	45625	50217	
8	1999	54339	26001	35612	58378	

4. Enter formulas to find the annual and quarterly totals.
5. Format the values in Comma style with no decimal places.
6. Spell-check the worksheet.
7. Delete the AutoCorrect entries you made in this exercise (Qtr and Tot).
8. Add the standard header with your name, filename, and date, and center the worksheet horizontally on the page.
9. Save the workbook as *[your initials]***7-sales.xls** in your Lesson 7 folder and close it.
10. Use the Open dialog box to rename the file *[your initials]***7-sales.xls** as *[your initials]***7-14.xls**.
11. Print the worksheet from the Open dialog box.

EXERCISE 7-15

Find and open a file, find and replace data, spell-check a worksheet, and print a workbook from the Open dialog box.

The Beautiful Belle Company's product sales analysis should be for the year 1999, not 1998. In addition, the company president wants to change the terms "Men" and "Women" in the worksheet to "Males" and "Females."

1. Find and open the file **Compare2.xls**.
2. Replace the column label **Men** with **Males**.
3. Replace the column label **Women** with **Females**.
4. Replace all occurrences of **1998** with **1999** (including the weekly dates where the year is not displayed).
5. Spell-check the worksheet.
6. Check the dates in cell A23 to verify the change in year.
7. Add the standard header with your name, filename, and date.
8. Save the workbook as *[your initials]*7-15.xls in your Lesson 7 folder and close it.
9. Print the worksheet from the Open dialog box.
10. Open the file *[your initials]*7-15.xls and save it as *[your initials]*7-15.htm.
11. Close the workbook.

EXERCISE 7-16   Challenge Yourself

Find and open a file, replace labels, spell-check a worksheet, and use the Open dialog box to rename and print a worksheet.

In this exercise, you create a six-month sales comparison for Sun Soft sales based on men and women. Unfortunately, you key in an incorrect six-month period and several spelling errors. So you enter the correct six-month period and correct your spelling errors. In addition, you use the Open dialog box to copy, rename, and print the worksheet.

1. Sketch on paper a worksheet for a six-month sales comparison for Sun Soft sales based on men and women. Create a title, column labels for comparison, and monthly row labels with the months Jun., Jul., Aug., Sept., Oct., and Nov. Include a place for totals for the months and for gender.

LESSON 7 ■ SPELLING, FIND/REPLACE, AND FILE MANAGEMENT   EXCEL **231**

2. Transfer your sketch to Excel and format the title and labels accordingly.
3. Insert the data in Figure 7-13 and format the numbers in Comma style, no decimals. Correct the row labels as shown.

FIGURE 7-13

	Women	Men
Jul. ~~Jun~~	2500	4200
Aug. ~~Jul~~	5000	4000
Sep. ~~Aug~~	6500	2000
Oct. ~~Aug~~	5500	2000
Nov. ~~Sept~~	6000	2800
Dec. ~~Nov~~	5600	4000

4. Create formulas that calculate month totals and gender totals.
5. Key **Results indcate that theer is moer brand loyelty among wemen than men** two rows below the last row of data. (You correct the misspellings in the next step.)
6. Spell-check the worksheet. Make the necessary corrections.
7. Create the standard header with your name, filename, and date, and center the worksheet horizontally.
8. Rename Sheet1 **Compare** and rename Sheet 2 **User Information**.
9. In the User Information worksheet, create documentation, which includes the following:

   File Information (With the following subheads: **Created by**, **Date created**, **Date revised**, **Revised by**, **Contact for help**)

   Purpose/Description of Worksheet *[Use a paragraph form]*

   Instructions to User *[Add special instructions needed by the user to enter data correctly]*

10. Style the documentation for easy reading and spell-check your work.
11. Add the standard header to the documentation worksheet and print it. Make the Compare worksheet active.
12. Save the workbook as *[your initials]***7-compare** in your Lesson 7 folder and close it.

13. Use the Open dialog box to rename the file *[your initials]*7-16.xls.
14. Print the worksheet *[your initials]*7-16.xls from the Open dialog box.
15. Open the file again and create a formula printout with grids and row and column headings.
16. Close the workbook without saving it.

NOTE: When you turn on formulas for printing the data you keyed, the results of the comparison get cut off as well as the title, which has been standard up to this point.

Unit 2 Applications

UNIT APPLICATION 2-1

Sketch a worksheet. Enter labels in a new Excel worksheet, create and enter formulas, center and print the worksheet. Display formulas and create a custom header. Print in landscape orientation showing column and row labels with gridlines.

The Beautiful Belle Company wants to construct a worksheet that calculates the difference between first quarter monthly sales for men and women for two of its products: Pacifica and Taos. The worksheet should also calculate the difference in total sales.

1. Sketch the worksheet giving it a title (**Pacifica vs. Taos Sales**), column labels (**Pacifica**, **Taos**, and **Difference**), and row labels (see Figure U2-1). Use F for formulas, but note that differences should only be figured in the two subtotal rows and the total row.
2. Open a new workbook.
3. Key the title and labels into the worksheet. Format the labels using bold or italic and center-alignment where necessary.
4. Key the data as shown in Figure U2-1 in appropriate rows and columns.

FIGURE U2-1

		Pacifica	Taos	Difference
Men	January	7,985	16,544	
	February	2,697	9,800	
	March	10,655	9,402	
	Subtotal			
Women	January	9,557	20,550	
	February	10,665	14,675	
	March	9,418	16,550	
	Subtotal			
Total	January			
	February			
	March			
	Total			

5. Create formulas that calculate the men's subtotal for "Pacifica" and "Taos." Calculate the subtotal difference for the two products in this section.
6. Create formulas that calculate the women's subtotal for "Pacifica" and "Taos." Calculate the subtotal difference for the two products in this section.
7. Create formulas that calculate the totals for January, February, and March. Calculate the total subtotal difference for the two products in this section.
8. Format all values in Comma style, no decimals.
9. Preview the worksheet.
10. Add a standard header including your name, filename, and date. Center the page horizontally.
11. Delete the blank worksheets.
12. Save the workbook as *[your initials]*u2-1.xls in a new folder for Unit 2.
13. Print the worksheet.
14. Create a formula printout with grids, row and column headings, and a landscape orientation.
15. Close the workbook without saving it. Submit the worksheet sketch, the normal worksheet, and the formula printout.

UNIT APPLICATION 2-2

Copy using drag and drop, the toolbar, the Fill command, AutoFill, and keyboard shortcuts. Freeze column titles and insert data. Create a custom header. Open and dock the Auditing toolbar and trace precedents for a cell.

Complete a worksheet that compares Pacifica and Taos product sales in the second quarter for two consecutive years.

1. Open the file **PacTaos.xls**.
2. Copy cells B8 through B20 to cells G8 through G20 using the drag-and-drop method.
3. Key the 1999 product data as shown in Figure U2-2 (on the next page).
4. Freeze column titles.
5. Copy the formula in cell E8 to cell J8 using the Copy button and the Paste button.
6. Using the Fill command, copy the formula to cells J9 through J11.
7. Use the drag-and-drop method to copy the formulas in cells J8 through J11 to cells J13 through J16.

UNIT 2 ■ APPLICATIONS　　　　　　　　　　　　　　　　　　　　EXCEL **235**

FIGURE U2-2

	G	H	I
		Pacifica	Taos
8	April	11,600	10,650
9	May	13,500	8,401
10	June	14,877	11,650
13	April	15,400	19,680
14	May	19,102	12,120
15	June	21,241	15,611

8. Create a formula that subtotals men's 1999 "Pacifica" sales.
9. Copy the formula in cell H11 to cell I11 using AutoFill.
10. Copy both of these formulas to subtotal women's sales using the Copy and Paste commands.
11. Using drag and drop, copy the formulas for calculating the monthly totals for April 1998 to April 1999.
12. Select cells H18 through H20 and calculate the totals for the remaining months using Fill, Down.
13. Select cells H18:I20 and Fill, Right.
14. Create a grand total for 1999 "Pacifica" sales for the second quarter and copy it to cell I22 using AutoFill.
15. Copy the difference formula from cell J16 to J18 and then to J19, J20, and J22 in the "Second-Quarter Total" row using the Copy button and the Paste button.
16. Add a standard header including your name, filename, and date.
17. Save the workbook as *[your initials]***u2-2.xls** in your Unit 2 folder.
18. Activate the Auditing toolbar and dock it. Trace the precedents for cell D22.
19. Undock the Auditing toolbar and close it.
20. Print the worksheet, including the tracing arrow.
21. Create a formula printout in landscape orientation with gridlines, row and column headings, and a Page 1 of ? footer. (The tracing arrow is still present.)

22. Close the workbook without saving it.
23. Reopen the workbook and save it as *[your initials]*u2-2.htm, then close the workbook.

UNIT APPLICATION 2-3

Use AutoSum and AutoFill. Create range names and build formulas using names. Sort data by salesperson's last name. Rename worksheet tabs. Create documentation, spell-check, navigate the worksheet using names, create custom headers, and print formulas.

Create a worksheet that calculates commissions for Beautiful Belle's Southwest region and summarizes yearly sales, commissions, and net sales—that is, gross sales minus commissions.

1. Open the file **SW.xls**.
2. In cell C15, use the AutoSum button to add the column.
3. Use AutoFill to copy the SUM formula to cells D15 through J15.
4. Create the name **rt** for the constant **.07** to calculate quarterly commissions due.
5. Create formulas using the constant name in cells D5, F5, H5, and J5 to calculate the commission due for each quarter. To complete the columns, copy the formula using AutoFill.
6. Create the names **sq1**, **sq2**, **sq3**, and **sq4** for the total sales for each quarter.
7. Create a formula in cell B17 that calculates the total sales for the year. Use names in the formula.
8. Create the names **com1**, **com2**, **com3**, and **com4** for the total commissions for each quarter.
9. Use the commission range names to create a formula in cell B18 that calculates the total commissions for the year.
10. Create a formula in cell B19 that calculates the annual net sales—that is, gross sales minus commissions—for the Southwest territory.
11. Select the range A5:J14. Sort data by last name, ascending.
12. Rename the Sheet1 tab **Commission**.
13. Rename the Sheet2 tab **User Information**.
14. Key the data from Figure U2-3 into the User Information sheet. Place the data in the worksheet so it is easy to read. Include formatting that might make it easy to read.

UNIT 2 ■ APPLICATIONS   EXCEL **237**

FIGURE U2-3

```
User Information
Created by:        Your name
Date created:      Current date
Date revised:
Revised by:
Purpose            Calculate commission for SW territory based on
                   sales by quarter.
User Instructions  1. Note the range and constant names below.
                   2. The constant name rt is used for the commission
                      rate of .07.
```

15. After the last line of text from Figure U2-3, skip a row and paste all the names you created into the worksheet.
16. Spell-check the User Information worksheet.
17. In the Commission worksheet, use the Go To command to locate the cell named "sq4."
18. Add the standard header including your name, filename, and date to both worksheets.
19. Save the workbook as *[your initials]***u2-3.xls** in your Unit 2 folder.
20. Print the entire workbook.
21. Create a formula printout in landscape orientation of the Commissions worksheet. Use gridlines, row and column headings, and a Page 1 of ? footer. Do not fit this on one page. (*Hint:* Change the Adjust To under Scaling in the Page Setup dialog box to 100%.)
22. Close the workbook without saving it.

UNIT APPLICATION 2-4

Find and open a file. Replace labels, spell-check, and train AutoCorrect to recognize typos. Use AutoSum and AutoFill to enter formulas. Create a custom header and change print settings. Use the Open dialog box to copy a file and print a worksheet.

Find and adapt a workbook to total fourth quarter cream and fragrance sales for Beautiful Belle.

1. Open the file **Prdcts.xls**.

2. Spell-check the worksheet.
3. Train AutoCorrect to recognize the misspelled word **Otcober**
4. Edit "July" with **Otcober** in both cells where July appears.
5. Delete the AutoCorrect entry.
6. Use the Replace command to replace all occurrences of "August" and "September" with **November** and **December**, respectively.
7. Use AutoSum and AutoFill to enter formulas for the "Totals" rows and columns.
8. Replace "Third Quarter" with **Fourth Quarter**.
9. Add the standard header including your name, filename, and date.
10. Save the workbook as *[your initials]*u2-4.xls in your Unit 2 folder.
11. Create a formula printout with grids and row and column headings in landscape orientation. Fit the printout to one page using the Fit To option under Scaling in the Page Setup dialog box.
12. Close the workbook without saving it.
13. Use the Open dialog box to create a copy of *[your initials]*u2-4.xls in your Unit 2 folder.
14. Print the worksheet from the Open dialog box.
15. Delete the copy of your file.

UNIT APPLICATION 2-5

Design a worksheet. Check spelling. Copy and paste data and formulas. Create range names and create formulas using range names. Use AutoSum and AutoFill. Find and replace data. Create documentation and paste range names into a worksheet. Create custom headers, change print settings, and use the Open dialog box to copy and print a worksheet.

Imagine you are a product manager for the Beautiful Belle Company charged with projecting revenue for three new lines of shampoo being launched in the third quarter of the current year. You need to create an initial worksheet design for the third quarter and enter data. After you transfer the design to Excel, your boss needs to add information to the worksheet for fourth quarter projections; this information is not included in your initial design.

1. Sketch a worksheet that contains:
   - An appropriate title
   - A single-entry area "Quarter:" (remember, this is a label below the worksheet title and above the row headings, usually with a blank row above and below it)
   - Column labels for three types of shampoo

- Row labels for the third quarter (abbreviate these)
- A column and a row for product and month totals (Use F for formulas.)

2. Transfer the title and labels to Excel, formatting them as necessary. Key **Third** in the cell to the right of "Quarter:" in the single-entry area and enter the data in Figure U2-4.

FIGURE U2-4

	Jaz	Britely	Frezia	Total
Jul	5800	6800	6000	
Aug	3200	7200	4500	
Sept	2800	8400	3800	
Total				

3. Spell-check the worksheet and make necessary corrections.
4. Use AutoSum and AutoFill to create formulas that calculate the monthly totals.
5. Use AutoSum and AutoFill to create formulas that calculate the product line totals for the third quarter.
6. Create a formula that calculates the total projected sales for the three new products in the third quarter.
7. Format all numbers in Comma style, no decimals.
8. Copy the range that contains labels and data including the single-entry item and paste it into the worksheet beneath the third-quarter data.
9. In the pasted text, replace "Third" with **Fourth** and replace "Jul," "Aug," and "Sept," with **Oct**, **Nov**, and **Dec**, respectively.
10. Create the name **rt** for the constant **1.1** that you will use to calculate projected sales growth for the fourth quarter.
11. Create an appropriate range name for the first product value for "Jul."
12. Create an appropriate range name for the first product value for "Aug."
13. Create an appropriate range name for the first product value for "Sept."
14. Create formulas that use the range names for the first product in the third quarter and the constant name **rt** to calculate projected sales growth for the fourth quarter.
15. Create similar range names and formulas for the other two products.
16. Rename the worksheet tab **Projections** and name the Sheet2 tab **User Information**. Delete Sheet3.
17. Create user documentation on the User Information sheet and include a pasted list of named ranges.

18. Add the standard header with your name, filename, and date to both worksheets. Horizontally center the Projections worksheet on the page.
19. Save the workbook *[your initials]*u2-5.xls in your Unit 2 folder. Print the User Information worksheet only.
20. In the Projections sheet trace the dependents to the first shampoo sales projection for October.
21. Create a formula printout in landscape orientation with grids and row and column headings.
22. Turn off the formula display and close the Auditing toolbar.
23. Use Page Setup to change the print settings to print in portrait orientation without gridlines and row and column headings.
24. Save and close the workbook.
25. Use the Open dialog box to create a copy of the file.
26. Print the file **Copy of** *[your initials]*u2-5.xls from the Open dialog box.
27. Delete the file **Copy of** *[your initials]*u2-5.xls.
28. Submit the worksheet sketch, the normal worksheet, and the formula printout.

UNIT APPLICATION 2-6 ✓ *Making It Work for You*

Design a worksheet. Create formulas and copy and paste. Check spelling. Create custom headers and documentation. Print worksheet and formulas.

You have been hired for your first job and you have opened a checking account to deposit your weekly paycheck and maintain a record of your expenses. Create a worksheet that you will use to double-check the current balance in your checking account. Your worksheet should have, but is not limited to, columns for the date of your checking transaction, check number, payee, description, deposit amount, check amount, and current balance. Be sure to title the worksheet.

Create a preliminary sketch before you key the information. Next, build your formulas and supply a minimum of 10 checking transactions in addition to an opening balance. Typical checking transactions would be a paycheck deposit and checks issued for rent, utilities, food, and other living expenses. Use numbers that are easy to calculate. Format numbers in Comma style, two decimals. Create User Information. Add the standard headers to both worksheets and delete Sheet3. Center the check register horizontally on the page. Save the workbook as *[your initials]*u2-6.xls in your Unit 2 folder. Create a formula printout with grids and row and column headings in landscape orientation. Use a Page 1 of ? footer, if needed. Close the worksheet without saving it.

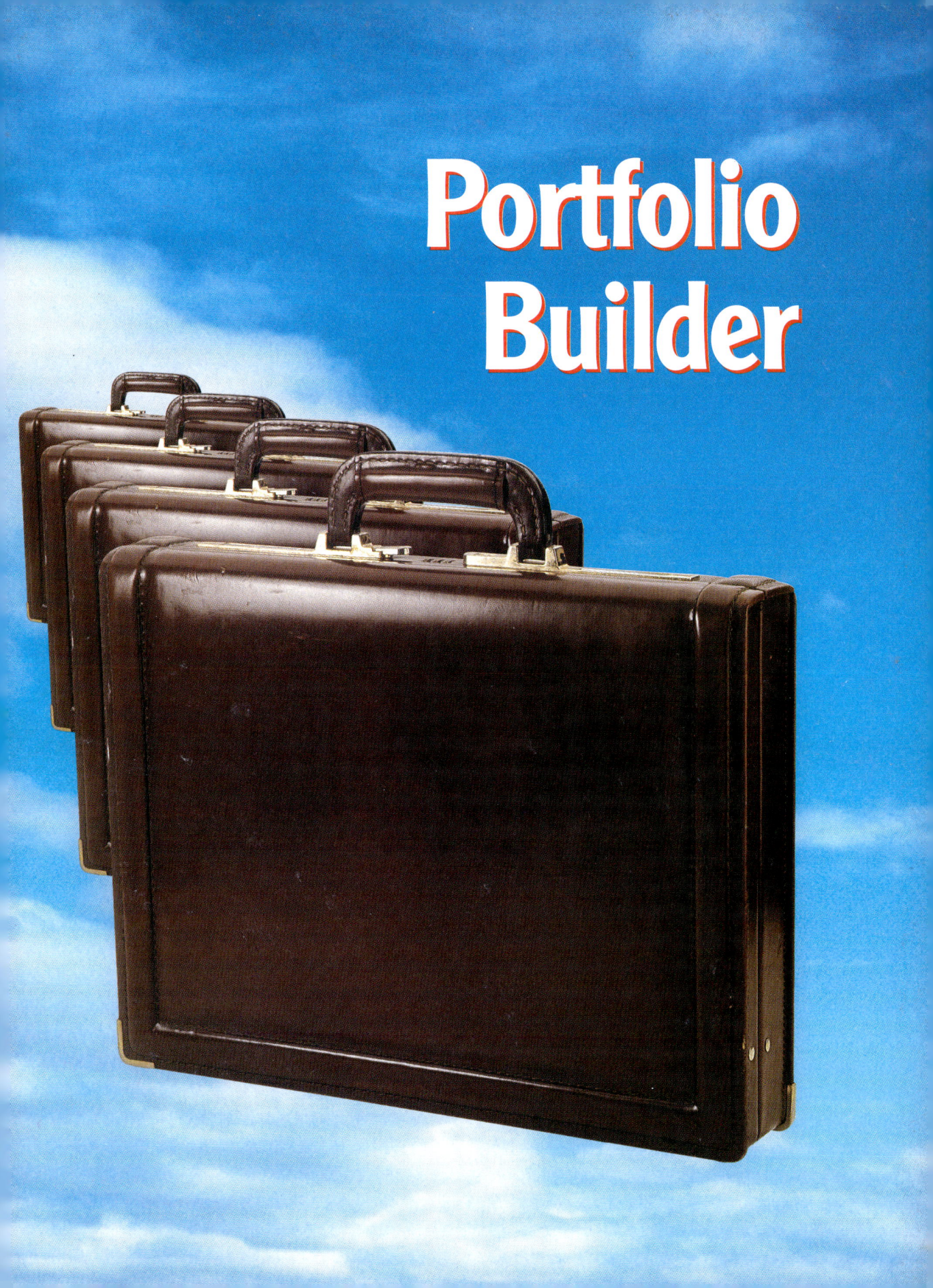

Portfolio Builder

List of Files Produced in the Portfolio Builder

Filename	Document
*[Your initials]*Res1.doc	Resume created using a Word Resume Template
*[Your initials]*Res2.doc	Resume created using the Word Resume Wizard
*[Your initials]*Prospects.xls	List of prospective employers
*[Your initials]*DocList.xls	List of documents to include in your Portfolio
*[Your initials]*CvrLtr.doc	Cover letter (From scratch or using Word's Letter Wizard)
*[Your initials]*AppInfo.doc	Information for use in filling out Employment Applications
10-15 additional documents	The documents listed in your Document List.

Optional Documents

Thank you letter

Contract Reference Sheet

Contract Reference Card

Portfolio Builder

OBJECTIVES By using this Portfolio Builder, you will learn how to:

1. Build a résumé.
2. Identify prospective employers.
3. Build a portfolio.
4. Target your résumé and portfolio.
5. Write a cover letter.
6. Fill out an employment application.
7. Prepare for a job interview.
8. Follow up an interview.

Finding a job is difficult—especially today in the midst of downsizing. The number of applicants often exceeds the availability of jobs. So you need to distinguish yourself from other people interested in the same job. You need to show a prospective employer what you can do.

This *Portfolio Builder* helps you build a résumé that will tell prospective employers about your work background. It also assists you in building a "representational portfolio"—a collection of your best work that you can show as evidence of your skills. The documents in your portfolio will be geared to specific employers. Finally, the *Portfolio Builder* leads you though the job-search process: including contacting prospective employers, filling out an employment application, and following up after interviews.

FIGURE P-1
The job-search process

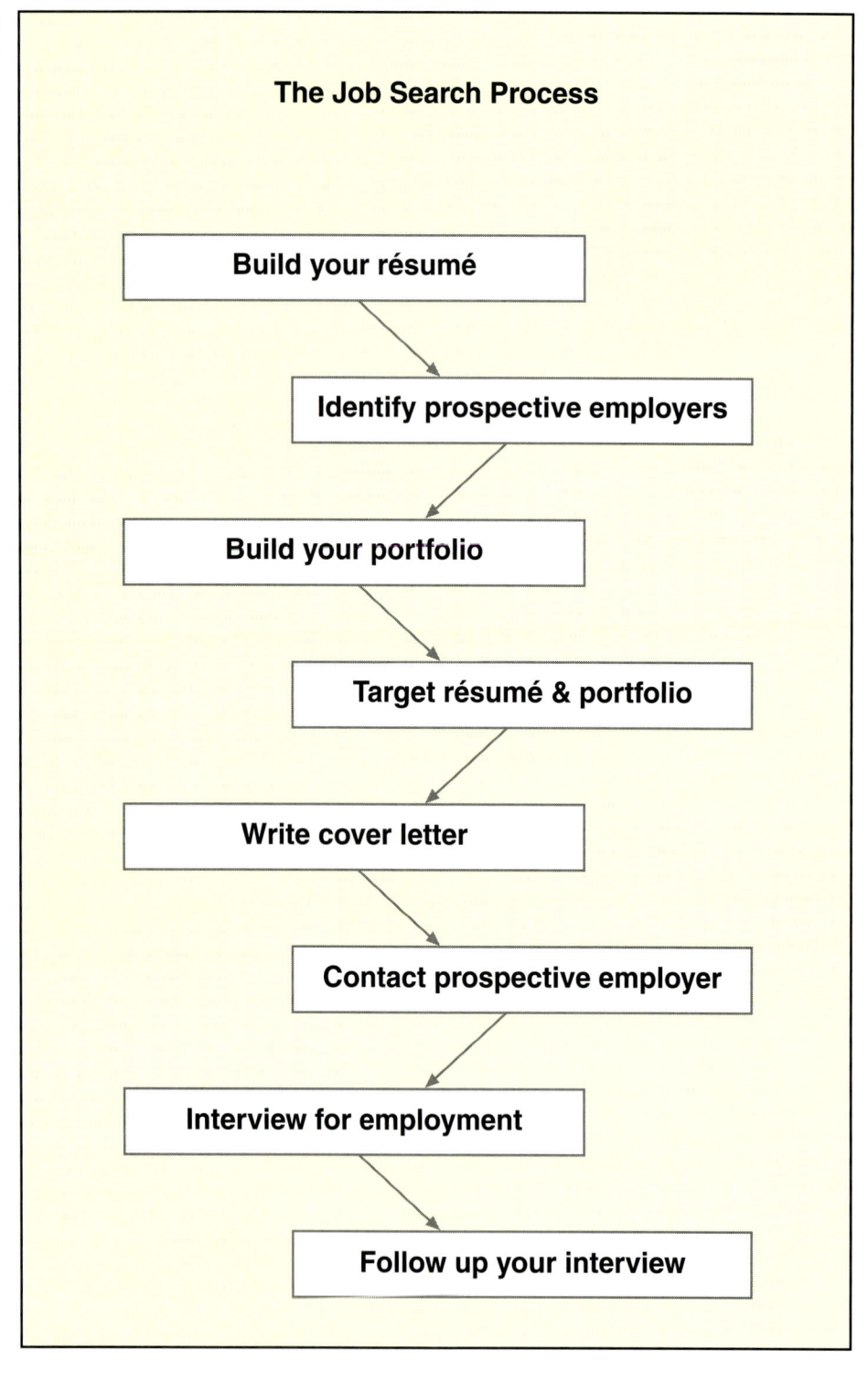

The Job Search Process

- Build your résumé
- Identify prospective employers
- Build your portfolio
- Target résumé & portfolio
- Write cover letter
- Contact prospective employer
- Interview for employment
- Follow up your interview

The *Portfolio Builder* will be helpful to you if you're planning to search for immediate employment. It is also a useful final project because it requires you to demonstrate skills you have gained from this course. Even if you're not looking for a job, it will help prepare you for an eventual job search.

Building a Résumé

A résumé is a representation of you on paper. It provides a first impression of you to a potential employer.

Building a résumé is an exercise in self-discovery. To create one, you must review your experience, identify your skills, and focus on a goal. Once you have created a résumé that states your strengths and objectives, you can begin the process of marketing yourself to prospective employers.

Although a good résumé will not guarantee a job, it is a primary tool in the job-search process.

There are three types of résumés:

- The *chronological* résumé is the traditional type of résumé. It lists your work history, starting with your most recent job. It includes a brief description of the position and your accomplishments. This is a "where you've been" type of résumé.
- The *functional* résumé highlights your skills or areas of expertise. It is a "what you can do" type of résumé.
- The *combination* résumé highlights your skill areas *and* lists the jobs you have held.

The following six pages illustrate these three kinds of résumés.

Chronological Résumé Description

Contact Information: Your name, address, and telephone number should appear at the top of the résumé. Spell out your address (do not abbreviate "Street" or "Avenue"). Include your ZIP code. Use a telephone number where you can be reached during the day or where a message can be left. Include other forms of contact, such as an e-mail address or fax number, if available. Don't use your current employer's telephone or fax number.

Job Objective: Your job objective represents the specific field or job title that you are pursuing. If you're targeting a specific job, tailor your objective to that position. Include the job type, the industry, and the geographical area in your objective (example: "Marketing position with a computer software vendor in the Chicago area"). To keep your options open, write a broader objective.

Work Experience: Describe the jobs that you have held, beginning with your most recent position. List the years of employment, company names and locations, and specific job titles. Include current and past jobs, part-time work, self-employment, volunteer work, and internships, as appropriate. The job description should focus on quantified achievements and specific skills.

Education: List the schools and training programs that you have attended. List your most recent education—school, degree or program, and date completed. Omit information about your high school if you have a college degree. Include any additional information, such as continuing education, seminars, or special course work that is related to your objective. This section can appear before **Work Experience** if you're a recent graduate, or if your education or training is your most important qualifying factor.

Additional Information: Your résumé can contain additional information that may be relevant to the job you are pursuing. For example, a section on computer proficiency can be included. You can also include **Activities**, **Professional Organizations**, or **Honors/Awards** as separate sections.

References: References are often not included on a résumé, but are provided separately if requested. Line up your references in advance, and list them on a sheet of paper. Include the name, address, telephone number, and title (if appropriate). You can ask a previous employer for a letter of recommendation, which you can then photocopy.

FIGURE P-2 Chronological résumé*

12 Juniper Drive
Any Town, State 00000
(000) 000-0000
E-mail: dmartin@xxx.xxx

Donald Martin

Objective   Seeking position as microcomputer salesperson in dynamic retail environment.

Work Experience

1996–Present	Electronics Depot	Any Town, State

Sales Associate
- Specialized in sales of computer hardware and software in busy retail outlet.
- Selected Salesperson of the Year for Midwest region.
- Established customer training program for computer sales that produced $80,000 in its first year.

1994–1996	Video Time	Any Town, State

Assistant Manager
- Managed video-rental store during most heavily-trafficked hours (evenings and weekends). Effectively handled as many as 250 customer contacts per day.
- Trained and supervised five sales assistants.
- Started "Old Time Cinema Club" that boosted sales of backlist videos by 50%.

1993–1994	Fairway Department Store	Any Town, State

Sales Assistant
- Assisted customers in busy Electronics Department.
- Handled more than $2,000 per day in cash sales.
- Completed sales training program.

Education

1997	**Fargo Technical College**	Any Town, State

- A.A., Microcomputer Systems Technology
- G.P.A. 3.93

Software/Hardware Training
- Proficiency in all Microsoft Office applications and PageMaker on both the PC and Macintosh computer.
- Can perform diagnostics on PCs and peripheral equipment, and can install/upgrade PC components such as network cards, memory chips, disk drives, and modems.

References   Available upon request.

*Created using a modified version of Word's Contemporary résumé style.

Functional Résumé Description

Contact Information: Your name, address, and telephone number should appear at the top of the résumé. Spell out your address (do not abbreviate "Street" or "Avenue"). Include your ZIP code. Use a telephone number where you can be reached during the day or where a message can be left. Include other forms of contact, such as an e-mail address or fax number, if available. Don't use your current employer's telephone or fax number.

Job Objective: Your job objective represents the specific field or job title that you are pursuing. If you're targeting a specific job, tailor your objective to that position. Include the job type, industry, and geographical area in your objective (example: "Marketing position with a computer software vendor in the Chicago area"). To keep your options open, write a broader objective.

Functional Sections: In a functional résumé, these sections provide the bulk of the information about you. Include two to four sections that describe a particular area of expertise or involvement. These areas should be directly related to the position you are pursuing. (In this résumé, the functional sections appear with the headings **Casework**, **Document Drafting**, and **Computer Skills**.) As an alternative to creating job-specific sections, create functional sections with the headings **Qualifications** and **Accomplishments**. Under these headings, list concise action statements that will catch the attention of a prospective employer.

Work Experience: A functional résumé lists your job history by date, company name and location, and title, beginning with the most recent position. Job descriptions are not included, as the résumé focuses on qualifications and skills, not work history.

Education: List the schools and training programs that you have attended. List your most recent education—school, degree or program, and date completed. Omit information about your high school if you have a college degree. Include any additional information, such as continuing education, seminars, or special course work that is related to your objective. This section can appear immediately below your **Objective** if you're a recent graduate, or if your education or training is your most important qualifying factor.

Additional Information: Your résumé can contain additional information that may be relevant to the job you are pursuing. For example, you can include sections with the following headings: **Activities**, **Professional Organizations**, **Honors/Awards**. The heading **References** may be listed at the bottom, followed by the text "Available on request" (see Chronological Résumé for more information).

FIGURE P-3 Functional résumé*

8809 Orange Terrace
Any Town, State 00000
Telephone (000) 000-0000
Fax (000) 000-0000

Lesley Brown

Objective	Paralegal position in computer or patent law
Casework	- Researched state and federal computer and patent laws. Wrote briefs for attorneys. - Prepared preliminary arguments and pleadings in computer law. - Obtained affidavits.
Document Drafting	- Drafted contracts under the supervision of an attorney. - Prepared tax returns, incorporations, patent filings, and trust agreements. - Prepared reports and schematic diagrams. - Assisted computer law specialists in preparing hardware and software patents, contracts, applications, shareholder agreements, and packaging agreements.
Computer Skills	- Word-processing software (Word). - Advanced use of database software (Access) and spreadsheet software (Excel). - Researched on-line databases using Internet search engines.
Employment	1995–Present Collimore & Hapke, Attorneys-at-Law Any Town, State **Legal Assistant**
Education	1998 York State Technical College Any Town, State **Associate Degree, Paralegal Technology**
Activities	Legal Eagles Public Library Volunteer coordinator of weekly youth discussion group that teaches basic law principles.

*Created using a modified version of Word's Professional résumé style.

Combination Résumé Description

Contact Information: Your name, address, and telephone number should appear at the top of the résumé. Spell out your address (do not abbreviate "Street" or "Avenue"). Include your ZIP code. Use a telephone number where you can be reached during the day or where a message can be left. Include other forms of contact, such as an e-mail address or fax number, if available. Don't use your current employer's telephone or fax number.

Job Objective: Your job objective represents the specific field or job title that you are pursuing. If you're targeting a specific job, tailor your objective to that position. Include the job type, the industry, and the geographical area in your objective (example: "Marketing position with a computer software vendor in the Chicago area"). To keep your options open, write a broader objective.

Functional Sections: Include two or three sections that describe a particular area of expertise or involvement, or that summarize your qualifications and accomplishments. Use concise statements that are easy to read.

Work Experience: As in the chronological résumé, list and describe the jobs that you have held, beginning with your most recent position. Include the years of employment, the company names and locations, and the specific job titles. You can include current and past jobs, part-time work, self-employment, volunteer work, internships, and so on, as appropriate. The job description should focus on quantified achievements and specific skills. Be careful not to repeat the same information here that you have listed in the Functional Sections.

Education: List the schools and training programs that you have attended. List your most recent education—school, degree or program, and date completed. Omit information about your high school if you have a college degree. Include any additional information that might be relevant, such as continuing education, seminars, or special course work. This section can appear above **Work Experience** if you're a recent graduate, or if your education or training is your most important qualifying factor.

Additional Information: Your résumé can contain additional information that may be relevant to the job you are pursuing. For example, you can include sections with the following headings: **Activities**, **Professional Organizations**, **Honors/Awards**. The heading **References** may be listed at the bottom, followed by the text "Available on request" (see Chronological Résumé for more information).

PORTFOLIO BUILDER EXCEL P-11

FIGURE P-4 Combination résumé*

ANNA LUPONE
1002 LOOKOUT POINT
ANY TOWN, STATE 00000
TELEPHONE (000) 000-0000
E-MAIL 00000@AOL.COM

OBJECTIVE

Corporate Word Processing Administrative Assistant

SUMMARY OF QUALIFICATIONS

◊ Four years experience in administrative/clerical support positions.
◊ Easily establish rapport with managers, staff, and customers.
◊ Proficient at analyzing statistics and market trends to develop accurate forecasts and effective sales presentations.
◊ Excellent problem-solving, project management, decision-making, and time management skills.
◊ Proven ability to prioritize and complete multiple tasks, independently and with little supervision.
◊ Bilingual: English/Spanish.

COMPUTER SKILLS

Operating Systems:	Microsoft Windows 98
Word Processing:	Word
Graphics:	PageMaker, PowerPoint
Database and Spreadsheets:	Access, Excel
Keyboard Speed:	85 wpm

PROFESSIONAL EXPERIENCE

1994–Present COCA COLA COMPANY Atlanta, Georgia
Administrative Assistant
◊ Analyze sales volume and profit.
◊ Finalize and package forecasting reports for annual sales of $100 million.
◊ Monitor monthly spending and reconciliation for $8 million budget.
◊ Manage $200,000 in advertising and promotional materials.

EDUCATION

1998 Blake Business Institute Any Town, State
A.S., Administrative Office Technology
◊ Dean's List, 4.0 GPA

REFERENCES

Available on request.

---

*Created using a modified version of Word's Elegant résumé style.

Choosing a Résumé Format

What type of résumé is right for you? Consider the following:

TABLE P-1   **Choosing a Résumé Type**

RÉSUMÉ TYPE	PREFERABLE IF:
Chronological	You have a history of steady work that reflects growth, and you are looking for a job in the same field or a related field.
Functional	You are new to the workforce, have gaps in your work history, or are changing careers.
Combination	You have some work history that is worth showcasing *and* want to highlight your marketable skills.

Be aware that the chronological résumé is the most traditional and conservative type of résumé. It is also the easiest to prepare. The functional and combination résumés, which use more innovative approaches, require greater thought, planning, and creativity.

Tips on Résumé Writing

When preparing your résumé, give yourself plenty of time, and keep in mind the following basics:

Content

- Everything in your résumé should support your job objective. Omit anything that doesn't.
- Be clear about what your skills are, both in your own mind and on paper. Your résumé should answer the question, "Why should I hire you?"
- Your résumé should convey the impression that you're focused. It should be targeted to a specific occupation or career field.
- Don't shortchange yourself. Emphasize any accomplishments, awards, and recognition you've received that supports your job objective.
- Mention promotions, raises, and bonuses, if appropriate, to prove your track record.
- Don't misrepresent yourself. Lying or exaggerating can only hurt—not help—you.
- Stress the positive—never include negative information about yourself. Your résumé should reflect what you *can* do, not what you can't.

Writing Style

- Strive for crisp, concise writing. Use short, easy-to-understand sentences.
- Use action words and phrases in your job and skill descriptions. For example, begin each description with words such as "Analyzed," "Administered," "Developed," "Initiated," "Organized," and so on.
- Use buzzwords and terminology that relate to the job you are pursuing.
- Proofread your résumé thoroughly for typographical, grammatical, or punctuation errors.

Appearance

- Your résumé should look professional. It should have an attractive layout, an easy-to-read format, and enough "white space" so that it is not too text-heavy.
- Use a good-quality printer to print your résumé. Avoid sending out photocopies, if possible.
- Limit your résumé to one page, unless you have substantial work experience that is relevant to your current job objective.

Getting Help

- Attend résumé and career workshops offered at your school or in your community.
- Read books about résumé writing to learn how to identify your skills, document your experience, and deal with special problems. Review résumé samples in such books.
- Ask someone whose judgment you trust to read your résumé before you send it out.

Résumé Templates and the Résumé Wizard

Word provides three résumé templates and a Résumé Wizard to help you create a résumé.

NOTE: Before using a résumé template or the Résumé Wizard, check the New dialog box in Word to see if they are available. If the templates have to be installed, use the Microsoft Office CD-ROM (Disk 1) to run the setup program. The Setup program location for these files is Microsoft Word for Windows, Wizards and Templates. You can also go to the Microsoft Office Web site (www.microsoft.com) and download wizards and templates.

P-14 EXCEL

■ **PORTFOLIO BUILDER**

EXERCISE P-1 Use a Résumé Template

The résumé templates allow you to create a chronological résumé based on one of three styles: Elegant, Contemporary, and Professional.

1. Choose New from the File menu, choose the Other Documents tab, and then double-click one of the résumé template icons.

   NOTE: To preview the template before choosing it, click the résumé template icon, and then view it in the Preview box.

FIGURE P-5
Résumé templates in the New dialog box

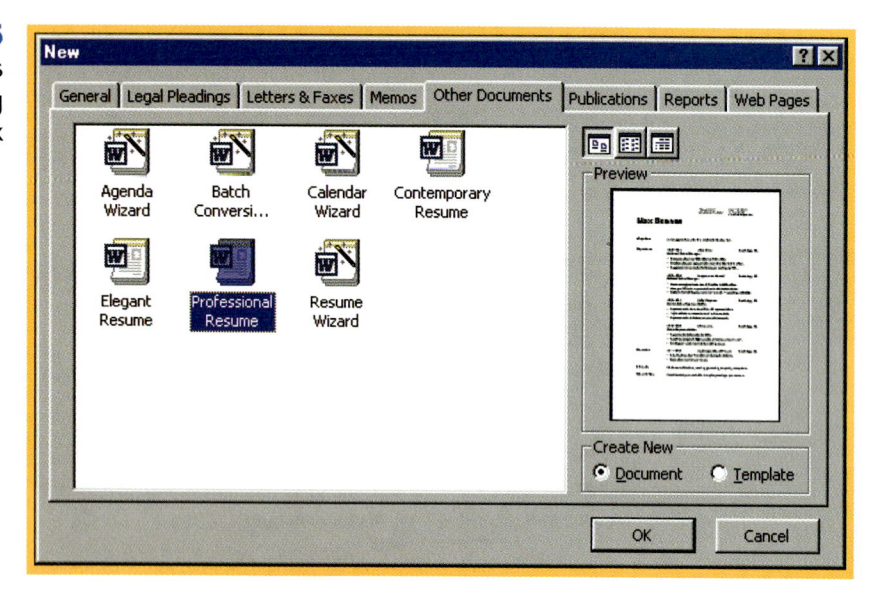

2. Replace all of the placeholder text in the document with your own information.
3. Make any formatting modifications. Save the document as *[your initials]***Res1.doc** and print it.

   NOTE: Use the Résumé Wizard or résumé templates as a basis upon which to build your résumé. Modify the layout and formatting of the résumé to make it unique. Remember, you don't want your résumé to look exactly like everyone else's.

EXERCISE P-2 Use the Résumé Wizard

The Résumé Wizard guides you through the steps needed to create a chronological or functional résumé using one of the three résumé styles.

PORTFOLIO BUILDER   EXCEL P-15

1. Choose New from the File menu, choose the Other Documents tab, and then double-click the Résumé Wizard icon. Click Next to start.
2. In the Style dialog box, choose a résumé style. Click Next to display the next dialog box.

FIGURE P-6
Choosing a résumé style

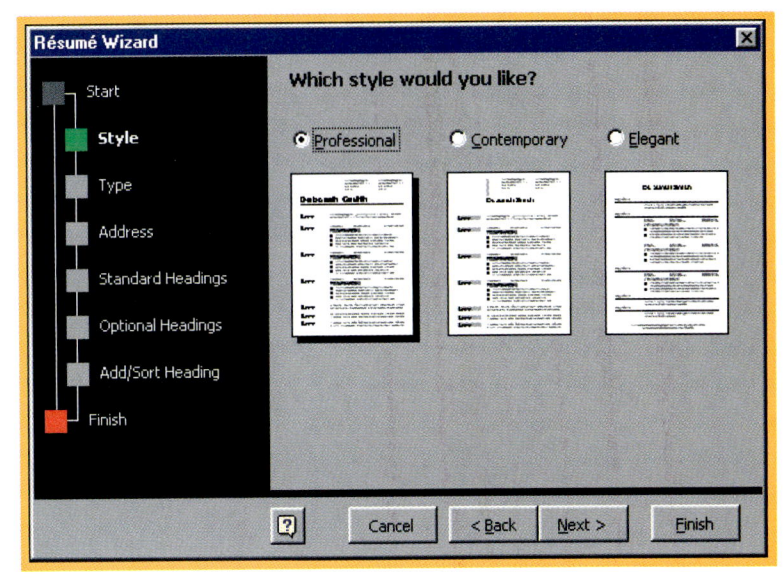

3. Choose the résumé type, and then click Next.
4. Enter your name and mailing address, and then click Next.

FIGURE P-7
Choosing headings for your résumé

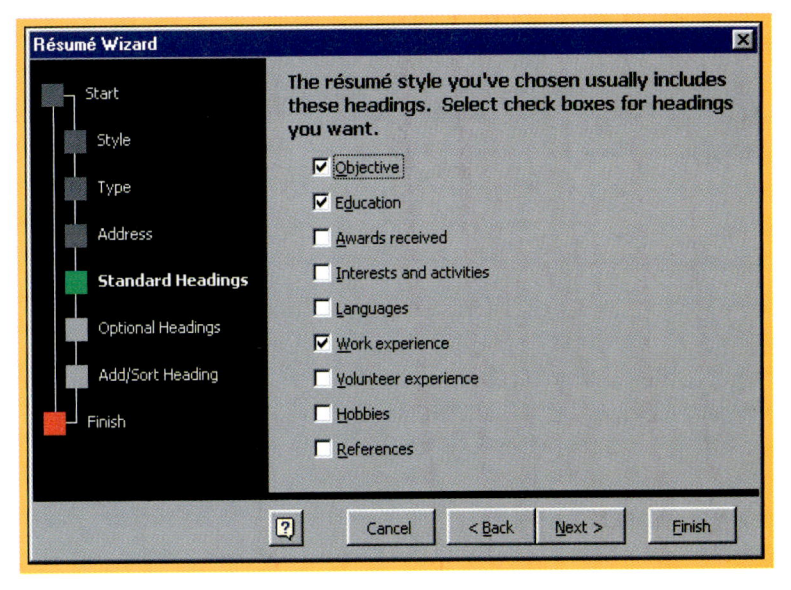

5. Choose the résumé headings you want, and then click Next.
6. Choose any additional headings you desire, and then click Next.

7. Add another heading or reorder your existing headings, and then click Next.
8. Click Finish to view the résumé.
9. At the Office Assistant prompt, choose an option or click Cancel.

TIP: You can click the Office Assistant option to create a quick cover letter at this point. The letter will contain sample text for you to replace with your own information. See the section "Writing a Cover Letter" in this Portfolio Builder to learn about cover-letter basics.

10. Replace the placeholder text in the résumé with your own information.
11. Make any modifications. Save the document as *[your initials]***Res2.doc**.

Identifying Prospective Employers

Now that you've prepared a résumé, it's time to think about who will view it. Your next step is to identify the companies in your area—and the people within those companies—who may be hiring people with your skills.

Always try to identify the manager in each company or organization who heads up the division, department, or group in which you hope to work. Avoid applying through a Human Resources staff member, if at all possible. In the Human Resources Department, it's easy to become just another applicant who receives no special attention.

Help Wanted Ads

Help-wanted ads can represent a useful way to research the hiring trends of a local company. Help-wanted ads are, however, less useful as a source of real employment opportunities. They should never be used as the primary focus of your job search. In fact, some experts believe that only 10 percent of all available jobs are listed in the newspaper.

Use the back issues of your local newspapers to find out whether a company has been hiring recently, what kinds of jobs have recently been advertised, and if a particular contact person was listed in the ad.

Networking

Talk to people who are in a position to provide information about job leads and the hiring process at particular companies. They can be friends, relatives, acquaintances—anyone who can put you in touch with a job contact. Try to identify the people within a company who have the power to hire you. Get the correct spelling of each person's name, official correct job title, department, company, and, if possible, a telephone number.

Company Research

An easy way to begin your company research is with the *Yellow Pages*. Use it to locate businesses in the field in which you're interested. (You may need to use the "Business-to-Business" section for some types of businesses.)

The business section of your local library contains reference books that can give you even more information about local companies. Some of the best sources are:

- *Standard & Poor's Register of Corporations, Directors, and Executives.* McGraw-Hill. (Volume 2 lists companies by location.)
- *The National Directory of Addresses and Phone Numbers.* Gale Research, Inc.
- *Million Dollar Directory.* Dun & Bradstreet.
- *Job Seeker's Guide to Private and Public Companies.* Gale Research, Inc.
- *Job Opportunities for Business and Liberal Arts Graduates.* Peterson's Guides, Inc.
- *Job Opportunities for Engineering, Science, and Computer Graduates.* Peterson's Guides, Inc.

Some of these sources are also available in easy-to-use software versions that allow you to search for particular companies based on specific criteria. Your local librarian can often provide help in locating information about specific companies as well.

Using the Internet

Many sources of company and career information are available on the Internet. Many companies operate their own Web site or home page, and some even list their job openings there. If a prospective employer is a large company, search the Internet based on the company's name. Often, promotional materials from the company (and available in a local public library) will indicate its Internet or Web site address.

Many Web search engines (such as Lycos, Excite, or Infoseek) offer career-oriented services. Search for such general keywords as "career," "employment," or "job." A targeted search using more specific keywords may produce results that prove more immediately useful to your job search.

You can also use your Internet browser to search for locations with appropriate keywords. For example, one recent search showed 600,000 matches for the keyword "career." Obviously, the more targeted your search of the Internet, the more useful it may be.

Specialized employment search engines on the Internet may prove useful. Because these services list jobs from across the nation (and around the world), they may be less useful for a local job search. A list of places to look for jobs on the Internet follows (remember that Internet options change rapidly, so this list may need to be updated and new options may be available):

- CareerPath
  Searches classified ads in U.S. newspapers
  www.careeerpath.com
- The Career Builder Network
  www.careeerbuilder.com
- CareerMosaic
  www.careermosaic.com
- E-Span Employment Database
  www.espan.com
- HotJobs
  www.hotjobs.com
- The Monster Board
  www.monster.com

EXERCISE P-3 Identify Prospective Employers

1. Identify at least five prospective employers. They may be located anywhere, but should represent the type of company for which you could imagine working.

2. For each prospective employer, obtain the name of a job contact. (This person would typically be a manager of the department, division, or group in which you would like to work.)

3. Key the list of prospective employers in a worksheet. Include the contact's name, department, company name, address, city, state, ZIP code, telephone number, and fax number. Save the worksheet as *[your initials]*Prospects.xls and then print it. You'll use this list throughout this *Portfolio Builder*.

PORTFOLIO BUILDER ■ EXCEL P-19

Building Your Portfolio

Your resume *describes* your experience and your skills. Your portfolio *demonstrates* your skills. It represents the best work that you can do. It also should be work with which a prospective employer can identify—that is, documents that the employer will understand.

The first step in building your portfolio is to decide what types of documents belong in it. Use the following checklist as a starting point to create a list of possible documents for your portfolio.

TABLE P-2   Possible Documents for Portfolio

DOCUMENT	COMMENTS
Worksheets and Tables	Create attractive stand-alone worksheets and tables. Include charts and maps.
Invoices	Check Excel's invoice template.
Purchase Orders	Check Excel's purchase order template.
Expense Statements	Check Excel's expense statement template.
Business Planners	Check Excel's Business Planner templates, including Income Statements, Cash Flow Forecasts, and Balance Sheets.
Profit & Loss Statements	Obtain information from annual reports available at public library. Possibly include charts.
Balance Sheets	Obtain information from annual reports available at public library.
Databases	Create an Excel database. Show data filtered in multiple ways.
Letters	Create business letters with the appropriate letter formatting. Attach or embed related worksheet, chart, or map.
Memos	Create business memos with the appropriate memo formatting. Attach or embed related worksheet, chart, or map.
Reports	Include graphics, index, table of contents, footnotes or endnotes, and embedded worksheet, chart, or map.
Brochures	Check Word's brochure template. Possibly show worksheets and charts.

continues

TABLE P-2   **Possible Documents for Portfolio (continued)**

DOCUMENT	COMMENTS
Newsletters	Check Word's Newsletter Wizard. Include graphics, special effects, and embedded worksheet, chart, or map.
Press Releases	Check Word's press release templates. Include an attached worksheet or chart.

NOTE: If any of these Wizards or templates are not installed on your computer, you can install them by using the Microsoft Office CD-ROM (Disk 1) to run the setup program. The Setup program location for the Excel files is Microsoft Excel for Windows, Spreadsheet Tamplates. The Setup program location for the Word files is Microsoft Word for Windows, Wizards and Templates. You can also go to the Microsoft Office Web site (www.microsoft.com) and download wizards and templates.

EXERCISE P-4   Develop a List of Documents for the Portfolio

1. Develop a list of 15 documents for inclusion in your portfolio. Use Table P-2 as a checklist, but also consider documents that you may have prepared in other courses related to your field of work. If you have work experience, list actual documents that you created. Use the following headings for your document list (see Figure P-8 on the next page):
   Number   **Type of Document**   **Description**
2. Save the list as *[your initials]***DocList.xls** and print it.
3. Finalize your document list by reviewing it with someone who is familiar with your job search area. Adjust the list as needed. Save and print it.

EXERCISE P-5   Build Your Portfolio

It isn't necessary to begin every document from scratch. In fact, it may not even be a good idea. Use material from your other courses, key material from brochures and newsletters that you might receive from a professional association, or recreate sample documents from people in positions similar to the one in which you are interested.

1. Create each of the documents listed in your document list.
2. Adjust every document to give it as professional an appearance as possible. Focus on formatting. Demonstrate the skills that you learned in this course.

PORTFOLIO BUILDER EXCEL P-21

3. Consult the appropriate style reference for your profession to check that your formatting is acceptable.
4. Spell-check, save, and print your documents.
5. Ask someone familiar with your future profession to review your documents and then modify them as necessary.
6. Save and print your documents again.

FIGURE P-8 Sample portfolio list for student seeking accounting clerk position

No.	Type of Document	Description
1.	Invoice	For bookkeeping or accounting services
2.	Database	Client database, filtered in various ways
3.	Accounts Payable	Client's Accounts Payable statement
4.	Account Receivable	Client's Accounts Receivable statement
5.	Employee List	Records of employees including date hired, years employed (with calculations)
6.	Purchase Order	For office supplies
7.	Loan Statement	Showing principal, annual percentage rate, and so on
8.	Check Register	Showing checks, deposits, and balance
9.	Cash Flow Statement	Showing cash receipts and cash disbursements
10.	Amortization Schedule	Showing various interest rates and payment periods
11.	Income Statement	Showing cash, accruals, and net income
12.	Balance Sheet	Showing assets and liabilities
13.	Chart	Showing sales over a 12-month period, for a presentation or handout
14.	Map	Showing states shaded to reflect sales, for a presentation or handout
15.	Report	Report with accompanying worksheet, including charts and maps

EXCEL — **PORTFOLIO BUILDER**

Targeting Your Résumé and Portfolio

So far you've created a résumé and a portfolio of documents that reflect something about you. Now it's time to *target* a specific company and tailor your portfolio, including your résumé, to that company.

EXERCISE P-6 — Target Your Résumé to an Employer

1. From your list of five prospective employers, choose one as your target. Review the information you've gathered about the company. If you feel you don't have enough information, collect additional material. Ultimately, you should be very familiar with the company—and the position—you've targeted.
2. Review Table P-3.

TABLE P-3 Targeting Your Résumé

TARGETING SUGGESTIONS

Objectives

- ☐ Change the job type to one that more closely resembles a job type available at the targeted company.
- ☐ Change the description of the industry or geographical area to one that more closely resembles those for the target company.

Chronological Résumé

- ☐ Reorder the bullets under a previous job in "Work experience" to emphasize skills that apply to the targeted position.
- ☐ Reorder or modify "Additional information" areas to emphasize skills that apply to the targeted position.

Functional Résumé

- ☐ Reorder or modify the "Functional sections" to emphasize skills that apply to the targeted position.
- ☐ Reorder or modify "Additional information" areas to emphasize skills that apply to the targeted position.

continues

TABLE P-3 Targeting Your Résumé *continued*

	TARGETING SUGGESTIONS
	Combination Résumé
☐	Reorder or modify the "Functional sections" to emphasize skills that apply to the targeted position.
☐	Reorder the bullets under a previous job in "Work experience" to emphasize skills that apply to the targeted position.
☐	Reorder or modify "Additional information" areas to emphasize skills that apply to the targeted position.

3. Based on the checklist shown in Table P-3, modify your résumé to increase its appeal to your targeted company.

NOTE: Modifying a résumé does not mean fabricating work experience. You can, however, increase your appeal to a specific employer by highlighting certain skills. You can also minimize potential problem areas through the design and format selected for your résumé (for example, by deciding to use a functional résumé rather than a chronological one).

4. Spell-check and save your résumé.
5. Print the final copy of your résumé on appropriate paper stock.

Choosing Paper

The most commonly used résumé papers are 20-pound bond or 50-pound offset (both weigh the same) in a linen (textured) or laid (flat) finish. A 24-pound paper is thicker, has more texture, and is usually more expensive than 20-pound bond or 50-pound offset papers. You might consider using 24-pound Nekoosa, Classic Linen, or Becket Cambric for higher-level positions.

Let your résumé speak for itself. Don't go overboard in selecting a paper that will make your résumé stand out. Such a strategy could backfire. Don't use colored stock, for example. Neutral stock in different shades of white, gray, or beige is recommended.

If you're uncertain about paper choices, visit a stationery store, an office supplies store, a printer, or a local copy shop. Buy enough paper to use for your résumés, cover letters, and follow-up letters. Your envelopes should match the stationery. Your portfolio documents shouldn't be printed on the same stock as your résumé, however.

EXERCISE P-7 Target Your Portfolio to an Employer

The job contact at your targeted company is likely to respond more favorably to your portfolio if you take the time to tailor it to the company. It shows that you made an effort to learn about your prospective employer. It may also provide more conversational opportunities in a job interview.

1. Review Table P-4.

TABLE P-4 Targeting Your Portfolio

	TARGETING SUGGESTIONS
☐	Use the targeted company's name in worksheet titles and its address where appropriate.
☐	Modify the contents of office documents so that they apply specifically to the targeted company.
☐	Do not change a report from one of your classes (other than to make any corrections your instructor may have recommended). It's a good idea to let the targeted company know that the report was submitted as a class assignment, especially if it relates to your chosen field.

2. Based on the checklist shown in Table P-4, modify the documents in your portfolio to increase their appeal to the targeted company.
3. Spell-check and save the portfolio documents.
4. Print the final copies of your portfolio documents. Use standard printer paper.

Writing a Cover Letter

It's been said that sending a résumé without a cover letter is like giving a gift without a card. It's incomplete and confusing, and it only decreases the value of the résumé that you've spent so much time preparing and fine-tuning.

The Cover Letter Recipient A cover letter should be addressed to the job contact at a targeted company—never to Human Resources or Personnel.

First Paragraph The first paragraph should explain what job you are applying for and why you are interested in it. Be as specific as you can. Describe how you heard about the job opening. If someone told you about the company or the job opening, mention the person's name (but make sure to get his or her permission first). Describe why the work of the department or company holds particular interest for you, but don't go overboard with superlatives or hype.

Second Paragraph Describe your credentials in the second paragraph. Don't repeat your résumé. Focus, instead, on the skills, experiences, or accomplishments that are most likely to appear relevant to the employer. If you're responding to an ad, incorporate language from the ad. If you've previously read a job description or had a discussion with the employer, try to use the language the employer used in describing the position. Mention two or three key credentials.

Third Paragraph Use the third paragraph to describe what you can do for the company. You need to show that you understand the employer's needs and that you have something to offer. In this paragraph (or as a separate paragraph), you should request a personal meeting. You could then indicate the time when it's easiest to reach you, whether the employer can contact you at work, and if you'll be following up with a phone call.

General Tips

- Your cover letter should be printed on the same paper as your résumé and should be printed in the same way.
- Do not use the letterhead of your current employer.
- Use the same typeface for both your cover letter and your résumé.
- Use the standard business letter format.
- Don't send your portfolio with your résumé and cover letter. The portfolio is generally shown in an interview, but it can be sent to a prospective employer who expresses an interest in viewing it.

EXCEL

FIGURE P-9 Sample cover letter

Donald Martin
12 Juniper Drive
Any Town, State 00000
(000) 000-0000

January 22, 2000

Ward T. Cleaver, Manager
The Computer Warehouse, Inc.
6 Old King's Highway
Any Town, State 00000

Dear Mr. Cleaver:

I am seeking a position as a microcomputer salesperson, and read in the *Any Town News* that The Computer Warehouse was opening a new store on Old King's Highway. I have visited The Computer Warehouse in Lincoln and was impressed with the variety of hardware and software carried by the store. The store's focus on customer service was also exceptional, both through its "Trouble-Free Technical Support" program and its wide range of software training courses.

As my enclosed résumé indicates, I specialized in the sales of computer hardware and software at the Electronics Depot on Main Street. Although the sale of computers and software constitutes only a small portion of the overall sales of the Electronics Depot, computer and software sales increased by 42 percent in the past year. Part of this increase was due to the Customer Training Program that I developed. In its first year, the program produced revenues of $80,000.

Opening a new store and training a new sales staff is a difficult prospect. With my proven background in sales and customer training, I feel I would be an asset to your sales staff and would welcome the opportunity to meet with you personally to discuss your staff needs. I will contact you in the next week to schedule an appointment at your convenience. Thank you for your consideration.

Sincerely,

Donald Martin

Enclosure

EXERCISE P-8   Write a Cover Letter

Using your word-processor application, write a cover letter to accompany your résumé.

1. Using the standard business letter style (if necessary, check the *Gregg Reference Manual*), write a cover letter for your résumé. Use the three-paragraph format described earlier.

2. Ask someone familiar with your résumé and with jobs in your chosen field to review your letter. Make any necessary modifications.

3. Spell-check the cover letter and save it as *[your initials]*CvrLtr.doc.

4. Print your cover letter using the same stationery as your résumé.

5. Print an envelope for your cover letter and résumé. If possible, use the same stationery for the envelope, cover letter, and résumé.

> **NOTE:** Some people believe that you should use a large envelope so you don't have to fold your résumé. Others recommend a standard business envelope.

> **TIP:** You can use Word's Letter Wizard to write a cover letter for your résumé. Choose New from the File menu, choose the Letters & Faxes tab, and double-click the Letter Wizard icon. Follow the steps to create the letter. Remember to choose the page design that matches your résumé, specify whether you're using preprinted letterhead, include "Mr." or "Ms." in the recipient's name area, and include an enclosure notation. After creating the letter, you can add, remove, or change letter elements by choosing Letter Wizard from the Tools menu.

Filling Out an Employment Application

Some companies require that every applicant, at every level, fill out an employment application. Other companies don't even use one. Generally, however, companies do use some form of an employment application. Whether you need to fill out such a form will depend on the company's internal personnel policies.

Often applicants are asked to fill out an employment application when they arrive at the company for an interview. To minimize stress in an already stressful situation, prepare for the employment application beforehand by creating a reference sheet that contains any information that might be included in the application and isn't found on your résumé. (Of course, you should refer to your résumé in filling out your employment application. Make sure to bring an extra copy for reference.)

Tips for Employment Applications

- Be as specific as possible when describing the position that you are seeking.
- Be careful when listing a required salary. A salary that is too high may eliminate you for some acceptable jobs, while a figure that is too low might weaken your negotiating position. Sometimes it is better to leave this line blank.
- Be prepared to list dates (month and year) for the schools you have attended. Some applications may also ask for your grade-point average and your class rank.
- Be prepared to list the following information for your previous employers: address, telephone number, name and title of supervisor, start date and end date (month and year), and a description of your duties.
- If some questions are not applicable to the job you are seeking, it is usually acceptable to write "Not Applicable" next to the question.

EXERCISE P-9: Create a Reference Sheet for an Employment Application

1. Review the "Tips for Employment Applications." Note any information that isn't covered by your résumé.
2. Key all information that you will need to fill out an employment application. Use any format that makes sense to you.
3. Save the file as *[your initials]***AppInfo.doc** and then print it.

Employment Interviews

Once you have contacted a potential employer and scheduled an appointment to meet, you'll need to prepare yourself to make a good impression in person. No matter how good your résumé or credentials may be, only the interview can, ultimately, land you the job.

The more interviews you go on, the better your interviewing skills will be.

> **NOTE:** If possible, avoid scheduling an interview on a Monday, which is often the most hectic day in a business environment.

Preparing Yourself

- Confirm your appointment the day before, and make sure you arrive at the interview on time.
- Become as familiar with the company as possible. Read articles about the company, if they are available, or talk to people who are, or have been, employed by the company. It's always flattering to a prospective employer when an applicant appears knowledgeable about the company in an interview.
- Approach the interview with a clear mental picture of your capabilities and your job objective. Review your résumé immediately before meeting the prospective employer. Think positively.

Presenting Yourself

- Come to the interview equipped with copies of your résumé, your references, and any recommendation letters you have gathered. Have your portfolio on hand, as well as a notepad and a pen.
- Look your best. Your attire and grooming are critical to making a good impression. Dress neatly and professionally, in a manner that is appropriate to the company you are visiting. If necessary, get help in selecting an interview outfit from someone who dresses well.
- Be yourself. Act as relaxed as you possibly can, sit in a comfortable position, and focus on the interviewer.
- Ask questions. Learn what you can about the job, the company, to whom (or to how many people) you'd report, and so on. If no job is available, or the job opening is not appropriate for you, ask for recommendations about other people in the company that you might contact.
- At the end of the interview, if you want the job, express your interest in it, and be ready to explain why the company should hire you.

Frequently Asked Interview Questions

The following are frequently asked interview questions. You may want to rehearse your answers before the interview. Never offer negative or unnecessary information to an interview question.

- Can you tell me about yourself?
- Why should I hire you?
- What are your major strengths? Weaknesses?
- What are your short-term goals? Long-term goals?
- Why do you want to leave your present job? (if employed)
- Why did you leave your previous job?
- What do you enjoy most (or least) about your current (or previous) job?
- Why do you want to work here?
- What salary do you expcct to receive?

Following Up the Interview

To be successful in the interview process, you should take two important follow-up steps:

- Send a "thank you" letter.
- Keep track of your contacts.

"Thank You" Letters

Always send a "thank you" letter within 24 hours after you've interviewed with someone. It creates a positive impression, shows that you have good follow-up skills and good social skills, and reminds the person of your meeting.

The letter should be short and friendly, thanking the person for his or her time and for any information he or she may have provided. You may want to mention something that reminds the person of who you are, in case many people have interviewed for the position.

Even if you know that the interview will not lead to a specific job offer, a "thank you" letter demonstrates your professionalism.

FIGURE P-10 Sample "thank you" letter #1

Dear Ms. Jones:

Thank you for the opportunity of interviewing for the sales position. I enjoyed meeting you and appreciate the information that you shared with me.

I am very interested in the position and believe I could quickly become a productive member of your sales team.

Thanks again for the interview, and I look forward to hearing from you.

Sincerely,

FIGURE P-11 Sample "thank you" letter #2

Dear Ms. Jones:

Thank you for the interview and the information you gave me yesterday. I really appreciate your recommendation that I meet with John Doe in the Marketing Department.

I have scheduled an interview with Mr. Doe and look forward to meeting him. If this contact eventually leads to a job offer, I will be most grateful.

Thanks again for your time and help.

Sincerely,

Keeping Track of Contacts

Be organized in your job search. Keep track of everyone who has received your résumé by creating a contact log.

FIGURE P-12
Sample format for contact log

Date Sent	Contact Name	Company	Telephone	Comments

In addition, develop a system for organizing your contacts so that you can follow up with telephone calls as appropriate. You can use a computer application of your choice or simple index cards to create the system.

If you use index cards, enter all pertinent reference information for each contact on the card. Place the cards in a box, and then sort them in the order that you want to contact the individuals. You can use tabs as date markers.

FIGURE P-13
Sample format for contact reference card

Company: _____

Contact Person: _____

Position: _____ Department: _____

Address: _____

Phone: _____ Fax: _____

Notes: _____
_____
_____

Appendices

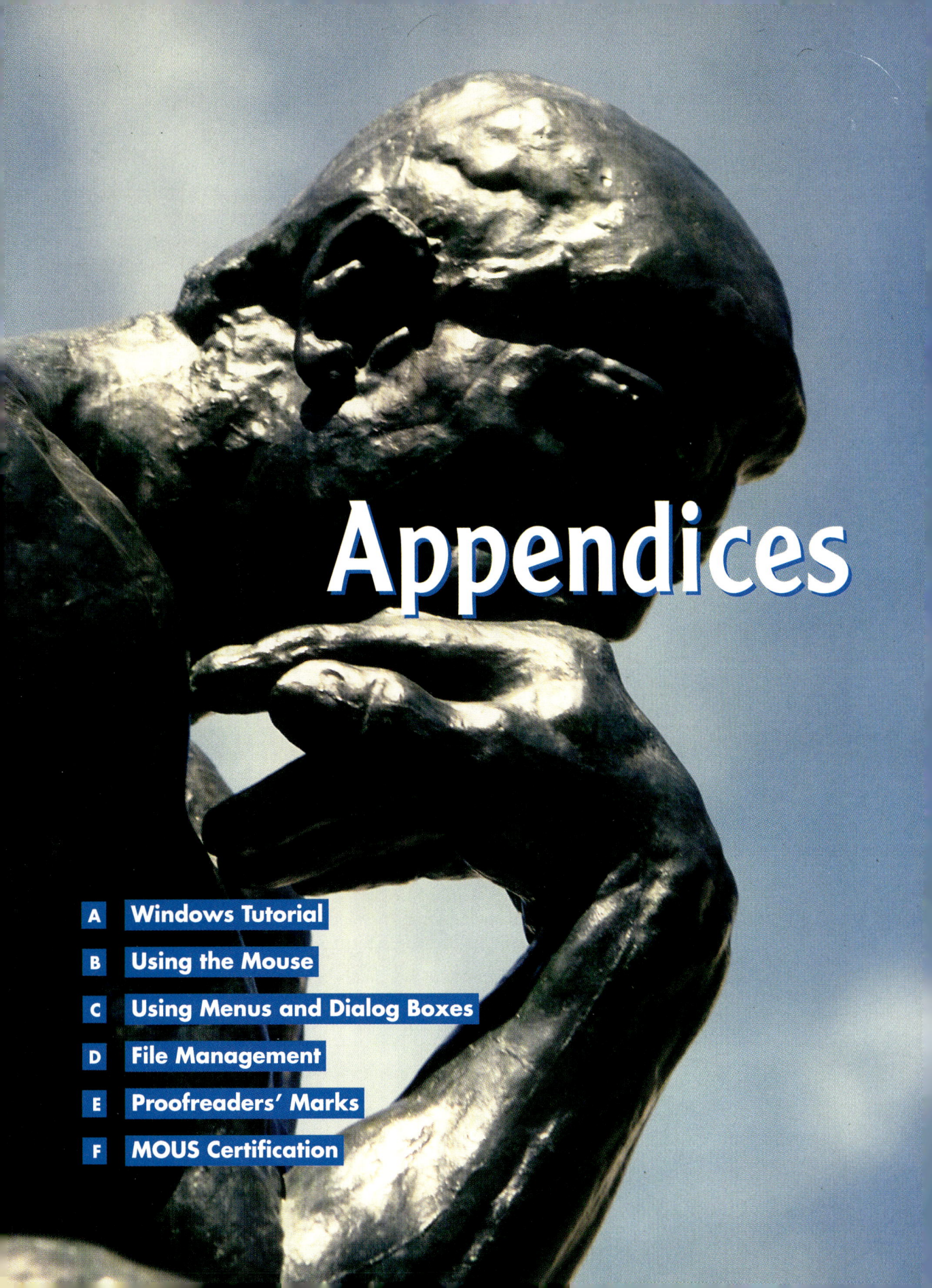

- **A** Windows Tutorial
- **B** Using the Mouse
- **C** Using Menus and Dialog Boxes
- **D** File Management
- **E** Proofreaders' Marks
- **F** MOUS Certification

APPENDIX A

Lesson Applications

If you're unfamiliar with Windows, we suggest you review this Windows tutorial.

If you never used Windows before, you may need help with basic Windows actions. At appropriate points in this Tutorial, a Note will guide you to Appendix B: "Using the Mouse" or Appendix C: "Using Menus and Dialog Boxes."

Starting Windows

Individual computers may be set up differently. In most cases, however, when you turn on your computer, Windows loads and the Windows desktop appears.

The desktop contains *icons*, or symbols representing windows. If you double-click an icon, the window represented by that icon opens. Two icons are especially important:

- My Computer
  Opens a window that contains icons representing each input and output device on your printer or in your network.

- Recycle Bin
  Opens a window listing files you've deleted. Until you empty the Recycle Bin, these files can be undeleted.

TIP: If you don't know how to use the mouse to point, click, double-click, or drag and drop, see Appendix B: "Using the Mouse."

Using the Start Menu

The Start button on the taskbar at the bottom of the desktop is probably the most important button in Windows. Clicking displays the Start menu from which you can perform any Windows task.

1. Turn on the computer. Windows loads, and the Windows desktop appears.

NOTE: When you start Windows, you may be prompted to log on to Windows or, if your computer is attached to a network, to log on to the network. If you are asked to key a user name and a password, ask your instructor for help.

2. Click on the Windows taskbar. The Start menu appears.

TIP: If you don't know how to choose a command from a menu, see Appendix C: "Using Menus and Dialog Boxes."

APPENDIX A ■ WINDOWS TUTORIAL   EXCEL **A-3**

FIGURE A-1
Windows desktop

Icons

Desktop

Pointer

Start menu

Start button

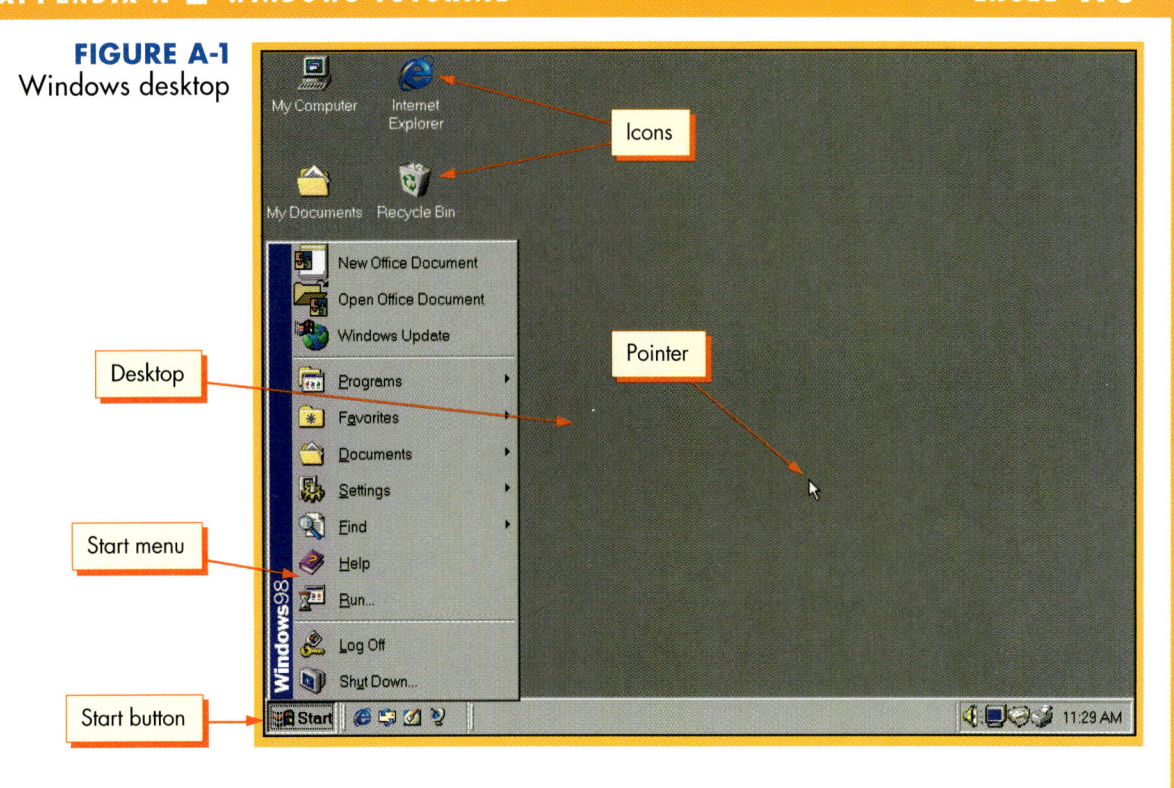

TABLE A-1 **Start Menu**

COMMAND	USE
New Office Document	Starts a new Office document of any type.
Open Office Document	Opens an existing Office document.
Windows Update	Connects to the Microsoft Web site for Windows updates.
Programs	Displays a list of programs you can start.
Favorites	Opens folders or connects you to Web sites that you designated as "favorites."
Documents	Displays a list of documents that you opened recently.
Settings	Displays a list of system components for which you can change settings.
Find	Helps you find a folder, a file, an address, a computer on a network; and helps you search the Internet.
Help	Starts Help. You can then use Help to find out how to perform a task in Windows.
Run	Starts a program or opens a folder when you type a command.
Log Off	Closes all programs, disconnects your computer from the network, and prepares your computer for someone else to use.
Shut Down	Shuts down or restarts your computer.

Using the Programs Command

The <u>P</u>rograms command is the easiest way to open a program.

1. Click [Start].
2. Point to <u>P</u>rograms. The <u>P</u>rograms submenu appears, listing the programs on your computer. Every computer has a different list of programs.

FIGURE A-2
<u>P</u>rograms submenu

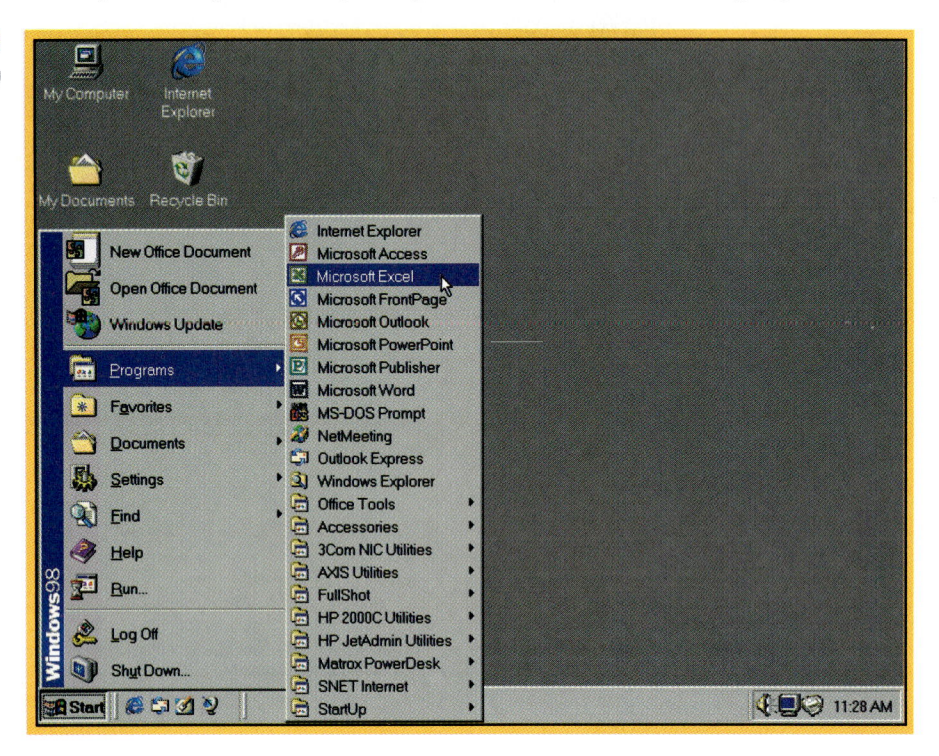

3. Point to the program you want to open and click. In a few seconds, the program loads and its first screen appears. Notice that a button for the program appears in the taskbar. Keep the program open.

> **NOTE:** Many items on the <u>P</u>rograms menu represent names for groups of programs. These group names have an arrow ▶ across from them on the right side of the menu. When you point to the group name, a submenu appears listing programs that you can click to select.

Using the Taskbar

A major feature of Windows is that you can work with more than one program at a time. The taskbar makes it easy to switch between open programs, and between open documents within a program.

The window in which you are working is called the *active* window. The title bar for the active window is highlighted, as is its taskbar button.

1. The program you opened in the preceding procedure should still be open. (If it's not, open a program now.) Open a second program using the Program command. Notice how the second program covers the first. The window containing the second program is now active. Its title bar is highlighted and its button on the taskbar is highlighted.
2. Click the button on the taskbar for the first program you opened. The program appears again.
3. Click the button on the taskbar for the second program to switch back to it.
4. Start a new blank document in the second program. Notice that each open document has its own taskbar button so you can easily switch between documents.

FIGURE A-3
Active window

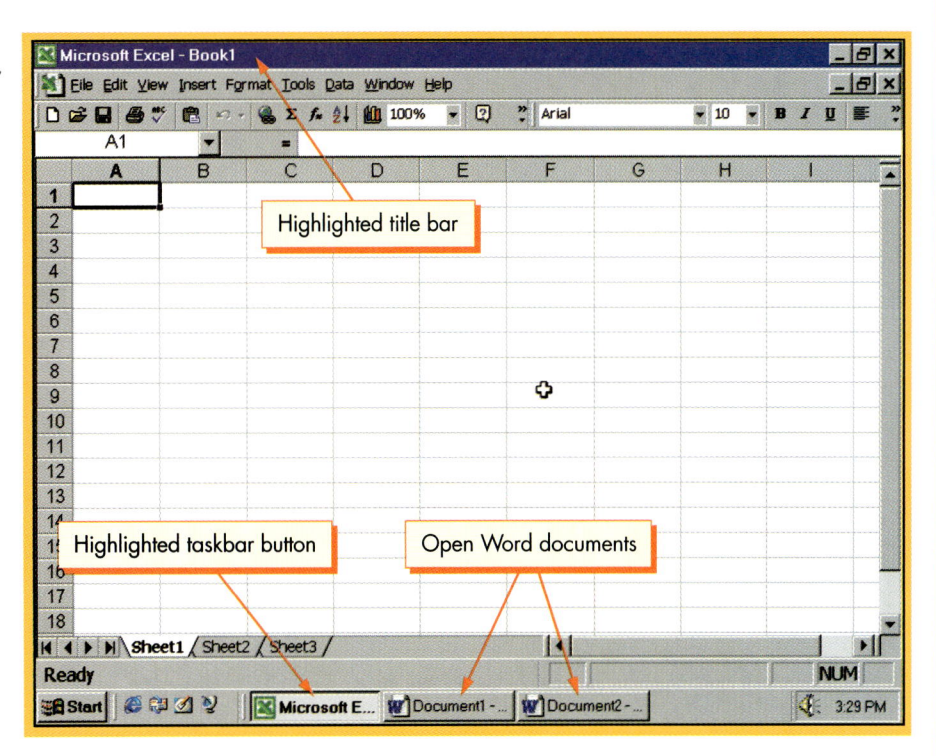

5. Practice using the taskbar to switch between program windows and document windows.

Changing the Size of Windows

In Windows it's easy to adjust the size of your windows using the pointer.
You can also use the Minimize button, the Maximize button, and the Restore button to adjust the size of windows.

TABLE A-2: Sizing Buttons

NAME	BUTTON	USE
Minimize button	[_]	Reduces the window to a button on the taskbar.
Maximize button	[□]	Enlarges the window to fill the desktop.
Restore button	[🗗]	Returns the window to its previous size. (Appears when you maximize a window.)

1. In the open window, click 🗗 at the right side of the title bar of the window. (If □ appears instead of _, the window is already reduced. In that case, go to step 2.)
2. Move the pointer to a window border. The pointer changes to a double-headed arrow ↔.

> **TIP:** Sometimes the borders of a window can move off the computer screen. If you're having trouble with one border of a window, try another border.

3. When the pointer changes shape, you can drag the border to enlarge, reduce, or change the shape of the window.
4. Make the window smaller. Notice that the other open program appears behind the currently active window.
5. Click the window that was behind the first window. It now appears in front of the first window because it has become the active window.
6. Click _ to minimize the active window to a button on the taskbar. The previous window becomes active.
7. Click the Close button ✖ at the top right corner of the window to close the window. The desktop should be clean.
8. Click a taskbar button for one of the other open windows. Close the window by clicking ✖. Close the remaining window. You have a clean desktop again.

> **NOTE:** When one document is open within a program, the document window contains two sets of sizing buttons and two close buttons, as shown in Figure A-4. The bottom buttons are for the document, the top buttons are for the program. When two or more documents are open within a program, each document window contains one set of sizing buttons and one close button.

Using the Documents Command

You can open an existing document using the Documents command on the Start menu. This command allows you to open one of the last 15 documents previously opened on your computer.

1. On the Start menu, point to Documents. The Documents submenu appears, showing documents that were previously opened.
2. Click a document. The document opens, along with the program in which the document was written (for example, if the document were a Word document, it would open within Word). A button for the document appears on the taskbar. You can now work on the document.
3. To close the document, click ☒ on the document window. Click ☒ to close the program window that contained the document.

FIGURE A-4 Close buttons

Click to close program.
Click to close document.

Using the Settings Command

You can change the way Windows looks and works using the Settings command. Be very careful when changing settings. Don't change them unless it's really necessary.

NOTE: Before changing any settings, talk to your instructor.

FIGURE A-5 Settings submenu

- Control Panel
- Printers
- Taskbar & Start Menu...
- Folder Options...
- Active Desktop
- Windows Update...

1. Open the Start menu, and point to Settings. The Settings submenu appears.
2. Click the option that relates to the settings you want to change. Close any open windows and clear your desktop.

TABLE A-3 Settings Options

OPTION	USE
Control Panel	Displays the Control Panel, which you use to change screen colors, add or remove programs, change the date or time, and change other settings for your hardware and software.
Printers	Displays the Printers window, which you use to add, remove, and modify your printer settings.
Taskbar & Start Menu	Displays the Taskbar Properties dialog box, which you use to customize the taskbar and add and remove programs on the Start menu.
Folder Options	Displays the Folder Options dialog box, where you choose the style for your folders (classic Windows style or Web style), and select folder and file characteristics.
Active Desktop	Displays a submenu with options to view your desktop as a Web page, customize your desktop, and update Web elements you added to your desktop.
Windows Update	Connects to the Microsoft Web site for Windows updates.

Using the Find Command

If you don't know where a document or folder is, you can use the Find command to find and open it.

1. On the Start menu, point to Find. The Find submenu appears.

FIGURE A-6
Find submenu

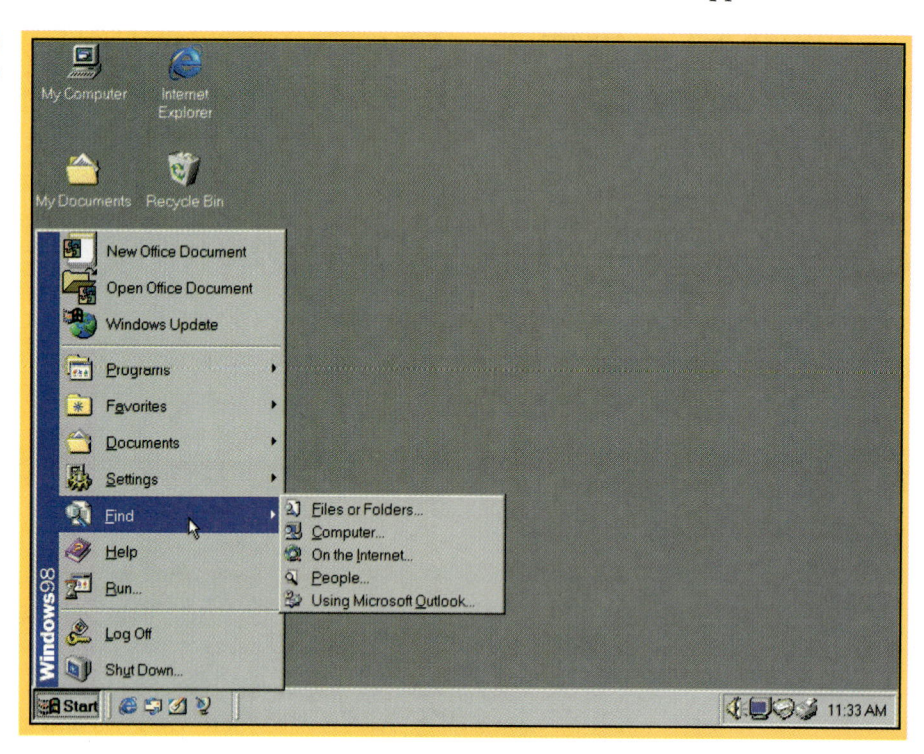

2. Click Files or Folders. The Find: All Files dialog box appears.

FIGURE A-7
Find: All Files dialog box

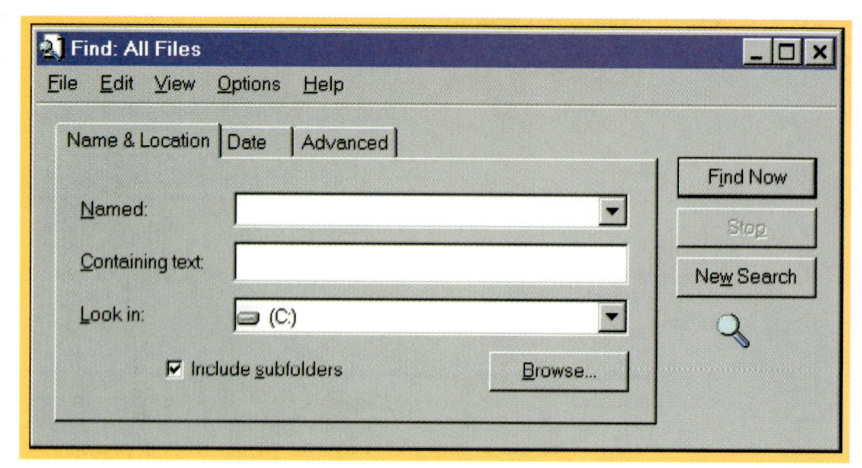

3. In the Named box, key the name of the file or folder you want to find.
4. Click the arrow next to the Look In box to specify where to search. (You could also click Browse.)

> **TIP:** To search files for specific text, use the Containing Text box. To narrow the search further, use the Date and Advanced tabs in the dialog box.

5. Click Find Now to start the search. Any matches for the file are shown at the bottom of the dialog box.
6. To open a file that was found, double-click the filename.

> **TIP:** If you set your Folder Options to Web style, you can single-click the filename, just like a hyperlink, to open the file.

7. When you finish viewing the file, close all open windows and clear your desktop.

Using the Run Command

If you know the name of the program you want to use, you can use the Run command to start it. This command is often employed to run a "setup" or "install" program that installs a new program on your computer.

1. On the Start menu, click Run. The Run dialog box appears.

FIGURE A-8
Run dialog box

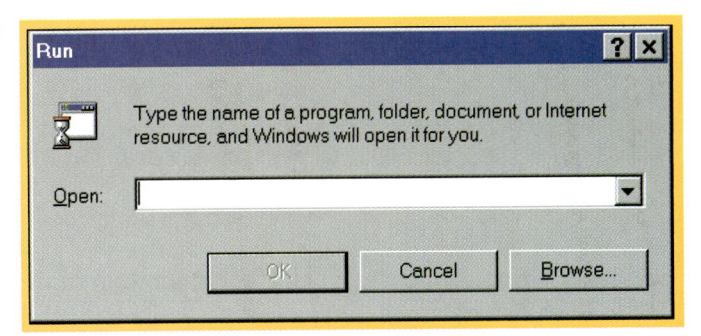

2. If you know the name of a program you want to run, key the name and click OK. The program you specified starts. Otherwise, you can click Browse to look for the program.
3. When you finish, close the program.

Displaying a Shortcut Menu

When the pointer is on an object or an area of the Windows desktop, and you click the right mouse button, a shortcut menu usually appears. This menu provides you with the commands that would be most useful in working with the object or area to which you were pointing.

FIGURE A-9
Shortcut menu for the desktop

1. Click a blank area of the desktop with the right mouse button. A shortcut menu appears with commands that relate to the desktop, such as arranging icons, displaying properties, and so on.
2. Click outside the shortcut menu to close it.
3. Right-click the time in the bottom right corner of the taskbar. Close the shortcut menu.
4. Right-click an icon to display its shortcut menu, then close the menu.

Exiting Windows

You should always exit Windows properly before turning off your computer. You can then be sure that your work is saved and no files are damaged. To exit Windows, use the Shut Down command.

1. On the Start menu, click Shut Down. The Shut Down Windows dialog box appears.

FIGURE A-10
Shut Down Windows dialog box

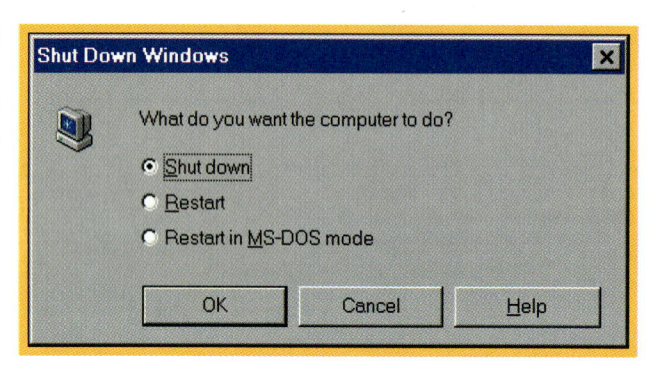

2. Choose Shut Down and click OK. Windows prompts you to save changes to any open documents. You can now turn off your computer safely.

NOTE: Occasionally, you may need to restart your computer. One instance in which this is necessary is when you add new software.

APPENDIX B

Using the Mouse

Although you can use a keyboard with Windows, you'll probably find yourself using the mouse. Typically, you roll the mouse on a *mouse pad* (or any flat surface). A *pointer* shows your onscreen location as the mouse moves.

To select items on the computer screen using a mouse, you usually press the left mouse button. (Whenever you're told to "click" or "double-click" the mouse button, use the left mouse button. If you should use the right button, you are told to do so.)

When using a mouse, you need to become familiar with these terms.

TABLE B-1　Mouse Terms

TERM	DESCRIPTION
Point	Move the mouse until the tip of the onscreen pointer is touching an item on the computer screen.
Click	Press the mouse button and then quickly release it.
Double-click	Press and quickly release the mouse button twice.
Triple-click	Press and quickly release the mouse button three times.
Drag (or drag-and-drop)	Point to an object, hold down the mouse, and move the mouse to a new position (dragging the object to the new position). Then release the mouse button (and drop the object in the new position).

The mouse pointer changes appearance depending on where it's located and what you're doing. Table B-2 shows the most common types of pointers.

TABLE B-2　Frequently Used Mouse Pointers

POINTER NAME	POINTER	DESCRIPTION
Pointer	▷	Used to point to objects.
I-beam	I	Used when keying, inserting, and selecting text.
2-headed arrow	↖↘	Used to change the size of objects or windows.
4-headed arrow	✥	Used to move objects.
Hourglass	⧗	Indicates the computer is processing a command.
Hand	☜	Used in Help to display additional information.

APPENDIX C

Using Menus and Dialog Boxes

Menus

Menus throughout Windows applications use common features. To open a menu, click the menu name. An alternative method for opening a menu is to hold down [Alt] and key the underlined letter in the menu name.

Menus are adaptive—they change as you work, listing the commands you use most frequently. To see *all* the commands on a menu, expand the menu by pointing to the arrows at the bottom of the menu (or wait a few seconds and the open menu expands).

TIP: If you open a menu by mistake, click the menu name to close it.

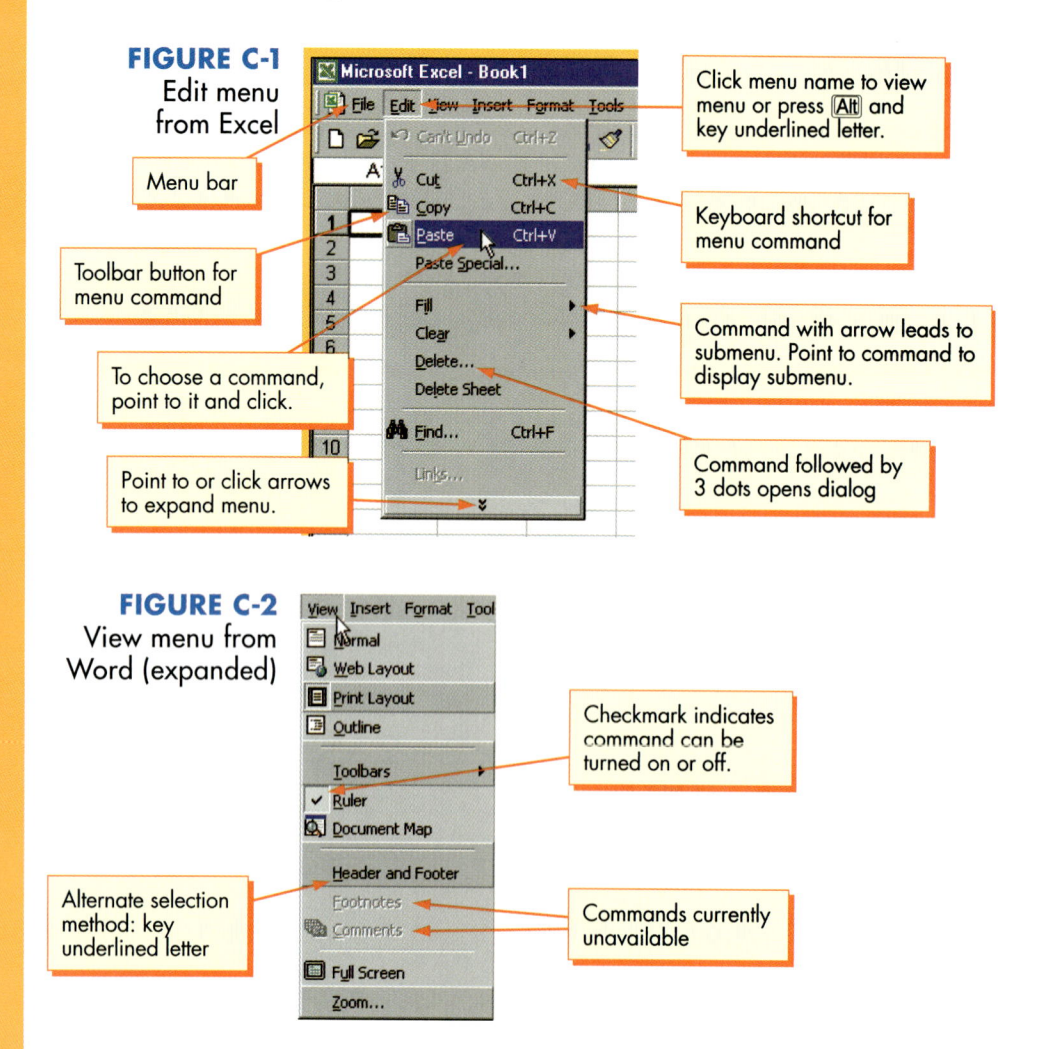

FIGURE C-1
Edit menu from Excel

- Menu bar
- Toolbar button for menu command
- To choose a command, point to it and click.
- Point to or click arrows to expand menu.
- Click menu name to view menu or press [Alt] and key underlined letter.
- Keyboard shortcut for menu command
- Command with arrow leads to submenu. Point to command to display submenu.
- Command followed by 3 dots opens dialog

FIGURE C-2
View menu from Word (expanded)

- Alternate selection method: key underlined letter
- Checkmark indicates command can be turned on or off.
- Commands currently unavailable

APPENDIX C ■ USING MENUS AND DIALOG BOXES EXCEL **A-13**

Dialog Boxes

Dialog boxes enable you to view all the current settings for a command, as well as change them. Like menus in Windows, dialog boxes share common features. The following examples show the most frequently seen features.

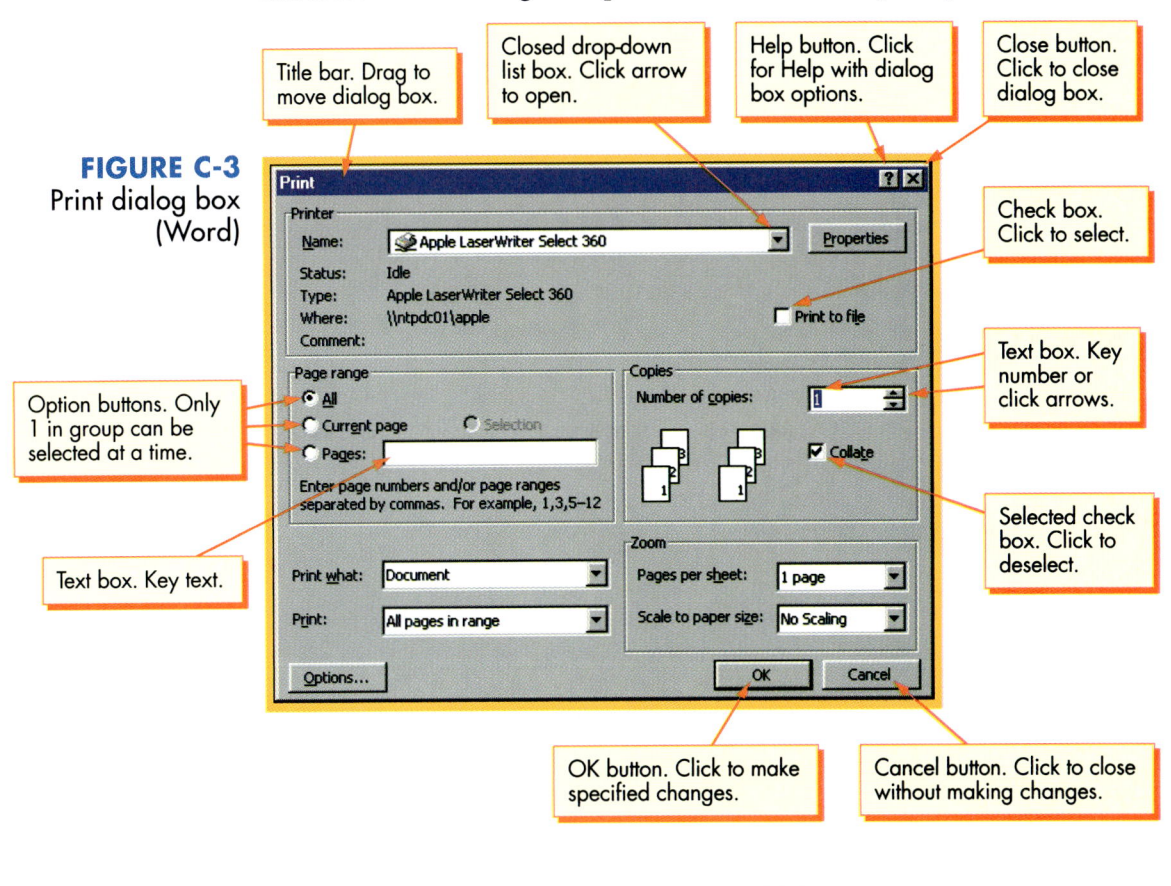

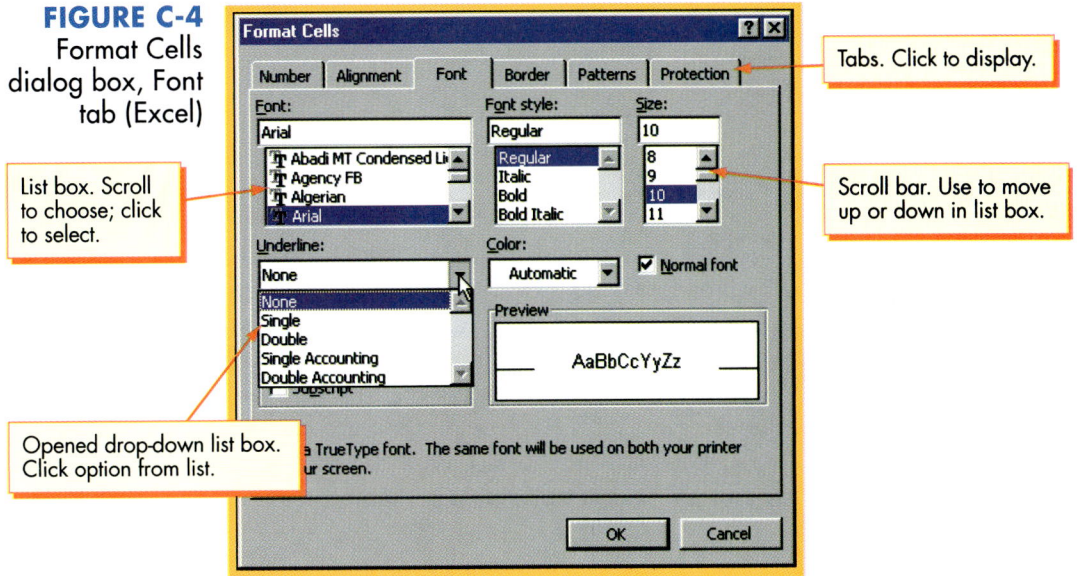

FIGURE C-3 Print dialog box (Word)

Callouts:
- Title bar. Drag to move dialog box.
- Closed drop-down list box. Click arrow to open.
- Help button. Click for Help with dialog box options.
- Close button. Click to close dialog box.
- Check box. Click to select.
- Text box. Key number or click arrows.
- Selected check box. Click to deselect.
- Option buttons. Only 1 in group can be selected at a time.
- Text box. Key text.
- OK button. Click to make specified changes.
- Cancel button. Click to close without making changes.

FIGURE C-4 Format Cells dialog box, Font tab (Excel)

Callouts:
- Tabs. Click to display.
- List box. Scroll to choose; click to select.
- Scroll bar. Use to move up or down in list box.
- Opened drop-down list box. Click option from list.

APPENDIX D

File Management

This Appendix briefly explains how information is stored in Windows. It also introduces one of the most useful tools for managing information in Windows—the Windows Explorer.

Files, Folders, and Paths

In Windows, the basic unit of storage is a *file*. The documents you create and use are files, as are the programs you use. These files are stored in *folders*, which can also contain other folders.

Windows supports filenames that can contain up to 250 characters. A filename also has a three-letter extension, which identifies the type of file. For example, the extension "doc" identifies a file as a Word document. The extension is separated from the filename by a period. For example: "Birthdays.doc."

> **NOTE:** In this course, we assume that your machine displays file extensions. If it doesn't, open Windows Explorer, select Folder Options from the View menu, click the View tab, and make sure that the following option is *not* selected: "Hide file extensions for known file types."

A file's *path* is its specific location on your computer or network. A file's path begins with the drive letter, followed by a colon and a backslash (example: c:\). The path then lists the folders in the order you would open them. Folders are separated by backslashes. The last item in the path is the filename.

For example: c:\My Documents\Letters\Reservations.doc

Windows Explorer

One of the most useful tools in Windows for managing files is the *Windows Explorer*, which gives you a view of your computer's components as a hierarchy, or "tree." Using Windows Explorer, you can easily see the contents of each disk drive and folder on your computer or network.

To open Windows Explorer, click the Start button [Start] with the right mouse button. Then click Explore on the Start button shortcut menu.

Table D-1 describes how to accomplish common file management tasks using Windows Explorer and shortcut menus.

APPENDIX D ■ FILE MANAGEMENT   EXCEL **A-15**

FIGURE D-1
Windows Explorer

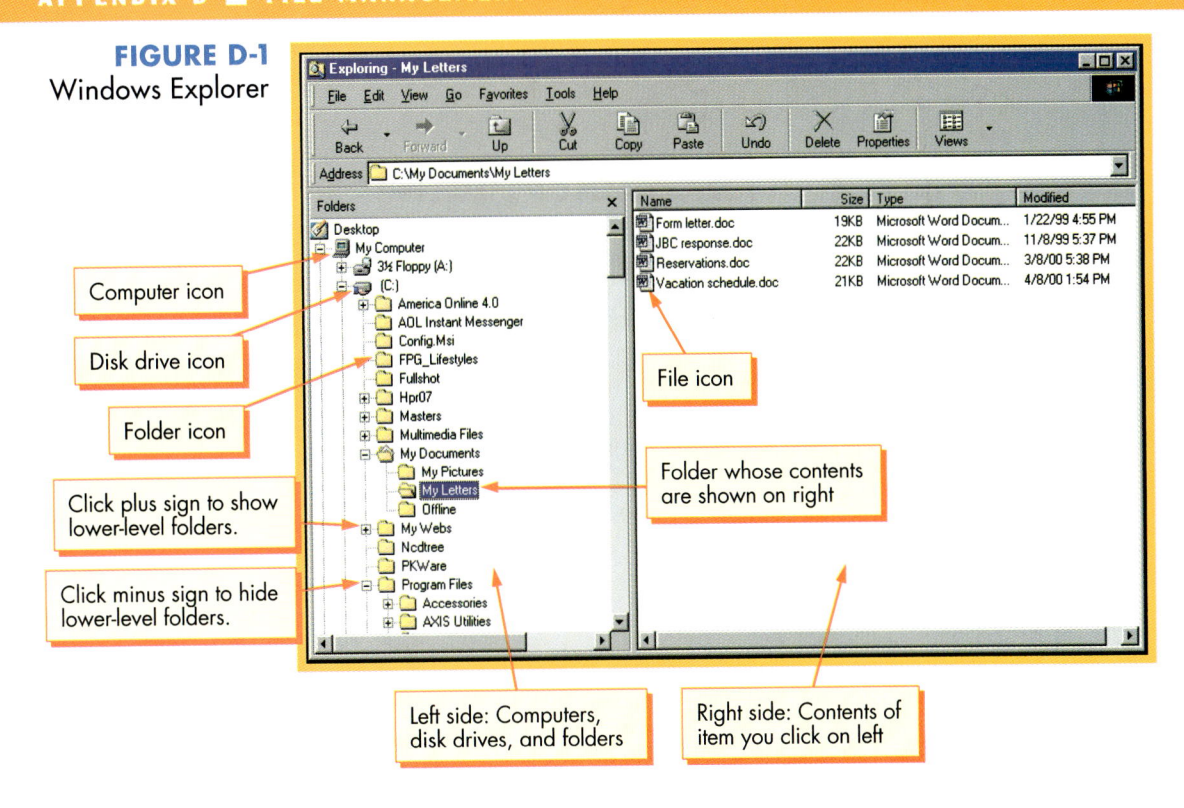

Callouts on figure:
- Computer icon
- Disk drive icon
- Folder icon
- Click plus sign to show lower-level folders.
- Click minus sign to hide lower-level folders.
- File icon
- Folder whose contents are shown on right
- Left side: Computers, disk drives, and folders
- Right side: Contents of item you click on left

TABLE D-1   Common File Management Tasks

TASK	HOW TO DO
Copy file or folder	Right-click file or folder to be copied and click Copy, then right-click folder in which you want to copy file and click Paste. (Alternative: Drag and drop a file from one folder to another.)
Move file or folder	Same method as above, but use Cut and Paste.
Delete a file or folder	Point to icon for file to be deleted and press [Delete].
Create a new folder	Choose New from File menu, and then choose Folder. Creates new folder at current position.
Copy file to floppy disk	Point to icon for file to be copied and click right mouse button. Point to Send To and click floppy disk drive in submenu.
Edit/rename file	Point to icon for file you want to rename, press right mouse button, and click Rename.
Open file	Double-click icon for file.
Print file	Point to icon for file to be printed, click right mouse button, and click Print.

APPENDIX E

Proofreaders' Marks

PROOFREADERS' MARK		DRAFT	FINAL COPY
¶	Start a new paragraph	ridiculous! ¶ If that is so	ridiculous! If that is so
⌒	Delete space	to gether	together
# ∧	Insert space	It#may be	It may not be
⟲	Move as shown	it is (not) true	it is true
∩	Transpose	beleivable is it so	believable it is so
○	Spell out	② years ago 16 Elm (St)	two years ago 16 Elm Street
∧	Insert a word	How much it? (is)	How much is it?
─⌐ OR ─	Delete a word	it may not be true	it may be true
∧ OR ⋀	Insert a letter	tempe⋀rture (a)	temperature
? OR ⋺	Delete a letter and close up	commitment to bu⌐ny	commitment to buy
─⌐ OR ─	Change a word	and if you won't (but) (can't)	but if you can't
....	Stet (don't delete)	I was very glad	I was very glad
/	Make letter lowercase	Federal Government	federal government
≡	Capitalize	Janet L. greyston	Janet L. Greyston
∨	Raise above the line	in her new book*	in her new book*
∧	Drop below the line	H2SO4	H_2SO_4

APPENDIX E ■ PROOFREADERS' MARKS

EXCEL **A-17**

PROOFREADERS' MARK		DRAFT	FINAL COPY
⊙	Insert a period	Mr⊙Henry Grenada	Mr. Henry Grenada
∧	Insert a comma	a large∧old house	a large, old house
∨	Insert an apostrophe	my childrens car	my children's car
∨∨	Insert quotation marks	he wants a loan	he wants a "loan"
=	Insert a hyphen	a first=rate job	a first-rate job
		ask the co=owner	ask the co-owner
—/M	Insert an em-dash	Here it is—cash!	Here it is—cash!
–/N	Insert an en-dash	Pages 1–5	Pages 1–5
___	Insert underscore	an issue of <u>Time</u>	an issue of <u>Time</u>
(ital)	Set in italic	(ital) The New York Times	*The New York Times*
(bf)	Set in boldface	(bf) the Enter key	the **Enter** key
(rom)	Set in roman	(rom) the *most* likely	the most likely
{ }	Insert parentheses	left today{May 3}	left today (May 3)
⌐	Move to the right	$38,367,000 ⌐	$38,367,000
⌐	Move to the left	⌐ Anyone can win!	Anyone can win!
ss [	Single-space	ss [I have heard he is leaving	I have heard he is leaving
ds [	Double-space	ds [When will you have a decision?	When will you have a decision?
+1ℓ#	Insert 1 line space	Percent of Change +1ℓ# / 16.25	Percent of Change 16.25
−1ℓ# →	Delete (remove) 1 line space	Northeastern −1ℓ# → regional sales	Northeastern regional sales

APPENDIX F
MOUS Certification

TABLE F-1   Level 1 ("Core") MOUS Activities Related to Lessons

CODE	ACTIVITY	LESSON
XL2000 1	**Working with cells**	
XL2000 1.1	Use Undo and Redo	3
XL2000 1.2	Clear cell content	2
XL2000 1.3	Enter text, dates, and numbers	1, 2
XL2000 1.4	Edit cell content	1, 2
XL2000 1.5	Go to a specific cell	1
XL2000 1.6	Insert and delete selected cells	3
XL2000 1.7	Cut, copy, paste, paste special and move selected cells, use the Office Clipboard	3, 5
XL2000 1.8	Use Find and Replace	7
XL2000 1.9	Clear cell formats	
XL2000 1.10	Work with series (AutoFill)	5
XL2000 1.11	Create hyperlinks	
XL2000 2	**Working with files**	
XL2000 2.1	Use Save	1
XL2000 2.2	Use Save As (different name, location, format)	1
XL2000 2.3	Locate and open an existing workbook	1
XL2000 2.4	Create a folder	2
XL2000 2.5	Use templates to create a new workbook	
XL2000 2.6	Save a worksheet/workbook as a Web Page	1
XL2000 2.7	Send a workbook via email	7
XL2000 2.8	Use the Office Assistant	1
XL2000 3	**Formatting Worksheets**	
XL2000 3.1	Apply font styles (typeface, size, color and styles)	
XL2000 3.2	Apply number formats (currency, percent, dates, comma)	3
XL2000 3.3	Modify size of rows and columns	
XL2000 3.4	Modify alignment of cell content	
XL2000 3.5	Adjust the decimal place	3
XL2000 3.6	Use the Format Painter	3
XL2000 3.7	Apply autoformat	
XL2000 3.8	Apply cell borders and shading	3
XL2000 3.9	Merging cells	
XL2000 3.10	Rotate text and change indents	
XL2000 3.11	Define, apply, and remove a style	

APPENDIX F ■ MOUS CERTIFICATION   EXCEL **A-19**

TABLE F-1 Level 1 ("Core") MOUS Activities *continued*

CODE	ACTIVITY	LESSON
XL2000 4	**Page Setup and Printing**	
XL2000 4.1	Preview and print worksheets & workbooks	1, 4
XL2000 4.2	Use Web Page Preview	1
XL2000 4.3	Print a selection	4
XL2000 4.4	Change page orientation and scaling	4
XL2000 4.5	Set page margins and centering	4
XL2000 4.6	Insert and remove a page break	
XL2000 4.7	Set print, and clear a print area	4
XL2000 4.8	Set up headers and footers	4
XL2000 4.9	Set print titles and options (gridlines, print quality, row & column headings)	4
XL2000 5	**Working with worksheets & workbooks**	
XL2000 5.1	Insert and delete rows and columns	3
XL2000 5.2	Hide and unhide rows and columns	
XL2000 5.3	Freeze and unfreeze rows and columns	4
XL2000 5.4	Change the zoom setting	4
XL2000 5.5	Move between worksheets in a workbook	1
XL2000 5.6	Check spelling	7
XL2000 5.7	Rename a worksheet	4
XL2000 5.8	Insert and Delete worksheets	
XL2000 5.9	Move and copy worksheets	
XL2000 5.10	Link worksheets & consolidate data using 3D References	
XL2000 6	**Working with formulas & functions**	
XL2000 6.1	Enter a range within a formula by dragging	2
XL2000 6.2	Enter formulas in a cell and using the formula bar	2
XL2000 6.3	Revise formulas	2
XL2000 6.4	Use references (absolute and relative)	
XL2000 6.5	Use AutoSum	2
XL2000 6.6	Use Paste Function to insert a function	
XL2000 6.7	Use basic functions (AVERAGE, SUM, COUNT, MIN, MAX)	2
XL2000 6.8	Enter functions using the formula palette	2
XL2000 6.9	Use date functions (NOW and DATE)	
XL2000 6.10	Use financial functions (FV and PMT)	
XL2000 6.11	Use logical functions (IF)	
XL2000 7	**Using charts and objects**	
XL2000 7.1	Preview and print charts	
XL2000 7.2	Use chart wizard to create a chart	
XL2000 7.3	Modify charts	
XL2000 7.4	Insert, move, and delete an object (picture)	
XL2000 7.5	Create and modify lines and objects	

TABLE F-2 Level 2 ("Expert") MOUS Activities* Related to Lessons

*Only selected Level 2 ("Expert") Activities covering common Office activities are included in this text.

CODE	ACTIVITY	LESSON
XL2000 E.6.1	Add and delete a named range	6
XL2000 E.6.2	Use a named range in a formula	6
XL2000 E.7.1	Hide and display toolbars	5
XL2000 E.7.2	Customize toolbar	5
XL2000 E.10.9	Use data validation	4
XL2000 E.12.2	Apply and remove worksheet and workbook protection	4

TABLE F-3

Lessons Related to MOUS Activities

LESSON	CODES*
1 What Is Excel?	XL2000 1.5, 2.1, 2.2, 2.3, 2.6, 2.8, 4.1, 4.2, 5.5
2 Creating a Simple Worksheet	XL2000 1.2, 1.3, 1.4, 2.4, 6.1, 6.2, 6.3, 6.5, 6.7, 6.8
3 Enhancing a Simple Worksheet	XL2000 1.1, 1.3, 1.4, 1.6, 1.7, 3.2, 3.5, 3.6, 3.8, 5.1
4 Designing and Printing a Worksheet	XL2000 4.1, 4.3, 4.4, 4.5, 4.7, 4.8, 4.9, 5.3, 5.4, 5.7, E.10.9, E.12.2
5 Copying Data and Using Toolbars	XL2000 1.7, 1.10, E.7.1, E.7.2
6 Naming Ranges and Sorting	XL2000 E.6.1, E.6.2
7 Spelling, Find/Replace, and File Management	XL2000 1.8, 2.7, 5.6

*MOUS Activity codes are abbreviated in this table.

Glossary

Active cell Cell that is current and ready to receive information. (1)

Block Group of adjacent cells (that is, cells that are next to one other). (2)

Cell address Location of a cell in a worksheet. A cell address is indicated by its column letter and row number. (1)

Cell Rectangle formed by the intersection of a row and a column. Cells can contain text, numeric values, or formulas. (1)

Character string Sequence of characters in a formula or text. (7)

Clipboard Temporary storage in the computer's memory. (3)

Constants Unchanging values used in formulas. (6)

Cut To remove cells or data in cells and placing it on the Clipboard. (3)

Docked toolbar Toolbar that appears in a fixed position outside the work area. (5)

Fill handle Small box in the lower right corner of an active cell. (5)

Floating toolbar Toolbar positioned over the work area. (5)

Formulas Instructions that tell Excel how to perform calculations. (2)

Hypertext Markup Language (HTML) File format that allows file content to be opened, viewed, edited, and printed using browser software. (1)

Label Text that can include any character, and cannot be included in calculations. (2)

Landscape page orientation Horizontal page orientation (11 inches by 8½ inches). (4)

Order of precedence Preset order in which mathematical operations in a formula are performed. (2)

Page orientation Print setting that is either 8½ inches by 11 inches (vertical page orientation, also called portrait page orientation) or 11 inches by 8½ inches (horizontal page orientation, also called landscape orientation). (4)

Panes Portions of worksheets. Panes allow you to see row and column labels as you enter data or formulas. (4)

Paste To move cells or data in cells from the Clipboard to a selected area on a worksheet. (3)

Places bar Vertical bar in the Open, Save, and Save As dialog box that contains recent or commonly used folders for easy access. (1)

Portrait page orientation Vertical page orientation (8½ inches by 11 inches). (4)

Print area Specific range of cells you want to print. (4)

Range name Name you give a range of cells. A range name can also be given to a single cell. (6)

Range Any group of cells specified to be acted upon by a command. (2)

Relative cell reference Cell reference in a formula that adjusts to a new position when you copy it. (5)

ScreenTip Text that identifies elements on the screen. ScreenTips are available for dialog boxes, menu commands, and button names. (1)

Source range Area of the worksheet from which you copy or remove data. (5)

Split bar Bar that splits the screen into panes. (4)

Split boxes Gray rectangular boxes that appear in the upper right corner of the document window above the vertical scroll arrow and at the far right of the horizontal scroll bar at the bottom of the document window. Split boxes allow you to split worksheets into multiple panes. (4)

Target range New location for data that you copy or move. (5)

Test data Easy-to-calculate numbers that you enter in a worksheet to test formulas. (4)

Value Entry that begins with a number or mathematical sign, and can be included in a calculation. (2)

Wildcard Symbol that stands for one or more letters or numbers. (7)

Workbook Excel worksheet, or group of worksheets, saved as a file. (1)

Worksheet Area in which text, numeric values, and formulas are entered. Worksheets contain a series of rows and columns. Worksheets are collected into workbooks, which can contain up to 255 worksheets. (1)

Zoom Option that changes the magnification of the display. (4)

Index

A

active cell, 14, 17–18, 43
   Name Box, 17
adding range names, 186–189
addition, 54
adjusting the decimal place, 89
ampersand, 137
apostrophe, 44
applying
   cell borders, 89–92
   number formats, 88–89
      comma, 121
      dates, 119
   text attributes, 89–92
      using Formatting toolbar, 90
applying and removing
   worksheet and workbook
      protection, 132–133
Arrow keys, 21, 23
asterisk, 214, 218
Audit arrows, 167
AutoCalculate feature, 61–62
   using to find a Sum, 62
AutoComplete feature, 47–49
AutoCorrect feature, 209, 211–213
   adding AutoCorrect entries for common
      typos, 212–213
   Replace Text As You Type, 212
AutoFill feature, 164–166, 171
   using to copy formulas, 164
AutoSum feature, 60, 121

B

blocks of cells, 49
   selecting block of cells
      using keyboard, 49–51
      using mouse, 51–53
      using Name Box, 53–54
borders
   applying cell borders, 89–92
      bottom border, 91–92
Borders palette, 92
browser, 29
buttons
   Address button, 221
   Align Right button, 90

Attach File button, 221
AutoSum button, 60, 121, 161
Bold button, 90
Borders button, 91
Cancel button, 26, 43
Center button, 90
Clear All button, 124
Clear Clipboard button, 168
Close button, 30, 31
Close Window button, 31
Comma Style button, 89, 121
Copy button, 159, 161
Create New Folder button, 46, 217
Cut button, 85
Date button, 137
Decrease Decimal button, 89, 121
Delete button, 220
E-Mail button, 221
Edit Formula button, 56
Enter button, 26, 43, 56, 60
File Name button, 137
Format Painter button, 90
Increase Decimal button, 89
Microsoft Excel Help button, 15
More Buttons button, 14, 15, 60, 84
Open button, 20, 217, 219
Open dialog box buttons, 217
Paste All button, 169
Paste button, 85, 159, 161
Percent Style button, 89
Print button, 30, 138, 141
Print Preview button, 134, 141
Redo button, 83
Remove All Arrows button, 168
Save button, 16
Search the Web button, 217
Sheet Name button, 137
Sort Ascending button, 194
Sort Descending button, 194
Spelling button, 210, 212
Start button, 11
tab scrolling buttons, 19
toolbar buttons, 14, 167
Trace Dependents button, 167
Trace Precedents button, 167
Undo button, 83, 169
Views button, 21
Zoom button, 129

C

calculating percentage changes, 57
cell borders, 89–92
    applying bottom border, 91–92
cell contents
    clearing, 46, 82
    completing entry, 47
    copying
        using AutoFill, 164–165
        using Fill, 163–164
    copying and pasting, 158–161
    cutting and pasting, 158–161
    dragging and dropping, 162–163
    editing, 46–47
    moving, 158–161
    overwriting, 160–161
    restoring, 47
cell formatting
    copying, 161
cell references
    adjusted after drag and drop, 162
    adjusted after Fill, 163
    blocks of cells, 58
    cell ranges, 58
    checking references in formulas
        after moving data, 88
    creating names for, 188–189
    entering by clicking cell, 56
    finding data in worksheet, 214–216
    for Go To command, 26
    groups of cells, 58
    keying, 53, 55, 58
        to identify range, 58
    relative cell references, 161
    single cell, 58
    used in formulas, 55
cells
    active cell, 14, 17–18, 43
    blank cells, 82
    blocks of cells, 49–54
    cell address, 17
    copying cell values, 161
    copying formulas to adjacent cells, 164
    deleting cells, 82–83
    entering data, 49–54
    go to specific cell, 21–26
    group of selected cells, 49
    if not enough room for data, 121
    inserting cells
        entire column, 80
        entire row, 80
        multiple cells, 81–82
        single cell, 79–80
        using Insert menu, 161
    locked cells, 132
    moving selected cells, 77–83, 160–161
    naming cells, 185–188
        group of cells, 187–188
        individual cell, 186–187
    overwriting cell by mistake, 44
    selecting block of cells
        using keyboard, 49–51
        using mouse, 51–53
        using Name Box, 53–54
    selecting cells by content, 124–125
    validating data in cells, 123–124
centering print area on page, 136
changing
    active cell, 17–18
    data in worksheets, 27
    number of decimals displayed, 89
    page orientation, 135
    print area, 139–140
    range names, 189–190
    zoom setting, 129
character string, 213
checking formulas
    entering test data, 120–121
checking spelling, 208–211
clearing
    cell contents, 46, 82
    print area, 139
Clipboard, 85, 158, 166, 219
closing
    toolbars, 171
    workbooks, 20–21, 31
colon, 58, 59
columns, 17, 22
    column headings, 14, 117
        printing with headings, 141
    column titles, 90
    column widths, 140
    deleting columns, 82–83
    freezing and unfreezing, 127
    inserting entire column, 80
    inserting multiple columns, 81–82
    row and column labels
        entering, 47–49, 118–120
        keeping in view, 125–128
    selecting multiple columns, 77–79
command summaries
    AutoCorrect, 220

AutoSum, 63
closing, 31
cutting and pasting, 92
defining and pasting names, 195
displaying formulas, 141
editing formulas, 63
exiting, 31
filling right, filling down, 171
finding and replacing, 220
Go To address, 31, 195
inserting and deleting cells, 92
page setup, 141
printing, 31
protecting workbooks and worksheets, 141
saving, 31
sorting, 195
spell-checking, 220
undoing and redoing, 92
constants, 188
  listing constants, 191
    naming constants, 185–189
      creating names, 188–189
constructing basic formulas, 54–57
Copy and Paste commands, 159–161
Copy mode, 160–161
copying
  cell formatting, 161
  cell values, 161
  files, 219–232
  formulas
    copying to adjacent cells, 164
    using AutoFill, 164–166
    using buttons, 161
    using drag-and-drop, 162
    using Fill, 163–164
  text attributes
    using Format Painter, 90–91
copying and inserting
  cells, 160–161
copying and pasting
  being specific about what is pasted, 161
  cell contents, 158–161
    only certain aspects of, 161
  cell formatting, 161
  formulas, 161
  source range, 159
  target range, 159
  using buttons, 161
  using Edit menu, 159–160
  using keyboard, 160–161
  values, 161

creating
  custom header, 137
  folders, 45, 217
  formulas, 55–57
  formulas including names, 188–189
  user documentation, 130–132
  worksheets, 17
customizing toolbars, 169
Cut and Paste commands, 85
cutting and pasting
  cell contents, 158–161

D

data
  copying
    using drag-and-drop, 162
  copying and pasting
    using buttons, 161
    using Edit menu, 159–160
    using keyboard, 160–161
  data entry areas, unlocking, 132
  Data Sort, 185
  editing data, 42–47
  entering data, 42–47
    in selected cells, 49–54
  entering test data, 120–121
  finding and replacing data, 213–216
  if not enough room in cell, 121
  moving data, 85–88
    cell references in formulas, 88
    using Cut and Paste, 85
    using Drag and Drop, 87
    using Insert Cut Cells, 86
  replacing data, 215–216
  sorting information, 193–207
  validating data, 123–124
Data menu
  Sort, 193, 195
  Validation, 123
Data Sort command, 185
dates and date formats, 119
  changing date format of selected cells, 119
deleting
  cells, 82–83
  columns, 82–83
  files, 219–232
  range names, 189–190
  rows, 82–83
  text, 47

dialog boxes
  AutoCorrect dialog box, 211
  Confirm Password dialog box, 133
  Customize dialog box, 167, 170
  Data Validation dialog box, 123
  Define Name dialog box, 187, 188
  Find dialog box, 214, 218
  Find Fast dialog box, 218
  Go To dialog box, 25, 190, 191
  Go To Special dialog box, 124
  Insert dialog box, 85
  Insert Paste dialog box, 161
  Label Ranges dialog box, 188, 195
  Open dialog box, 21, 216, 219
  Options dialog box
    View tab, 130, 140
  Page Setup dialog box, 140
    Header/Footer tab, 136
    Margins tab, 136
  Paste Name dialog box, 192
  Print dialog box, 30, 134, 139
  Protect Sheet dialog box, 133
  Replace dialog box, 215
  Save As dialog box, 29
  Sort dialog box, 193
  Spelling dialog box, 210
  Zoom dialog box, 129
disks and disk drives, 20, 28, 45
display options, 128–130
displaying
  formulas, 141
  multiple toolbars, 166–169
displaying on screen
  row and column headings, 128
division, 54
docked toolbar, 169
docking a floating toolbar, 169
documentation, creating, 130–132
Drag and Drop feature, 87
dragging out of the way
  formula bar, 56
  toolbars, 169
  Validation Input Message box, 126

E

e-mail
  attaching entire workbook, 221
  preparing computer, 220
  sending workbooks, 220
  sending worksheets, 220
  system requirements, 220
Edit menu
  Clear, 46, 63
  Copy, 159, 171
  Cut, 92
  Delete, 82, 84, 92
  Delete Sheet, 132
  Fill, 163, 171
  Find, 214, 215, 220
  Go To, 25, 31, 124, 141, 190
  Paste, 92, 159
  Paste Special, 161
  Redo, 83, 92
  Redo Delete, 84
  Replace, 215, 216, 220
  Undo, 83, 92
  Undo Delete, 84
Edit mode, 46, 56
  keystrokes in, 47
editing
  cell content, 46–47
  data, 27, 42–47
Enter mode, 43
entering
  cell references, 56
  data, 42–47
    in selected cells, 49–54
  formulas
    automating calculations, 121–123
    using formula bar, 55
  functions
    using formula palette, 59
  header and footer, 136–138
  labels, 47
  range within formula, by dragging, 59
  SUM formula
    using Arrow keys, 59
    using AutoSum button, 60–61
    using mouse, 59–60
  test data, 120–121
entering text, dates, and numbers
  completing an entry, 43
  data, 42–47, 49–54
  dates, 119
  labels, 47
  numbers, 26–27, 42–47
  overwriting cell by mistake, 44
  text, 42–47
equal sign, 55, 56, 58
Excel. *See* Microsoft Excel
exiting Excel, 31
exponentiation, 54

F

file extensions, 21, 28–29
file management, 216–220
File menu
   Close, 20, 31
   Exit, 31
   Open, 20, 217, 220
   Page Setup, 135, 141
      Fit on the Page tab, 141
      Sheet tab, 141
   Print, 30, 138, 141
   Print Area, 139
   Print Preview, 134, 141
   Save, 16, 28, 31
   Save As, 28, 45
   Web Page Preview, 30
files, 27
   copying files, 219–232
   deleting files, 219–232
   file type, 29
   filenames, 28
      extension .doc, 28
      extension .htm, 29
      extension .xls, 28, 29, 220
      letters and spaces, 28
   finding files, 216–218
   HTML (Hypertext Markup Language)
      format, 29
   previewing files, 219
   protecting files, 132–133
   renaming files, 219–232
   searching for specific filenames, 217
Fill command, 163–164
fill handle, 164
finding
   data, 214
   files, 216–218
   Sum, using AutoCalculate, 62
   workbooks, 217–218
finding and replacing
   character string, 213
   data, 213–216
floating a docked toolbar, 169
floating toolbar, 169
folders, 28
   creating folders, 45
Format menu
   Cells, 119, 132
   Column, 45, 82
Format Painter
   using scroll bar, 91
   using to copy attributes, 91
formatting dates
   changing date format of selected cells, 119
formatting numbers
   as labels, 43
   basic formatting, 88–89
   comma style, 89
   percent style, 89
formula bar, 13, 22, 43, 56, 186
   dragging out of the way, 56
Formula Palette, 60
formulas, 54–57
   addition formulas
      building, 56
      keying, 55
   basic formulas, 54–57
   calculating percentage changes, 57
   checking formulas
      entering test data, 120–121
   constants, 188
   copying formulas, 161–165
      to adjacent cells, 164
      using AutoFill, 164–165
      using buttons, 161
      using drag-and-drop, 162
      using Fill, 163–164
   displaying formulas, 141
   entering formulas to automate calculations, 121–123
   moving formulas, 88
      checking cell references, 88
   multiplication formulas, 56
   order of precedence, 54
   printing formulas, 140–141
   SUM formulas, 58
   typical Excel formulas, 55
   using names in formulas, 188–189
Formulas option, 140
freezing and unfreezing rows and columns, 127
freezing panes, 127
functions, 54, 58
   AutoSum function, 60
   Function box, 56
   function names, 58
   SUM function, 121

G

go to specific cell, 21–26
gridlines
   displaying on screen, 128

grid of rows and columns, 17
printing with gridlines, 141
removing from screen, 129–130

H

headers and footers, 136–138
   removing from screen, 129–130
Help, 92
   Help topics and tips, 14–15
   Hide the Office Assistant, 43
   Office Assistant, 32
hiding
   toolbars, 171
HTML (Hypertext Markup Language) file
     format, 29

I

icons
   Excel shortcut icon, 12
   light gray icons, 15
   New icon, 15
   printer icon, 31
indicators, 14
Insert Cut Cells, 86
Insert menu
   Cells, 80, 92
   Columns, 80, 82, 92
   Copied Cells, 161
   Cut Cells, 86
   Name, 186, 190, 195
   Rows, 80, 92
inserting
   entire column, 80
   entire row, 80
   multiple cells, 81–82, 161
   multiple columns, 81–82
   multiple rows, 81–82
   single cell, 79–80

K

keyboard combinations, 18
keyboard commands, 18–21
keyboard shortcuts
   as shown on menus, 16
   closing workbook, 31
   copying and pasting, 159
   cutting and pasting, 85
   displaying formulas, 140
   exiting Excel, 31

inserting cells, columns, rows, 79
keying
   addition formulas, 55
   cell references, 53, 55, 58
     to identify range, 58
   data, 26–27, 42
     deleting errors, 26
   SUM formula, 58

L

labels, 43–44, 47, 117
   blank labels, 82
   quotation marks around, 188
   row and column labels
     entering, 47, 118–120
     keeping in view, 125–128
laptop, using, 80
locating and opening existing workbooks,
     20–21

M

margins, 42
   Margins tab, 136
   setting page margins and centering, 136
mathematical operators
   commonly used operators, 54
   exponentiation operator, 54
menu bar, 13–16
menus and menu commands, 16–17
   shortcut menus, 84–85
Microsoft Excel
   Excel window, 13
   exiting Excel, 31
   introduction to, 11–31
   starting, 11–17
   typical Excel formulas, 55
minus sign, 57
modes
   Copy mode, 160, 161
   Edit mode, 46, 56
     keystrokes in, 47
   Enter mode, 43
   Point mode, 56
   Ready mode, 47
moving
   between worksheets, 18–19
   cell contents, 158–161
   data, 85–88
     source range, 159
     target range, 159

INDEX   EXCEL   I-7

    using Cut and Paste, 85
    using Drag and Drop, 87
    using Insert Cut Cells, 86
  insertion point, 47
  selected cells, 77–83, 160–161
  to named ranges, 190
  toolbars, 169–171
multiplication, 54, 57

N

Name Box, 13, 17, 22, 53, 186
named ranges
  listing named ranges, 191
  moving to named ranges, 190
names
  changing range names, 189–190
  creating for cell references, 188–189
  creating for constants, 188–189
  deleting range names, 189–190
  function names, 58
  names in formulas, 188–189
  navigating using range names, 190–191
naming
  cells, 185
  constants, 185, 188–189
  functions, 58
  groups of cells, 187–188
  individual cell, 186–187
  ranges, 186–188
  workbooks, 28–29
  worksheet tabs, 125
navigating
  between worksheets, 18–19
    keyboard commands, 19
  using range names, 190–191
  within worksheets
    using keyboard commands, 22
    using scroll bars, 24
nesting expressions, 54
numbers
  changing number of decimals displayed, 89
  formatting numbers
    basic formats, 88–89
    in comma style, 89
    in percent style, 89
numeric keypad, 80

O

Office Assistant, 14–15, 32, 63, 92, 167
Office Clipboard, 165–166

opening
  workbooks, 20–21
  worksheets, 19
order of precedence, 54
orientation, portrait or landscape, 135
overwriting and inserting
  using Copy and Paste, 160

P

page orientation, 135
Page Setup options, 135
panes, 125
  four-pane split, 128
  freezing panes, 127
  splitting worksheets into panes, 126–127
parentheses, 55, 58
passwords
  form of, 133
  Password text box, 133
Paste Special, 161
pasting
  certain aspects of cell contents, 161
  everything except borders, 161
  formatting, 161
  validation, 161
  values only, 161
pasting range names into worksheets, 191–192
percentage changes, 57
Pick From List feature, 47–49
Places bar, 20
Point mode, 56
pointers
  arrow pointer, 87, 134, 162
  black cross pointer, 164
  drag-and-drop pointer, 87, 162
  Format Painter pointer, 91
  four-headed arrow pointer, 128, 169
  I-beam pointer, 46
  magnifier pointer, 134
  mouse pointer, 15, 48, 87, 128, 162
  split pointer, 128
  white-cross pointer, 18, 46, 87
previewing and printing
  worksheets and workbooks, 30–31, 133–134
    Print Preview, 134
    Web Page Preview, 30
print options, 140
  gridlines, 140
  row and column headings, 140

printers, 30
   designated printer, 30
printing
   changing print area, 139–140
   clearing print area, 139
   Entire Workbook option, 31
   formulas, 140–141
   page orientation, 135
   previewing workbook, 133–134
   print areas, 139
   print options, 140
      gridlines, 140
      row and column headings, 140
   printing with grids, 141
   printing with headings, 141
   setting up for printing, 133–139
   workbooks, 138–139
   worksheets, 30–31
Programs menu
   Microsoft Excel, 12
protecting files, 132–133
   Protect Sheet, 133
   Protect Workbook, 132–133

Q

quotation marks around label, 188

R

raising value to a power, 54
range, 58
   identifying range, 58
   sort range, 193
range names, 186–192
   adding, 186–192
   changing, 189–190
   deleting, 189–190
   navigating using, 190–191
   pasting into worksheets, 191–192
   valid and invalid, 186
Ready mode, 47
relative cell references, 161
removing
   gridlines from screen, 129–130
   headers from screen, 129–130
renaming
   files, 219–232
   worksheets, 125, 133
replacing data, 215–216
reshaping toolbars, 169–171

restoring previous cell contents, 47
reversing last action, 83
revising formulas, 55–57
rows, 17, 22
   deleting rows, 82–83
   entering row labels, 47–49, 118–120
   freezing and unfreezing rows, 127
   inserting entire row, 80
   inserting multiple rows, 81–82
   keeping row and column labels in view, 125–128
   row headings, 14
      printing with headings, 141
   selecting multiple rows, 77–79

S

saving
   workbook, 27–30
      as Web Page, 29–30
   worksheet
      as Web Page, 29
screen
   displaying gridlines, 128
   displaying row and column headings, 128
   parts of Excel screen, 13
   removing gridlines, 129
   removing headers, 129
ScreenTips, 15
scroll bars, 14, 21, 24–25
selected cells, deleting, 82–83
selected cells, inserting, 79–82
selecting
   block of cells
      using keyboard, 49–51
      using mouse, 51–53
      using Name Box, 53–54
   cells by content, 124–125
   display options, 128–130
   multiple columns and rows, 77–79
      using keyboard, 78–79
      using mouse, 78
sending workbook via e-mail, 220
sending worksheet via e-mail, 220
setting page margins and centering, 136
setting print titles and options, 116
   gridlines, 140
   Page Setup dialog box, 140
   printing with grids, 141
   printing with headings, 141
   row and column headings, 140
   setting print titles, 116

setting up for printing, 133–139
setting up headers and footers, 136–138
sheets and sheet names, 18–19, 125
   deleting sheets, 132
shortcut menus, 84–85
sorting
   Data Sort command, 185
   information in worksheets, 193–207
source range, 159
spell-checking, 208–211
   entire worksheet, 209–210
   range in worksheet, 210–211
   spell-checking options, 209
spelling
   AutoCorrect, 209
   automated dictionaries, 208
split boxes and split bars, 125, 128
splitting worksheets into panes, 126–127
starting Microsoft Excel, 11–17
status bar, 14, 43, 56
subtraction, 54
SUM formula
   cell references
      block of cells, 58
      single cell, 58
   entering formula
      using Arrow keys, 59
      using AutoSum button, 60–61
      using mouse, 59–60
   keying formula, 58
   range, 58
SUM function, 58–61, 121

T

tab scrolling buttons, 14
target range, 159
test data, 120
text
   deleting text, 47
   editing text, 46
   entering text, 42–47
text attributes
   alignment, 90
   applying, 89–92
      using Formatting toolbar, 90
   bold, 90
   centered, 90
   copying using Format Painter, 90–91
   italic, 90
   number styles, 90
title bar, 13

titles, worksheets, 116
toolbars, 13
   closing toolbars, 171
   customizing toolbars, 169
   displaying multiple toolbars, 166–169
   docked toolbar, 169
   docking a floating toolbar, 169
   floating a docked toolbar, 169
   floating toolbar, 169
   moving toolbars, 169–171
   reshaping toolbars, 169–171
      floating toolbar, 169
   table of Excel toolbars, 165–166
   toolbar buttons, 14
   using Excel toolbars, 165–184
toolbars, by name
   Auditing toolbar, 166, 168
   Clipboard toolbar, 166, 168
   E-Mail toolbar, 221
   Expanded Formatting toolbar, 88
   Formatting toolbar, 14, 89
   Standard toolbar, 14, 121
Tools menu
   AutoCorrect, 211, 212, 220
   Find, 217
   Options, 87, 129, 140, 164
   Protection, 132, 141
   Spelling, 210, 220

U

Undo and Redo commands, 83–84, 190
unlocking data entry areas, 132
using AutoCorrect, 211–213
using AutoFill
   to copy formulas, 164
using AutoSum, 60–61
using basic functions
   SUM function, 58–61
using data validation, 123–124
using Format Painter
   to copy attributes, 90–91
   using scroll bar, 91
using named ranges in formulas, 188
using names in formulas, 188–189
using Office Assistant, 14–15, 32, 63, 92, 167
using Save, 16, 27–31
using Save As, 28
   different format, 29
   different location, 28
   different name, 28
using shortcut menus, 84–85

using Undo and Redo, 83–84
using Web Page Preview, 30

V

validating data, 123–124
validation message box, 124
values, 42, 161
View menu
   Toolbars, 166
   Zoom, 129, 141
View options, 140
View settings, 21, 28

W

Web pages, 29
wildcard, 214
Window menu
   Freeze Panes, 127, 141
   Remove Split, 126, 127
   Split, 126, 127, 141
   Unfreeze Panes, 127
windows
   Excel window, 13
   multiple panes, 125–128
   Window menu, 126
Windows Explorer, 21, 28
Windows taskbar, 11
workbooks, 17
   attaching entire workbook to e-mail, 221
   closing workbooks, 20–21, 31
   distributing to other people, 220
   files, 27
   finding workbooks, 217–218
   naming workbooks, 28–29
   opening workbooks, 20–21
   previewing workbooks, 133–134
   printing workbooks, 133–139
   saving workbooks, 27–30
worksheets, 13–17
   building worksheets
      using Copy and Paste, 158–161
   centering on page, 136
   changing data in, 27
   controlling appearance of, 14
   designing worksheets, 116–118
   distributing to other people, 220
   entering labels and values, 43–45
   finding and replacing data, 213–216
   keying data in worksheets, 26–27
   magnification of display, 128
   moving between worksheets, 18–19
   multiple panes, 125
   naming worksheet tabs, 125
   navigating between worksheets, 18–19
   navigating within worksheets
      using keyboard commands, 22
      using scroll bars, 24
   opening worksheets, 19
   pasting range names, 191–192
   planning worksheets, 116–125
      on paper, 116–118
      putting on screen, 118–125
   printing worksheets, 30–31
   renaming worksheets, 125
   reversing last action, 83
   sorting information, 193–207
   spell-checking
      entire worksheet, 209–210
      range in worksheet, 210–211
   splitting worksheets into panes, 126–127
   structure of worksheet, 116
   titles, 116
   worksheet documentation, 131
   worksheet tabs, 14, 18, 19
   worksheet titles, 119
World Wide Web, 217

Z

Zoom
   changing zoom setting, 129
   magnifying and reducing display, 129
   Zoom box, 129
   Zoom options, 128

Photo Credits

Pages 2 and 5, PhotoDisc, Inc.;
Pages 6 and 9, Telegraph Color Library/FPG.